Once upon a Time in Beirut

A Journey to the Heart of the Middle East

CATHERINE TAYLOR

BANTAM
SYDNEY AUCKLAND TORONTO NEW YORK LONDON

ONCE UPON A TIME IN BEIRUT
A BANTAM BOOK

First published in Australia and New Zealand in 2007
by Bantam

National Library of Australia
Cataloguing-in-Publication Entry

Taylor, Catherine (Catherine Helen).
Once upon a time in Beirut: a journey to the heart of the Middle East.

ISBN 978 1 86325 520 2 (pbk.).

1. Taylor, Catherine (Catherine Helen). 2. Journalists – Australia – Biography. 3. Public opinion – Lebanon – Beirut. 4. Lebanon War, 2006. 5. Beirut (Lebanon) – Social life and customs. 6. Lebanon – Politics and government – 1991–. I. Title.

303.660956925

Transworld Publishers,
a division of Random House Australia Pty Ltd
100 Pacific Highway
North Sydney, NSW 2060
www.randomhouse.com.au

Random House New Zealand Limited
18 Poland Road, Glenfield, Auckland

Transworld Publishers,
a division of The Random House Group Ltd
61–63 Uxbridge Road, Ealing, London W5 5SA

Random House Inc
1745 Broadway, New York, New York 10036

Author photograph by Paul Blackmore
Typeset by Midland Typesetters, Australia
Printed and bound by Griffin Press, South Australia

10 9 8 7 6 5 4 3 2 1

For Yasmine and Joseph; and for Matthew,

who shared every step of the way

CONTENTS

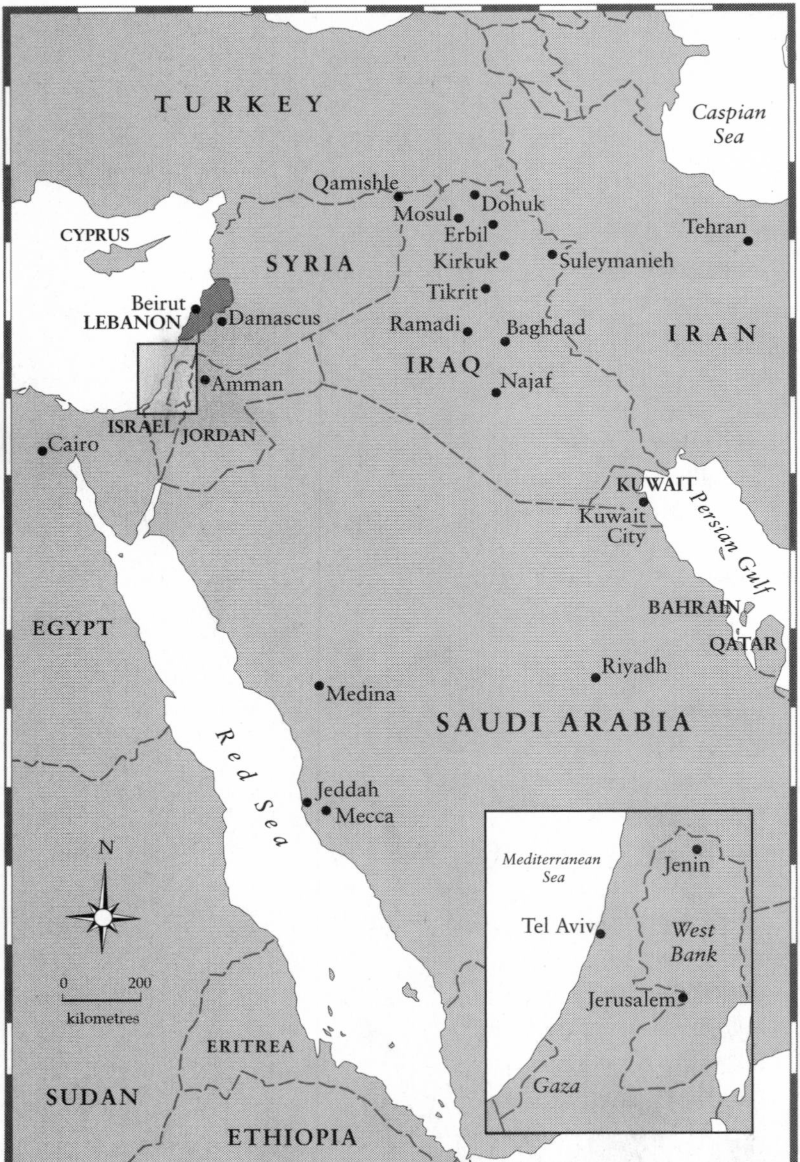

The Middle East

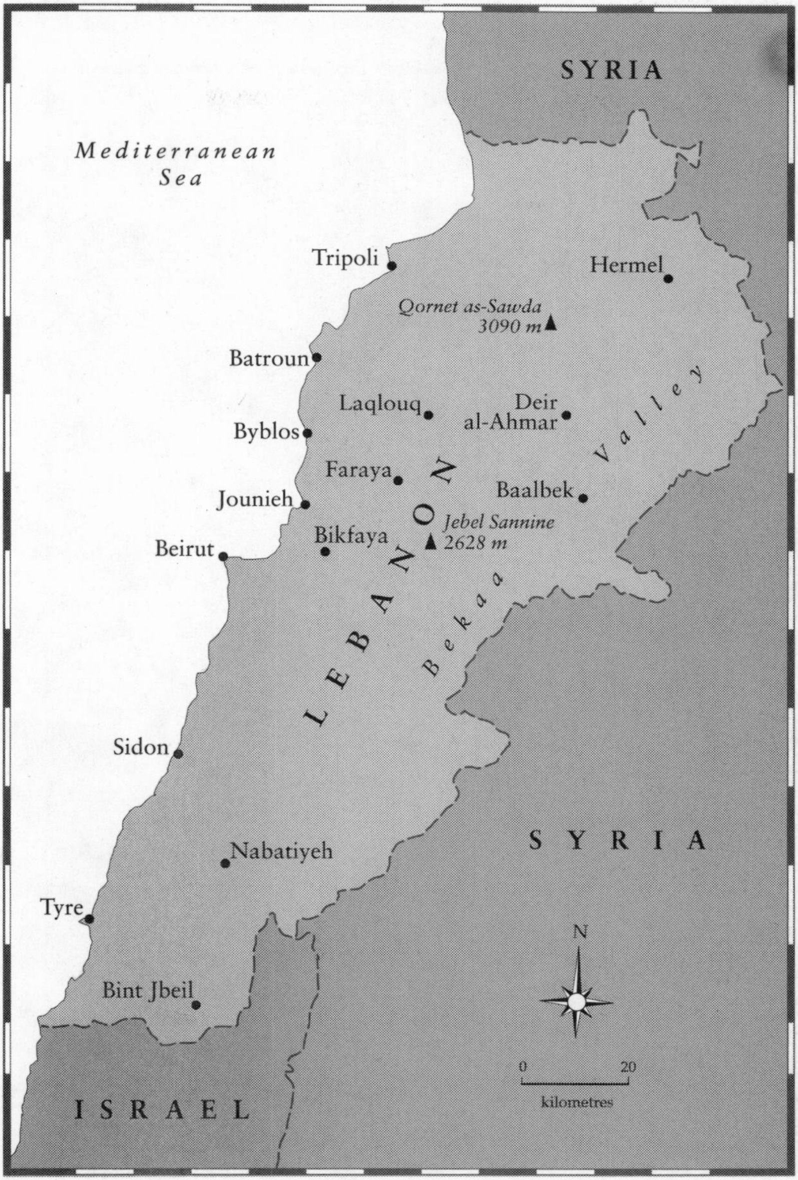
SYRIA
Mediterranean Sea
Tripoli
Hermel
Qornet as-Sawda 3090 m
Batroun
Laqlouq
Deir al-Ahmar
Byblos
Faraya
Baalbek
Jounieh
Jebel Sannine 2628 m
Bikfaya
Beirut
LEBANON
Bekaa Valley
Sidon
SYRIA
Nabatiyeh
Tyre
N
Bint Jbeil
0
20
kilometres
ISRAEL

Lebanon

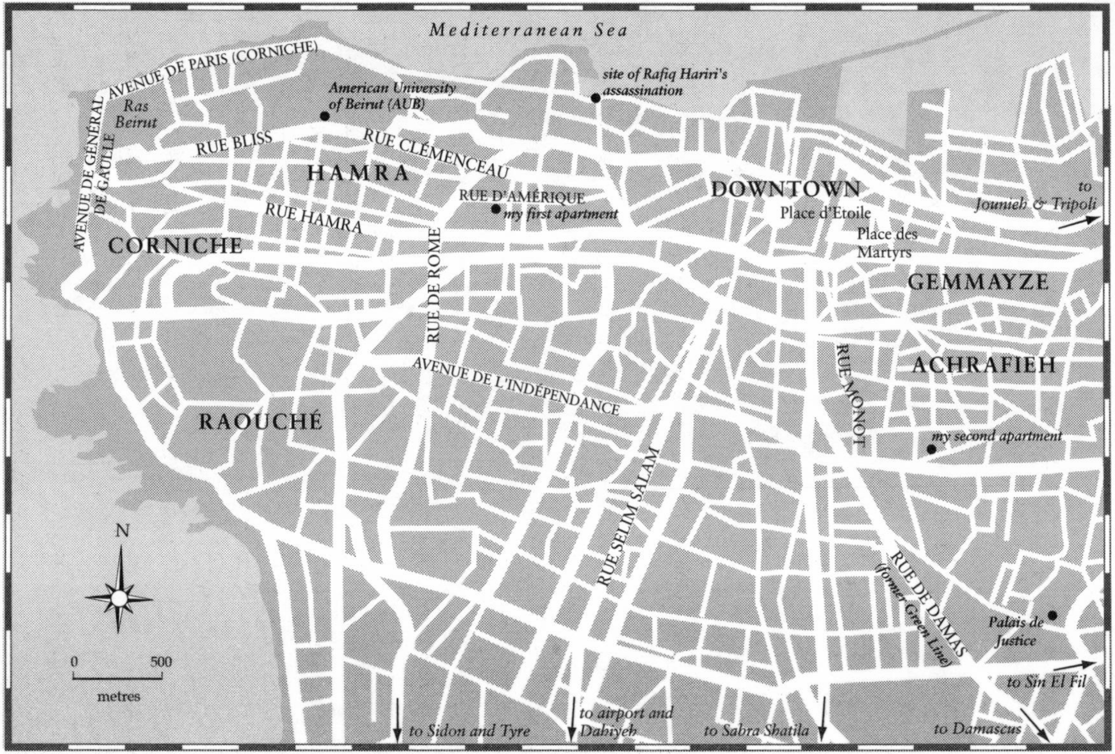
Mediterranean Sea
AVENUE DE PARIS (CORNICHE)
AVENUE DE GÉNÉRAL DE GAULLE
Ras Beirut
American University of Beirut (AUB)
site of Rafiq Hariri's assassination
RUE BLISS
RUE CLÉMENCEAU
HAMRA
RUE HAMRA
RUE D'AMÉRIQUE
my first apartment
CORNICHE
RUE DE ROME
DOWNTOWN
Place d'Etoile
Place des Martyrs
to Jounieh & Tripoli
GEMMAYZE
ACHRAFIEH
RUE MONOT
AVENUE DE L'INDÉPENDANCE
RAOUCHÉ
my second apartment
RUE SELIM SALAM
RUE DE DAMAS (former Green Line)
Palais de Justice
to Sin El Fil
to Damascus
to Sabra Shatila
to airport and Dahiyeh
to Sidon and Tyre
N
0
500
metres

Beirut

AUTHOR'S NOTE

I began to write this book while I was pregnant in Beirut and had to abandon the reporting jobs that had been taking me to remote and sometimes dangerous places. Those first days of writing were after 9/11 and the war in Iraq, when the Middle East had become a feared and vilified place. On trips back home to Australia I was cornered at parties and overwhelmed with agitated questions: 'But what is it *like* there?'; 'Aren't you *scared*?' I would often feel alarmed and confused by the disconnect between the sense of fear people felt towards the region and the reality of my daily life there, which was surrounded by kind and generous friends and acquaintances – of all religions – and people who faced their country's and their own problems with great courage. I was constantly humbled by the way in which I would be warmly welcomed into strangers' homes, be they in Tehran, Riyadh, Baghdad, Ramallah or Beirut, and would wonder what sort of hospitality they would have received in Sydney. So my earliest inspiration to write this book arose from a desire to show what it is 'like there'.

The Middle East is not an easy place to distil. But I hope

I have given a voice to some of the people of the region, to reveal something of the complexity of their lives, away from the preconceptions we have come to fall back on so easily in the West.

Some of the characters described in the following pages, though not of course those of public figures, have pseudonyms or are amalgamations of several people. This was done to offer privacy so that opinions and emotions could be more honestly expressed. Otherwise, all events, encounters and conversations are true.

As there is no agreed method of transliteration from Arabic to English I have chosen the most common spellings, or those I believe best convey the correct pronunciation of the words.

My thanks go first to the people in Lebanon and the Middle East who opened up their lives to me, fed me and kept me company; for their warmth and generosity, which truly matches the legend.

Thanks also to my parents (for your huge love and for never baulking when I needed your consummate babysitting talents); to my sister Alexandra (for the richness of family to return home to); to my agent, Tara Wynne (for solid advice and support); at Random House thanks to Sophie Ambrose and Catherine Hill (for seeing me through with enormous patience and skill). To Paul Blackmore (for being the first to convince me I had a book in me), and Jane Southward (for getting me started), Garth Nix (for advice and contacts), Bani McSpedden (for a place to write), Loubna Dimachki (for a precious friendship and encouragement at a critical moment), Whitney Harris, Mathilde de Hautecloque, Susan Gray, Donna Malouf and Aline Matta (for perfectly timed opinions). And finally my thanks to Matthew Carney, my constant support, who has inspired this book in so many ways.

PROLOGUE

There were people crawling out of the rubble, chalky and pale, covered with a layer of white dust from the crushed stone of the houses that had collapsed around them. It was July 2006 and these images of war in Lebanon, yet more war, showed walking shadows, frail and devastated people who had been trapped for almost three weeks without food or water while fighting raged. A short ceasefire had been declared, not a resolution but a pause in the bombing that was long enough to allow them to creep to some kind of safety, to point to where their dead relatives and friends still lay.

On 12 July the Islamic group Hezbollah had kidnapped two Israeli soldiers and planned to use them as bargaining chips to secure the release of Lebanese and Palestinian prisoners held in Israeli jails. But Israel was not in a bargaining mood. The army responded with shocking force. For 34 days Hezbollah and Israel fought it out, and when it was over more than 1000 Lebanese were dead, tens of thousands more were homeless, and almost one million people had fled in fear and were now refugees, living in parks and school halls, churches and mosques across the country. The Israelis had suffered too – 160 dead, thousands injured – from Hezbollah's cache of smuggled Iranian rockets.

I watched all this from my living room in Sydney with my baby son, Joseph, just one month old, in my arms and my two-year-old daughter, Yasmine, holding up playdough shapes for me to admire from across the room.

I turned the television towards me and muted the sound. I didn't want Yasmine to see the horror on the screen or hear the cries of the people. I didn't want her to see it, but I was glued to the news, to the television, internet, anything.

One year earlier my husband, Matthew, and I had returned to Sydney after living in Beirut for more than four years. The Beirut we came to know was, most of the time, a sophisticated and fun-loving place, determined to recover from its past. Paradoxically, when you thought about its history, those years in Lebanon became some of the happiest of our lives together. Matthew and I had so often sat on the balcony of our apartment in Beirut and reminded each other to savour every glorious moment. Three years after we arrived I fell pregnant and our little girl was born there, and so the story of Beirut became somehow stitched forever into ours.

Now, this. I had walked through many of the towns and villages that were on the news each night, bombed. I knew the streets of southern Beirut that had been flattened into a kind of Ground Zero. I knew how hard the people of Lebanon had struggled to put their country back together after the end of the civil war in the early 1990s. Most of all, this was not the Lebanon I had known. The country was being torn apart again and it was heartbreaking.

PROLOGUE

My Middle Eastern adventure began in February 2001. Matthew and I had been married for only nine months when we moved to Beirut, on little more than a whim. We were both journalists – he worked as a television reporter and producer and I was a writer for newspapers and magazines – and we were drawn to the region by a craving for a good story and a traveller's hunger for a journey that would take us somewhere unexpected.

But I felt a deeper yearning that was hard to explain. Perhaps it was a sense of time passing, of being 30-something and feeling myself lurching towards the brink of a more accountable life. My life to date had been a whirl of travel and strange places – I'd lived in London, Melbourne, Hanoi and Ho Chi Minh City as well as my hometown of Sydney, and I'd travelled almost everywhere in between. In quiet moments I admitted to myself that I feared forgetting how to live courageously.

And week after week as I sat at my desk in Sydney with its view of over-familiar inner-city streets, churning out opinion pieces for *The Australian* newspaper's daily editorial column, that fear gnawed deeper. My thoughts were mechanical, crafted in the abstract, in sterile meeting rooms and under the pressure of deadlines. Did I care whether an *intifada* had begun in Israel and the Palestinian Territories? Did I care about AIDS in Africa and if pharmaceutical companies would provide drugs cheaply to poor countries to treat it? The world was out there and yet from my vantage point I felt disconnected and robotic. I wanted to feel passionate and engaged. A change was overdue, but what?

On a winter night in Sydney seven months before we boarded our plane to Beirut, Matthew returned from an assignment in Syria. He had spent more than a decade making current affairs documentaries at the Australian

Broadcasting Corporation (ABC) and Special Broadcasting Service (SBS) and a lot of that time had been spent travelling – filming with the Falantil resistance in the mountains of East Timor, with the Tamil Tigers in Sri Lanka, the boy soldiers in Sierra Leone. And now to Syria, where the country's leader of 30 years, Hafez al-Assad, had recently died. Matthew's story looked at the challenges his son Bashar faced as successor. When he arrived home a few weeks later with a suitcase bulging with Oriental goodies – a water pipe shaped like a snake and inlaid with silver, carpets and intricate woodwork from the rambling ancient *souk* in Damascus – an idea took hold in both of us: let's move to the Middle East.

We had both travelled the world and competed over who had been to more places (airports didn't count and you had to have been on the ground for more than 24 hours) but apart from Matthew's brief and recent trip to Syria, the Middle East remained unexplored by both of us. The fact that it was a region overflowing with newsworthiness, and therefore a place we envisaged that we could successfully base ourselves as journalists, added greatly to its appeal. But where to set up home? We were looking for a place that would be interesting to live and from where we could travel easily around the region for work.

Cairo, Dubai and Jerusalem were the usual choices of Middle Eastern base for foreign reporters, and for that reason alone we avoided them – we wanted to strike our own path. We considered Damascus – but Syria kept tight surveillance on foreigners in the country, and foreign reporters in particular, and we knew we would have trouble working efficiently. There was Amman, famously boring and without soul, if you believed its detractors. Forget it.

And then Beirut began to wend its way into our consciousness. First it was a travel documentary on television, switched on by chance, that showed off ski fields, great restaurants and swanky boutiques and filled us with curiosity. Then it was a friend who had returned from a holiday to Lebanon enthused about the place, the complicated and fascinating history, the friendliness of the people, Beirut's Mediterranean lifestyle and worldly outlook. Lebanon was at the fulcrum of ancient trading routes and its people looked west just as eagerly as they looked to the east. It seemed that this quality would make Beirut an easy place to live. Post-war reconstruction was well under way, and we loved the fact that we could replace Sydney's ocean-side location. Somehow, that was that: the choice was made.

Nevertheless, Beirut was hardly a traditional launch pad into wedded bliss. Despite the isolated rave reviews, its reputation as a war zone, as a place of Islamic fundamentalism, was overwhelming, and most people screwed up their faces, disbelieving, when we told them where we were headed: 'Will you have to cover your head?' 'Is it even *safe*?'

I could only give vague answers. I had little real idea what sort of world I was stepping into and I couldn't have cared less. I parroted information I had picked up during voracious last-minute reading: 'Beirut is one of the most liberal cities in the Middle East'; 'The civil war was over a decade ago'. And finally, exasperated, when others failed to embrace my excitement over the adventure ahead: 'Look, *I will be fine*.'

So we packed up and got on the plane, as simple as that. We would be filing stories for our old employers back in Sydney and then freelancing for other as yet unknown new ones. We had no idea where we would be living, who our friends would be, what stories we would find or whether we had made the worst decision of our lives. It was an old-fashioned quest for adventure, a journey of faith.

As I sat so far away in Sydney that morning, sifting through a head full of memories of Beirut that clashed with the images on the screen, it occurred to me that I had enjoyed an island of time, a fairytale era of hope that had bloomed briefly in Lebanon between the end of the civil war and this short and bloody summer war of 2006.

My first memories of Beirut are of a dynamic tangle of contradictions: ancient and contemporary, pre and post war, Muslim, Christian, East and West, secular and devout, eye-popping wealth that rubbed against desperate poverty. In the middle of it all, the city drew its energy. Once upon a time, in Beirut, I found an unlikely place to call home.

PART ONE

CHAPTER 1
ARRIVAL

Darkness was falling. As the plane banked and slid towards Beirut I could only imagine what lay below us. The Mediterranean Sea was all around and through the fading dusk light it appeared to me like undulating velvet. The plane dipped and swayed above the Lebanese coastline and the dark hulk of a mountain chain was just visible in the last glow of sunset.

We were descending rapidly now and yet the lights of the city remained unseen, lying somewhere to the southeast. The aeroplane had sunk so low it seemed to skim the surface of the water and then, without warning, Beirut sprawled beneath us so suddenly it made me catch my breath.

From the window I could make out a Palestinian refugee slum abutting a dense urban sprawl that stretched to the very edge of sheer stone cliffs. Swimming pools studded coastal rock ledges like strange jewels. Cars and people were moving on a criss-cross of neon-lit streets that twisted between high-rise apartment blocks. From the air, this ravaged city looked chaotic and shabby – but alive.

A crush of people waited in the arrivals hall and I felt

a moment of doubt as Matthew and I pushed through the mob of unfamiliar faces. My palm sweated slightly against the plastic handle of my suitcase. Airports have always been my least favourite part of the ritual of travel. They are often both the (uncertain) first and the (bittersweet) last taste of a new place, yet rarely an authentic one. They frequently attract the desperate and the insincere, and I had long ago decided to stop feeling resentful when I was overcharged by airport taxi drivers.

Our taxi from Beirut International Airport (half rebuilt, unexpectedly gleaming and efficient) was a rattletrap Mercedes-Benz from the early 1980s – a model, I soon discovered, as distinctive to Beirut as yellow cabs to New York. The driver was a tanned, wiry fellow with a cigarette jammed between his teeth. He loaded our many bags into the boot and tied down the lid with a piece of string, unfazed by the trembling pile he had created, and manoeuvred the overflow into the passenger seat. Matthew and I climbed into the back, glad to have some protection from Beirut's cold winter night. I wrapped my arms around me, drummed my feet on the floor of the cab and tried to keep warm.

A figure hurried towards us from the darkness, opened the car door and flung himself into the driver's lap. The two men exchanged greetings and we took off, with the driver's side door held open and the hitchhiker's legs suspended in the night air by the force of acceleration. I stayed silent, looked over at Matthew and smiled, thrilled by the recklessness of it. When I remember the moment now it seems to somehow mark the beginning of our adventure.

The taxi left the airport via a loop of road that passed the site of the former US Marine Barracks – destroyed by a suicide truck bomber in 1983, during Lebanon's civil war when the place was a chaos of every kind of unspeakable violence. Ahead of us was a security checkpoint manned by a lone soldier. He signalled for us to stop by waving his gun in the beam of the headlights and then leaned into the car, looked Matthew and me up and down, and spoke quickly in Arabic. The driver nodded grimly and pulled the car to the dark side of the road. The hitchhiker got out and gave a wave goodbye as he dissolved into the night.

But I was in no mood for farewells. Everything I'd ever read about Beirut, or imagined, was concentrated in that moment. The word 'kidnap' hovered darkly at the edges of my mind. The driver got out and walked around to the back of the car and I must have looked alarmed, because he said 'No problem!' and smiled brightly. I was not placated. I'd read about this: how the kidnappers said, 'Don't worry, just come with us for five minutes', and then you were left chained in a basement for endless, terrifying years.

'What the hell is happening?' I asked Matthew, suspicion rising.

'I don't know. It's fine.' He was tense, unconvincing.

We were stuck in that moment I'd played over and over in my head: if I was in a dangerous situation would I think fast enough to save my life? Should we cut and run? Should we wait it out?

And then the driver returned carrying a magnetic plastic sign with the word 'Taxi' written in red. He slapped it on the roof of the car, raised his eyebrows sheepishly. The engine kicked back into life, a cassette tape of Fairouz – Lebanon's most famous, most adored diva – snapped into the deck. '*Hawa* Beirut,' she sang in that haunting, yearning way she was so famous for. 'O love of Beirut, O love of days. They will come back, Beirut, the days will come back.' Several strings of prayer beads were looped around the rear-vision mirror and they swung wildly as we picked up speed.

We were heading for the Mayflower Hotel in the heart of the Hamra district – a shopping and commercial area in the mainly Muslim west of the city that had taken over as a sort of de facto city centre when fighting claimed Beirut's heart. The hotel turned out to be a family-run place with a British gentlemen's club feel – not exactly what I had expected for my first night in the Middle East. There was even an English-style pub, the Duke of Wellington, with framed prints of hunting scenes and English wildflowers on the walls. Irish peacekeepers from the United Nations – dispatched to monitor tensions between Israel and Hezbollah along Lebanon's southern border – were on R&R and sat drinking dark beer on claret-coloured chesterfield sofas set around an open fire.

I woke the next morning to a room decked out in bottle green and chintz and panelled wood. Hungry for a sense of place, I slid open the glass doors to the balcony and breathed in the smells of Beirut: diesel fumes, low tide, roasted meat. Car horns and the crash of jackhammers at a nearby construction site ricocheted through narrow, tattered streets. A group of taxi drivers loitered on the corner and smoked cigarettes, read the newspaper. Shop owners gathered intermittently in groups to chat and sip coffee together on the footpath, and hurried back inside when a customer appeared.

The uncertainty of the night before was fading and in its place a feeling of excitement welled. I felt I had come too far to turn back now and the finality of it made me bolder. I stood in the brisk morning air, mentally loosening the knots that tied me to my Sydney life, when the ethereal wail of the call to prayer floated out from a mosque somewhere in the distance. I closed my eyes, and I was smiling.

As I sat at the breakfast table later on that first morning, feasting on crescents of fresh grapefruit, croissants, *fuul* (a stew of kidney-shaped beans, olive oil and lemon juice) and strong black coffee, I was caught off guard by the civility of the place. It seemed at odds with Beirut's reputation for brutality and madness, and it occurred to me, as I bit into my *pain au chocolat*, that Lebanon's rich history had been obscured in the minds of most outsiders by the legacy of its civil war.

It would require another book to properly explain that war, which raged from 1975 until 1991 and then continued to simmer for another two years. And it would probably take another lifetime to find two Lebanese with the same view on the subject. But the basics: Lebanon was a French colony from the break-up of the Ottoman Empire until 1944. The country's Christians had been favoured by the French and after Independence they retained most of the political and economic power. The Muslims were restive and there were sporadic clashes. In 1958, civil war brewed but was quickly put down with American intervention.

By 1975 things were more complicated. Lebanon's multifaceted population of 18 different religious sects, from Jews to Catholic and Orthodox Christians, Sunni and Shi'ite Muslims and Druze (an ancient offshoot of Islam that believes in reincarnation), packed into a population of less than four million, offered a glut of differing grievances that were ripe for manipulation by outside forces.

Most significantly, since 1948, when Israel was created, Lebanon became stuck in the middle of the battle between Palestinians and Israelis. Three waves of Palestinian refugees – 1948, 1967, 1973 – arrived in Lebanon, creating internal pressure on infrastructure and politics. Then the Palestinian Liberation Organisation (PLO) relocated to Beirut, where it waged its war against Israel from across Lebanon's southern border. While in Lebanon, the PLO and its leader, Yasser Arafat, sided with Lebanon's coalition of leftist Muslim militias against the right-wing Christian militias. When Palestinians were blamed for attacking a Maronite Catholic church, the Phalange, a powerful Christian political party and militia founded by the Gemayel family, retaliated by attacking a busload of Palestinian civilians. In April 1975, full-scale civil war ensued.

Then things got even more complicated. Regional and international powers were attracted by the anarchy and the opportunity it offered to use Lebanon as a theatre in which to pursue their own political agendas in the Middle East. Over the course of the war, Israel and the Palestinians, Syria, Libya, Egypt, Iran, Iraq, Saudi Arabia, the US, France and Russia all found ways to use Lebanon as a plaything to pursue their interests. There were so many militias with so many different agendas, and there was always foreign money for weapons, and there was always a new reason to hate. For 17 years the war raged on and any idea of a Lebanese state ceased to exist. The militias and the warlords and their revolving club of foreign benefactors controlled the country. By the end of the war the Christian militias fought Christians, and Muslims fought Muslims, in ever-changing combinations.

In 1991 an Arab-brokered peace accord was signed and, with 150,000 Lebanese dead, the country's long war was declared over.

Three important things had happened. Firstly, Lebanon was politically occupied by Syria, which controlled Lebanese politics from behind the scenes, and militarily occupied by Israel, which controlled a swathe of land in the south of the country. The second important thing to come out of the war was the creation of the Shi'ite group Hezbollah as a potent political and military force. And thirdly, Lebanon's Christians were forced to cede some of their political power.

Lebanese politics continue to be defined by sectarianism:

the president is always a Maronite Christian – not a Catholic, not a Greek Orthodox or any other kind of Christian, but only a member of Lebanon's indigenous Maronite order; the prime minister is always a Sunni Muslim; and the parliamentary speaker is always a Shi'ite. But there was never any formal reconciliation. It was agreed that a general amnesty would protect Lebanon's mafia politicians and militia warlords from punishment, and 17 years of competing agendas and bitter memories were packed away and covered up (although never *really* forgotten), and the Lebanese just got on with it in their own dysfunctional way. Somehow, that thing called Lebanese culture, the Lebanese spirit, continued to survive. Maybe it was just pragmatism, maybe it was exhaustion with war, maybe it was the great love the Lebanese had for their destroyed country that united them? It was impossible to tell.

But life started again, slowly at first – infrastructure was in chaos, pollution was jaw-dropping, entire blocks of the city were uninhabitable, packs of wild dogs roamed the old centre of town, abandoned boulevards were choked with trees and the remnants of snipers' nests – and the Lebanese more or less got back to what they did best: being the most liberal and most democratic Arab state in the Middle East.

Parliamentary elections were held for the first time in 20 years. A year later Rafiq Hariri was appointed as Lebanon's new prime minister and a new era had begun. Hariri was a career businessman rather than a career politician, and one of the world's richest men. He brought with him a plan to lure international investors and rebuild his destroyed homeland.

This was the Lebanon that Matthew and I stepped into that February. War had been over for almost exactly a decade and Hariri's reconstruction plan was in full swing. But the fighting had gone on for so long that for those who knew the country only from news reports, Lebanon had become defined by the conflict that tore it apart. What remained was an image of a shattered and lawless place.

To an earlier generation Beirut was just about the hippest city on the Mediterranean; a favourite getaway for Brigitte Bardot and Marlon Brando and their hangers-on, who loved it for its elegant, freewheeling lifestyle and endless summer. That first day in Beirut, I stopped at the hotel reception desk to flip through a wooden box of old postcards, many left over from the 1960s and early 1970s. That past was now in front of me, rendered in sentimental Technicolor images of women in bikinis waving from the bow of speedboats, with *Bienvenue au Liban* written in swirling embossed gold script. There were pictures of gracious cedar trees, snowfields and splendid Roman ruins. Streets of fine Ottoman buildings and the jet set laying bets at a glittering casino. These were not the usual Middle Eastern stereotypes – no camels, no sandy deserts, no dark *souks* with pyramid-shaped piles of brightly coloured spices. This was the Lebanon Gibran Khalil Gibran wrote of so longingly. It was the Lebanon of milk and honey. It was the Paris of the Middle East.

But did it exist only on old postcards? I was keen to see for myself what remained of this other Lebanon and to find out if that same spirit was fuelling the country's revival. Matthew and I had given ourselves two magical weeks to settle in – find a place to live, come to grips with Beirut – and in those early days we did little else but walk. The usual routine was to leave shortly after breakfast with vague landmarks in mind, but our real goal was to get a feel for the city.

Central Beirut covered a small area and was stuffed into a nose-shaped promontory fringed by the Corniche, a long promenade that hugged the Mediterranean coast. It was easy to walk from the clash and din of Hamra through the reconstructed city centre (just starting to live again when we arrived) and on over the old frontline to east Beirut, which was now mostly Christian, with pockets of rich and poor living side by side. From these points the city continued to sprawl: south to the Dahiyeh, a mash of working-class, mostly Shi'ite suburbs dominated by supporters of Hezbollah; and north and east into the Christian areas, where Beirut crept along the base of mountains that rose sharply from narrow beach-fringed flatlands. Beach clubs dotted almost the entire length of Lebanon's coast, north to south, and different places hosted music festivals throughout the year. If you continued inland, up into the mountains, you hit the ski fields, modelled on European resorts, with plenty of bars and restaurants for a vibrant *après-ski* life.

But even within Beirut's apparently Christian or Muslim halves I was constantly tripping over invisible scars from the war that marked out territory won or lost. The best way to identify those fault lines was by the political posters, which would shift depending on the affiliations of the residents and with them the entire tone and feel of the street. I learned to identify the green, red and white posters of Amal, a Shi'ite party and political competitor of Hezbollah, which had a yellow flag decorated with a green silhouette of a fist clutching a Kalashnikov rifle and rising from the words 'Party of God'. I came to tell the difference between the political and religious leaders associated with each group: Hezbollah's Sayyad Hassan Nasrallah and Amal's Musa Sadr. I could match the image of Lebanon's assassinated wartime president Bashir Gemayel – in his retro get-up of aviator sunglasses and short-sleeved Lee Cooper shirt – with the Phalange Maronite Christian militia.

Parts of Beirut seemed suspended in time and, after the

gloss of Sydney, the fading scars of war felt overwhelming. I walked across Damascus Road, on the old frontline, past abandoned buildings with gaping holes hollowing their sides. Sprays of bullet marks scored old walls; trees grew from the ruined balconies of deserted apartment blocks; sandbags snipers once used to steady their weapons were still in place on the derelict floors above. Families made homes in buildings with entire walls sheared off; the minutiae of their lives visible as I went by.

There were other hardships: a butcher's shop, empty of meat, with a pair of old shoes displayed incongruously in the window next to a sign that said 'For Sale'. An old man, rumpled, earnest, weaving through a knot of city traffic, holding up gardenias threaded along a loop of string to the windows of expensive cars, and being impatiently ignored then waved away.

Every landmark was haunted, heavy with memory, and it didn't take much to imagine a gunfight or a kidnap around each new corner. Matthew and I would draw each other close to brace against imagined horrors, and wonder how Beirutis lived with the weight of recollection; the knowing.

But among it all life continued and after a while a frayed beauty started to emerge. I began to see the city with romantic eyes: corner shops unchanged since the 1970s, with blinking neon signs in old-fashioned fonts, their crinkle-faced owners tucked into dusty, darkened corners puffing on French cigarettes. Old men, friends forever, hunched smiling over a backgammon set. Amid the drabness of forgotten buildings were flashes of colour that hinted at rebirth. A hairdressing salon had opened in the ground floor of one of Beirut's most famous ruins – a dramatic corner block left exactly as it must have been the day the war ended; hip bars peeked from behind broken balustrades. Women teetered on expensive heels, expertly negotiating unstable ground. I even saw a McDonald's restaurant with a valet parking service.

The result was a head-spin of contradictions – pre-war, post-war, Christian, Muslim, rich, poor, East, West. 'You can have any reality you want in this place,' Matthew said as we walked.

The old city centre – the frontline where most of the fighting had taken place – had been rebuilt and, to me, it was a revelation: a confection of elegant Ottoman and French colonial buildings, painstakingly reconstructed so that their custard-coloured stone facades glowed above newly cobbled streets. When we arrived the place was still more or less empty, like a beautiful and abandoned Hollywood set. Nearby, there was a nightclub, built underground in the shape of a coffin, and on the site of a war era massacre. In the early hours of the morning the roof lifted off, opening the dance floor to the sky, and the place was so avant-garde it had earned a spot on a list of the world's Top Ten Clubs.

I worked out from reading the local English language newspaper, *The Daily Star*, over my morning coffee at the hotel each day that a lot of Beirutis raged about the picture-perfect image of Beirut, which mocked the heartbreak of what had gone before. It was true that the colonnaded streets and steadily growing numbers of chic shops and expensive cafés bore little resemblance to the pre-war neighbourhood that had welcomed everyone, rich or poor, and had housed the hard-working heart of the city.

When you walked around you could still see fenced-off ruins marking out past civilisations that had occupied Beirut. When the rubble of war was scraped away, ruins from the Bronze Age, Canaanites, Phoenicians, Egyptians, Greeks, Romans, Byzantines, Arabs, Ottoman Turks, Crusaders and French colonialists were found. I took heart from this archeological treasure trove. To me, it was a reminder that Beirut had remade itself many, many times before.

In the evenings Matthew and I would leave our hotel and walk down Rue Hamra looking for Beirut's latest version. We would stop at Modca, an old café on a corner with tables on the footpath. Modca was one of the most famous cafés in Hamra, a favourite hangout for students and professors from the university nearby. It wasn't hard to imagine it in its heyday when everyone said Rue Hamra was 'the Champs-Elysées of the Middle East' (the Lebanese couldn't resist endless comparisons between Beirut and Paris), packed with boutiques and promenading families. Rue Hamra had lost much of its prestige – it was chaotic but no longer chic – but Modca was the sort of place that inspired loyalty. It was always full of noise and cigarette smoke and people reading newspapers and writing notes; regulars who sat at the same table, ordered the same thing. And even though we had only been going there for a few days we liked to think that Modca had also become 'our' place. There weren't that many foreigners in Beirut, even travellers were relatively rare, and so the waiters quickly came to know our faces and we'd be welcomed with that effusive Lebanese hospitality, a unique combination of deference and pride and an odd knack for mixing two or three languages in the one sentence: '*Ahlan, ahlan wa s'ahlan monsieur, madam.* Please take a seat.'

We'd find a table and order the local beer, Almaza, from these attentive trilingual waiters dressed in black with long white aprons, French bistro style. Our beers would be accompanied by sliced carrots, salted and dipped in lemon juice, and plates of yellow beans, peanuts and pumpkin seeds. We'd practise eating the pumpkin seeds the way the Lebanese did it – split delicately between the teeth and extracted invisibly inside the mouth with the tongue so that the shell could be removed politely. I never mastered it and instead chewed on the lot, shell and all, and pretended I was enjoying the tough fibrous crust with its coating of baked-on salt.

As the night wore on and we tired of Modca, we would wander further and slip behind a little opening cut into a corrugated-iron roller door and inside a drab arcade to Chez André, an impossibly tiny bar that everyone said was one of very few places to continue trading right through the war. There were always posters for an upcoming art exhibition or musical recital or film festival, and the latest important sporting match, whatever it was, was always on the television. The crowd was a mish-mash of local bohemians and stray visitors, returned Lebanese expats. Chez André sold Heineken on tap and baguettes filled with spicy Armenian sausage – *basterma* and *sojuk* – that everyone also said made your sweat stink. But it was fabulous for soaking up all the alcohol and for munching between games of darts, and it went perfectly with the warm, oozing slices of *haloumi* cheese that were endlessly coming off the grill.

One night as we were walking the backstreets on our way home to the hotel, hankering guiltily after another drink (we were already drunk), we spotted an uninspiring little place called American Dream. The name intrigued me. Incongruous, I thought through my beer haze as we walked up a flight of stairs from the street and inside.

The bar looked unchanged since before the war – an abstract mural hung on one wall and the rest of the place was decorated with brown carpet and metal stools with brown vinyl padded seats and an electric guitar signed by some once-famous Lebanese band. There was a sign outside advertising 'Pub Drink and Dine' but the back of the bar, which must once have been a buzzing late-night diner, was empty.

We didn't care about the lack of food, style or fellow patrons. It was well after midnight. We were drunk – on beer, on the thrill of this strange new city – and we weren't ready to give the night away. We had come for the whisky.

There were two men behind the bar, probably in their fifties, and they looked surprised to see us. I was beginning to realise that my long dark hair, in certain lights, in certain outfits, allowed me to almost pass as a local. 'You are half Lebanese?' people would sometimes ask me. But when I was with Matthew we could never be anonymous. His freckled skin, blue eyes and head of wild light-brown curls made him stand out as an *ajnabi*, a foreigner. And this was not a bad thing. Modca had taught us that the Lebanese were often effusive in their hospitality, and it was the same tonight. Both men rose to welcome us as we walked in and gestured towards two bar stools. Despite the lack of customers the bar was well stocked. Matthew spotted his favourite whisky and we ordered one each. The huge serves reached the rim of the tumbler.

Henri, who owned the place, didn't take long to introduce himself. He opened a packet of cigarettes and pushed them across the bar towards us. 'Please, take one,' he encouraged, and we did, out of politeness and because it was late and we were drunk and, anyway, everyone smoked in Beirut. As we sipped our drinks and let the smoke from the cigarettes curl into the dark corners of the bar, we began to talk, filling Henri in on who we were, where we were staying, our plans (to hunt down story leads, network and travel and interview and turn it all into films and articles for our audience back home and elsewhere). And slowly our cigarettes burnt to the stub and the level of our whisky began to sink until we were swishing the shells of melting ice around the bottom of our glasses.

'On the house!' Henri called out, and poured another shot with a flourish. He pulled the bottle high and twisted it just as the whisky was about to overflow. Frank Sinatra was on the stereo singing 'New York, New York'. Henri pulled out a plastic bag full of apples, his private stash, and put two or three in front of us on a plate with a knife. 'From the apple tree in my garden in Bikfaya,' he said, and I recognised the name of the town from my reading – a Christian village famous for its fruit trees and hot springs. But, like almost everywhere in Lebanon, it was also famous for its politics. Bikfaya is the hometown of the Gemayel family, founders of the Phalange and source of two Lebanese presidents.

I picked up one of the apples and began to slice through the skin, peeling it away in a long coil. 'So what was this place like before the war?' I asked Henri. The bar seemed so empty and forgotten I was looking to make sense of why anyone would have opened it in the first place.

'I bought it in 1962,' Henri said and lit another cigarette. 'It was pumping then. But you know, the big years were 1967 until 1975.' He let out a long whistle and widened his eyes, rubbed his fingers together in an expression that was supposed to suggest money for nothing. 'But even during the war, business was good.'

I remembered what a Lebanese friend had told me back in Sydney: how he would come to Beirut for holidays with his family during the war, when he was about 20. Madness, but people did it. How his sisters would go shopping during the day, and duck behind metal screens lined up along the street when they heard the whistle of an incoming mortar or the boom of a bomb nearby. Then, when it was over, they'd go right back to shopping. At night, my friend would head to Hamra and go to the bars and clubs. At curfew time the bar manager would yell out that you had to either leave now or stay until dawn. My friend would always stay, locked down in one of Hamra's many bars, and he told me how the pounding of the music used to drown out the sound of the bombs.

I told Henri the story and he nodded, yes, it was true. 'That is how we lived!' he said. He told me about a supermarket that tried to always ship in crates of caviar and champagne to go with the essentials: bread, milk, cigarettes. During the tough days everyone needed the essentials, and when the bombing relented everyone wanted the luxuries. Henri's face was all at once a mixture of nostalgia and sadness for what the war had cost everyone.

'What are you going to do?' I asked him gently. My eyes scanned the empty room and he caught my meaning: surely he couldn't go on like this.

'When you go outside, look around you,' he said. He explained that the entire block had been razed, save for a group of five or six buildings, including the one where we were now sitting, that were joined together terrace-style and made up the corner of the block. 'Whoever wants to develop this land needs my building,' he said. 'I am waiting for the developers to give me an offer.'

'How much do you think they are worth?' I asked, smiling at evidence of this wily business savvy that the Lebanese were so famous for. He threw out a few figures, scandalous amounts, and certainly enough to make coming to work in an empty bar night after night well worth his time.

'And then it's back to Bikfaya to retire in the mountains

and grow apples,' I said, laughing, as I bit into the crisp flesh of the fruit.

Henri ignored my joke. 'When my mother died,' he said, 'I saw her birth certificate and found out for the first time that she was born in America.'

He paused to let the importance of the detail sink in: if his mother was born in the US it meant Henri was eligible for an American passport. In a country so racked by uncertainty, so vilified that visas to Western countries could take weeks to be issued and were never guaranteed, access to a second passport offered a precious means of escape. It could be as simple as smoothing the way to get visas for a holiday in the West during summer. But the thing that no one wanted to admit, because the thought of it was too painful to contemplate out loud, was that a foreign passport could parachute a family out of conflict if things blew up again.

Henri continued: 'I immediately applied for American citizenship.' He took a drag of his cigarette and shrugged. Of course he applied. It would have been madness not to. 'I went there a couple of times,' he said, and feigned nonchalance. 'If I am able to sell my land for a good price then I will have enough money to go over there and live for a while and apply for citizenship for my son.'

The name of Henri's bar began to resonate with new meaning. His American dream wasn't just a cheap marketing trick, an excuse for Frank Sinatra on the stereo. It hinted at the uncertainty that lingered inside every Lebanese: what would happen if war came back again?

Well after midnight Matthew and I said goodnight to Henri. We rugged up against the cold and walked slowly back to the hotel, arm in arm. In the half-light – winter dark lit by street lamps and glowing shop windows and the glimmer that reached us from high-up apartments – we wound our way through Hamra's backstreets. That night, Beirut in the early hours seemed almost tranquil. Lebanon had entered a new era, I decided, and I felt privileged and excited to be experiencing these days of peace.

CHAPTER 2
SETTLING

Two weeks passed like this; walking and drinking. As our world slowly expanded, hotel life began to grate. It was time to search for a new home. I found an advertisement in the newspaper and when I called, Mrs Medawar answered the phone. 'Meet me at Le Vendome hotel,' she said. Matthew and I found her lounging on an expensively upholstered chaise longue in the lobby. She bustled us into her tiny jalopy; the front passenger seat was missing and empty packets of French cigarettes and empty bottles of Evian mineral water were scattered about. We zoomed to a place her sister owned in Achrafieh, in the mostly Christian east of Beirut. The apartment was on one of the upper floors of the building and had sweeping views over a disused rail yard and out across the city's jumbled, jagged skyline. 'There's a room for the maid,' she announced and opened a door beside the kitchen to reveal a space only a little bigger than a cupboard. I thought she was joking, but she wasn't.

The apartment was bright and airy and, in spite of the crazy built-up outlook, the view was strangely spectacular. It felt exhilarating to be so high, with Beirut laid out in front of me. 'You should see it at night,' Mrs Medawar said, sensing my enthusiasm. 'The lights are on all over the city. It's beautiful,' and she swept her arms wide, theatrical.

She spoke to her sister in French – dismissing Arabic as 'for the servants' when I asked why. It was a common view among many of the Christian upper class, who liked to claim their heritage could be traced to the ancient Phoenicians rather than the Arabs. This position was underlined by rejecting the Arabic language. The two women settled on a price: US$1000 per month. I tried to haggle. It was customary, expected, and even though I privately thought it wasn't a bad price (the apartment was furnished and included water and satellite television) there was no doubt a local could have got it cheaper.

I began my charade: long slow exhale, eyebrows set in a sceptical expression, mock outrage at the price. I paused for effect, then began to systematically point out the apartment's flaws – the second bedroom was rather small, the lift was tiny and looked as if it would break down at any minute, the building had no concierge and no parking.

Mrs Medawar listened patiently, knitting her brow in a show of concern. And then, far more practised than I was in the art of bargaining, she politely commenced her rebuff. 'Catherine,' she said, smiling, assured, 'I like you. You are nice. You are young. You are clean.' She paused to think and then her face brightened as she hit upon a final compliment designed to soften me further: 'You are Australian!' The pause was melodramatic and she waited several beats before she delivered her verdict. 'But my best price is *mille dollars par mois*.'

We thanked her and decided to keep looking – more out of pride than any genuine dissatisfaction with the apartment. Surely she could have saved our dignity with a modest discount?

We found a place with beautiful views of the Mediterranean Sea, but the flat had been destroyed by over-eager decoration: the ever-popular faux Louis XIV furniture (which wags described as Louis de Lebanon) and three-centimetre-thick bright green shag-pile carpet. There was a place in the mountains, prized for its wild valley view and cool summer climate. But it was now February, the middle of winter, and the weather had reached almost blizzard conditions. Unbearable! Inside, it was decked out like a North American hunting lodge – all bottle green leather and dark wood and a collection of deer antlers mounted on the walls.

In the end we rented a place on America Street, surrounded by reminders that during the 1930s, when Lebanon was governed by French colonialists, the area had been the heart of the embassy district. America Street – or Rue d'Amerique, as it said next to the Arabic on the street sign – intersected with Rue de Rome and Rue de Mexique. But the embassies had long-since moved on.

Our new apartment was in a small custard-coloured Art Deco block, built during the French Mandate. On each side were Lebanese houses, more than 100 years old and built during the time the Ottoman Empire had extended throughout the Middle East. They had red tiled roofs and peaked arched windows and hugged our block like antique bookends.

The apartment was accessed via a gate covered with creeping vines and along a stone pathway, past two small statues of cherubs playing harps. A wide staircase with a wrought-iron balustrade corkscrewed up through the centre of the building and our apartment was on the first floor. The rooms were large and airy, painted white, with brass chandeliers suspended on long chains from high ceilings and terrazzo tiles on the floor. Each window had wooden shutters, painted the colour of butterscotch, and there were two little curved balconies that hung above the street. From the roof terrace we even had glimpses of the sea.

Amir, our landlord, had revived the gardens belonging to the two old Lebanese homes and they fringed our block on two sides. There was a row of ageing fig trees, and an avocado tree (that bore fruit for the first time that year) nestled among a riot of hibiscus, frangipani, bougainvillea, magnolia and acacia. Two pet tortoises and an army of cats roamed freely. The gardens each had decorative stone fountains and one was filled with carp: flashes of white and orange in a soup of green slime. A jasmine vine twisted around the railings on one of the balconies.

The area, Clemenceau, was in Beirut's mainly Muslim western half, a short walk from the buzz of the Hamra district's main street, but refreshingly – and unusually for Beirut – free of the weight of one religion or nationality. It was a secular pocket, with Shi'ite, Sunni, Druze, Christian, Armenian, Syrian all crowded close. Clemenceau was still considered well-to-do, but there were small indignities now: most of the grand mansions had gone, and in our street alone there were seven vacant lots, overtaken by squatters and cheap car parks, waiting for the developers to move in.

There was a time when Beirut had been full of colonial-era apartment buildings and traditional old red-tiled villas set in large tropical gardens. But in the 1960s a fever of development took hold. Many old villas were demolished to make way for cheap, shoddily built apartment blocks. During the war the damage was consolidated: more of the old places fell into disrepair, and when the fighting ended the cost of fixing them was prohibitive. For reasons I never understood, the value of land in Beirut was high. The vacant lots in our street were said to be worth US$2 million each. In the face of such compelling economics, the graceful, crumbling old villas didn't stand a chance.

This made the saving of our apartment and the adjoining villas and their grounds all the more precious. One afternoon, a few days after we moved in, I joined Amir for a tour of the place. We were both in our early thirties and yet Amir seemed to come from another era. He had a fragile, elegant beauty about him and an aristocratic air that seemed too refined for the present, so I wasn't surprised when he told me that as well as his love for the garden he was passionate about saving Beirut's old homes. He had wrangled with his father for the money to restore the family's old places, full of memories, where he had spent chunks of a war childhood and adolescence, back and forth between Beirut and refuge in London and Canada. He had promised to oversee the work, and to make sure the apartments and villas were rented so they paid their way.

The restoration job was enormous. There was damage from a Syrian mortar that had exploded in the back of one of the old homes during the civil war, plus 100 years of rising damp, neglect, age. Amir had scoured the city to find original light fittings, door frames, the red and green glass that was typically fitted into the peaked arched windows and gave the old villas a cathedral dignity. He checked old photographs to match the paint, lifted mouldy carpet and hired experts to scrape and buff the old tiles back to their original gleam. Bringing the villas and apartments back to life took months, even though they were better off than most because they had been rented continuously throughout the war. Amir and his family were very proud of that.

As we wandered Amir picked at stray leaves and at the crunch of dead flowers; cleaning, preening, protective of what he had saved.

'What kind of people lived here during the war?' I asked him.

'A French journalist used to live on the top floor,' Amir told me. 'He had a big dog that used to scratch at the doors and even now you can see the marks from its claws. He kept the dog to protect him from being kidnapped.'

I thought that was a rather strange welcome to offer a new tenant, a journalist to boot. 'Who did he work for?'

'I can't remember,' Amir said. 'But one day the journalist came home and found that the dog was dead. It had been poisoned.'

'By who?'

'He guessed by whoever was doing the kidnapping. And so he started to worry that maybe he was being watched.'

'You mean he thought he was a target? So what did he do?'

'Well, he bought a rope and tied it to the back balcony with the idea that if anyone came for him he could escape out the back of the flat.'

'Wow,' I said, very interested now. 'So did they? Did anyone ever come for him?'

'No. But they took a guy from the old house, the Irish one, the teacher, what was his name?'

'You mean Brian Keenan?'

'Yes, Brian Keenan.'

Brian Keenan had arrived in Beirut in 1985 to teach English at the American University of Beirut. He was one of the best-known hostages, imprisoned for years in a series of dungeons and concealed rooms with the journalist John McCarthy. A profound friendship grew between the working-class Irishman and the upper-class Englishman that sustained them through the beatings and the darkness. I had read *An Evil Cradling*, the book Keenan wrote about his experience, and I remembered his description of the old house and how he had walked through its garden in the moments before his kidnap, soaking it in, calmed, at peace. Oblivious of what was to come.

> I left the villa, walking through the long garden that fronted it and separated it from the street. I stopped as I always did to look at three or four carp which swam in the fishpond with its fountain, which is so much a part of a typical [Oriental] villa . . . I had come to understand the importance of the garden in Arab culture as a source of peace, of rest, a place for meditation, a kind of sanctuary, and this garden had become the same for me.

I looked around the garden, the lusciousness of it, a real oasis of peace and beauty in a city that had been stripped from time to time of both, and it was almost impossible to imagine that something so horrific had happened here. For weeks afterwards, every time I left my apartment I thought, this nondescript little patch of road is where he was taken. Yet it was forgotten, submerged beneath time passed, beneath the burden of so many other, larger, tragedies. I wondered how Keenan would feel if he returned now. Perhaps it would be comforting to see life being lived, people on the street, smiles on their faces.

For Rue d'Amerique was a busy street, often crammed with traffic, horns blaring. The footpaths were full of people walking back and forth to the maternity hospital up the road, with armfuls of flowers, of pink and blue balloons; or to the Armenian university around the corner. All of Lebanon went past my window: well-dressed women in tight clothes and high heels; families of Druze in their traditional costume – baggy gathered pants, cummerbund and white cap for the men, and a long, flowing black coat topped with a snowy white, sheer linen veil for the women; Muslim women in *hejab* – some in coats that were dowdy and black, others dressed in stylish ice-cream tones with matching skirt and scarf; Syrian workers from the building site down the road.

A parade of vendors passed calling out for business. One sold mops, brooms and brushes; another pushed a cart that held a giant pot of boiling water in which he cooked up fresh corn-on-the-cob; another regular sold *kaake* – loops of bread covered in sesame seeds – from an elaborate wooden frame balanced on the handlebars of his bicycle. My favourite was the coffee seller who wore an oversized, embossed silver pot in a harness on his back. The coffee was poured through a piece of plastic tubing into tiny ceramic cups that he clinked together to attract customers.

The street was home to an eccentric cast of residents, of which we had unwittingly become a part. Amir's brother, quiet and scholarly, lived below and spent hours every day practising complicated concertos on the piano. Affaf, Amir's childhood nanny, with her too-thick glasses and squinty expression, still cared for the two brothers, and from early morning the wonderful smell of her cooking started creeping under the door and spiralling up the stairwell until I couldn't help myself but knock at her apartment door to beg for left-overs and cooking lessons. When the village farmers passed – in Beirut for the day selling cans of freshly pressed olive oil from their mountain farms, or vats of homemade *labneh*, a kind of yoghurt, or slabs of salty *haloumi* cheese – Amir or Affaf would knock on my door and encourage me to buy. 'Very good!' Affaf would say in her broken English, and the salesman would pour a few centimetres of the olive oil into a glass and urge: 'Drink! Drink! It's like wine.'

A few doors away lived Susan, an English expatriate who came to Lebanon just before the war and stayed and stayed, and now lived alone with a gang of pet cats and a jaw-dropping stash of years of collected treasures kept in piles against the walls, and taught yoga for a living. As the weather got warmer she would teach us – Amir, Matthew, Dina (a photographer who rented the villa next door) and myself – in the garden near the fishpond. I would know when Susan had arrived because I'd hear her calling 'Yoga time!' Her high-pitched and very English accent floated to me across the lawn and through the courtyard and into my bedroom. I'd lie on the grass with the others and try to tie myself into knots, while Amir's cats looked on, and above us crimson bougainvillea clashed against bright blue sky.

There was Ahmad, the son of a well-known Shi'ite politician, who never strayed too far away from politics – although he fought it enthusiastically, and from time to time I actually believed that he was genuine when he said he avoided political life. But it was in his blood and he hovered on the sidelines, helping out at his father's electoral campaigns, liaising with important foreign embassies, lobbying passionately for his country and its future. He spent the rest of his time designing and opening little restaurants and bars that could have been in New York or Paris or London, and throwing fabulous parties for crowds of friends and acquaintances in the apartment he had transformed from a blackened shell into a showcase of modern design. At Ahmad's parties everyone danced and stayed too late. They were all about cocktails on the terrace, an almost endless buffet, lounging on the banquettes smoking cigarettes, political gossip and influential guests who kept their bodyguards stationed at the entrance.

We had other political neighbours too: Walid Jumblatt, warlord-turned-politician and leader of the Druze, had a beautiful mansion up the road. A lazy labrador was always lying in the driveway.

In the empty lot on the corner lived an extended family of Syrians – in Lebanon to provide cheap labour at building sites. My Syrian neighbours had landscaped their vacant lot and turned it into an impressive compound. I enjoyed watching their progress from the kitchen window. In one corner was a collection of corrugated-iron shacks that were used for shelter. Another corner had been planted with vegetables in neat rows. And the remaining land was used as a football field by scruffy kids.

The car park on the empty lot directly opposite my apartment was run by Abu Khalil. The going rate all around the city was 1500 Lebanese lira (LL) for a space, about one American dollar. Abu Khalil lived in a basic one-room dwelling fashioned out of an old shipping container tucked into a corner of the car park. The roof was reinforced with plastic sheeting and lengths of chipboard that had warped in the wet, all held in place with broken lumps of breeze block and old tyres. He had a simple existence and yet there was an elegance to it. He often set up chairs and a small table in the shade between the cars, and invited friends for tea, which he poured with great flair from a silver teapot. On summer evenings he heaved a banana lounge onto the roof of his home and lay back, smoking cigarettes, watching the darkening sky.

I loved how the Lebanese lived so much of their lives in public. It was a world away from my Sydney life, where I didn't even know all the residents of my small apartment block. My balcony in Beirut offered almost no privacy, but a spectacular view of the comings and goings below us. In return, I felt quickly drawn into the hum of the street and it soothed my yearning for a sense of home.

There had been barely a moment of real homesickness, but still, there was an urge to find a place to fit in this new city. Little routines began to take on great significance, like signposts guiding me, helping me to tame Beirut's chaos of strangeness and make it feel like home.

About once a week Matthew and I walked along Rue Hamra – past old cinemas that were once the height of fashion but were now either boarded up or obliged to make a living playing reruns of old Egyptian films – and up one of the side streets to a little coffee roastery. An old-fashioned coffee roaster stood at the back of the shop and beans clattered through it as we waited. The place was filled with the heady scent of fresh coffee beans and we'd take refuge from it outside with a takeaway espresso served in a brown plastic cup. We sipped slowly as we waited for our bag of coffee to be prepared. After that first visit the owner took our name and wrote next to it in his book a recipe for the sort of coffee we liked. The recipe stipulated a coarse grind. This was important. Much of the coffee for sale elsewhere in Beirut was ground to a fine powder so it was suitable for making Arabic-style coffee in a pot, but when mixed with hot water it made a muddy sludge that clogged up my Italian espresso percolator.

It was around this time, a month or so after we arrived in Beirut, that I began to think seriously about learning Arabic. My meanderings around the city with Matthew had presented little need for language – we were lost, and happy to be lost. Where English did not suffice, I had plugged the gaps with my schoolgirl French.

One day I decided to try a Lebanese pizza, *mana'oushi*, to snack on as I walked home from buying the weekly coffee supply. Stalls selling these pizzas were all around the city. They were usually simple places with a large brick oven and a glass cabinet that was filled with uncooked pizzas waiting to be thrown deep into the furnace. The pizzas were served rolled around a fresh salad of mint, olives, slices of cucumber and chunks of tomato. When spread with *zaatar*, a thyme mixture, they were a favourite for breakfast. Before ordering I consulted a phrasebook for a few words of Arabic, and when it was my turn I took a breath and smiled and launched crudely into this strange foreign tongue. 'Want cheese pizza,' I said with another smile. '*Bideh pizza jibneh*.'

The man behind the counter was young, maybe 20, and he looked at me with slight irritation. I was crushed. He hadn't understood, I thought, and began preparing to try again. I imagined the words with different emphasis or accent. But he spoke first. 'Look, would you like to speak English or French?' he said, in confident English. We finished the transaction in English and I couldn't shake the feeling that rather than charming him with my attempts at his language, I'd somehow insulted him.

I discovered more and more Beirutis (like Amir, my landlord) who spoke fluent English, French and Arabic. I began to listen in to café conversations and discovered people spoke all three languages at once, cherry-picking the most appropriate word or phrase from whatever language they preferred and mixing up their sentences. At other times I'd hear one person speak Arabic and then another in the group reply in French, a third in English.

The problem was that this made Beirut possibly the worst place in the Arab world to learn Arabic. Instead, I began to learn a little supply of Arabic words that I could use to make a joke, to get out of a sticky situation, to show off and make me sound like I knew far more than I really did. After a month or so in Beirut I had distilled my language learning into a few essentials. My personal dictionary of Lebanese Arabic read as follows:

***Yalla*: Let's go!** One of my favourites. Good for almost any situation when it's time to wrap something up and move on. The Lebanese end almost every telephone conversation by saying '*Yalla*, bye!'

***Haram*: Forbidden.** Technically a religious word used to denote things banned in the Qur'an. But also used to tease someone you've discovered over-indulging, or to halt inappropriate behaviour.

***Khalas*: Enough, it's settled.** If you're over it, *khalas* will stop it. If something has been finalised, *khalas* ends the negotiation.

***Schwey*: Little.** A favourite word to use in a taxi when I didn't know how to describe my precise destination. It was always *schwey*, a little further.

***Shu*: What's going on?** Chatty and familiar and a good way to extract the latest.

***Insha'allah*: If God wills it.** A fabulous answer when you don't want to give an answer, apart from its religious meaning, of course.

***Habibe* or *habibte*: Dear one.** The Arabic classic, an intimate way to greet a good male or female friend.

***Yanni*: More or less; you know.** The translation could vary wildly depending on the situation, but this was another effective way of stalling the need to answer questions, or being vague with your answer, or punctuating a sentence and giving you time to think.

My new language skills were far from the yearned-for fluency, but it was a start. I put my humiliation at the *mana'oushi* stand behind me and launched myself back on the unsuspecting Lebanese public. Luckily, this time my audience was far more sympathetic.

Diagonally opposite my new home was a small shop that sold everything from balls of fresh *labneh* bobbing in vats of olive oil to pickled turnip, stained a bilious pink, to accompany plates of *mezze*. Nada looked after the place during the day, and in the evening, when she went home to the kids, her husband, Asmat, took over. When business slowed, he pulled a chair onto the footpath and set up his water pipe and a small oil-burner to make coffee. 'Sister, come and drink *café*,' he would call out, and sometimes I'd join him.

We drank shots of strong, bitter coffee from tiny ceramic cups and I attempted conversations in English and broken French, bolstered with my few words of Arabic. Asmat's friends from the neighbourhood stopped for a chat or a smoke. The pace was slow and inclusive and I thrilled at being a part of it. I would amble back up the street to home and fall asleep to the sound of dice clattering on a backgammon board.

But life in Beirut also included certain eccentricities that had to be overcome. It was a post-war country after all and to live sanely required developing a numbness to some things. The blackouts – regular, unannounced – sucked me into a void of pacing, waiting, everything on hold. I took long candlelit baths, snuggled in bed and read. But candlelight quickly lost its romantic appeal.

I never really understood why the blackouts were so frequent. Was it that the electricity supply was never enough and had to be rotated through the city? The substations that had been bombed by Israel a few years before were not up to full capacity? Lebanon was in such debt it was rationing the fuel that ran the power stations? Was it some political plot in which the constituents of certain areas got a better service than those in others? It could have been any number of reasons. Everyone had a theory and it was impossible to separate truth from conspiracy. After a while I stopped bothering and the blackouts just became a boring, ordinary reality. I left the apartment and sat in a café and read. Or I visited a friend with a generator or one who lived in a suburb where the power was still on. What else was there to do?

If it wasn't unreliable electricity, then it was too-frequent construction. Our street was constantly being torn up and resealed – inexplicable, except for the corruption theory; someone was making money, lots of it. One week it was the plumbing; the next it was a plan to elevate the footpaths; after that a scheme to put metal posts along the newly raised footpaths at regular intervals to prevent cars parking across them.

But the biggest adjustment of all was the military presence that hovered everywhere around the city. I couldn't work out if it was due to fear of clashes breaking out again at any time, or whether it was just habit. Lebanese police, decked out in camouflage fatigues with giant M16 rifles slung over their shoulders, slouched on various corners around the city and I felt the hairs stand up on the back of my neck every time I walked past them.

Relations between Israel and Lebanon remained tense. Lebanon didn't officially recognise Israel, and any map bought in Beirut showed the country to Lebanon's south as Palestine, not Israel. The Lebanese army made sure to keep well away from the border; it was no match for the US-funded and well-armed Israel Defence Force (IDF). Instead, the IDF faced off against Hezbollah's guerrillas, armed by Syria and Iran. Compared with the IDF, Hezbollah's arsenal of rockets and rifles was insignificant, but its guerrilla tactics and willingness to die on the job made the group's fighters formidable opponents. Nevertheless, the Lebanese army did a good job of appearing to be in control. Military jeeps packed with a rabble of soldiers frequently cruised the streets on the way to or from some exercise or other. Military helicopters did regular aerial sweeps of the city, especially when there was a foreign dignitary in town or an upcoming national event. It was surreal to be relaxing at an outdoor café, sipping espresso, and to be shaken into the present by the thud, thud of a chopper and then look up to see four or five of them in formation, each with snipers hanging from the sides.

By the standards of the civil war Lebanon was now a peaceful place, but low-level conflict was depressingly frequent. Some mornings I would wake to learn Israel had bombed a Syrian communications tower a few kilometres away, or a famous warlord had been blown to bits in a car bomb, or a plot to assassinate the US ambassador or bomb a popular supermarket had just been foiled. Other days it was a trading of fire – Katyusha rockets and mortar rounds – on the border between Hezbollah and Israel, and for a moment Matthew and I would feel anxious. What if the scuffle escalated into a wider conflict? But the café wisdom seemed to be that neither side would be so stupid. Israel had only just withdrawn from southern Lebanon after a failed 22-year occupation. More committed attempts to eradicate Hezbollah – bombing campaigns in 1993, in 1996 – had always ended without success. Surely history couldn't repeat itself so soon?

Nevertheless, I became jumpy. The sound of a car backfiring could convince me there'd been some sort of explosion up the road. The man who drove a vegetable van up and down our street, advertising produce and prices through a megaphone, began to sound like he was recruiting for an angry political rally. The boom and crack of fireworks being let off at weddings, ricocheting back and forth off tall city buildings, sounded spookily like a mortar round.

I got used to these things and laughed at myself. But one night I woke around 2 a.m. to a noise of such power it couldn't be dismissed as the imagination of a nervy foreigner. There was a whoosh, boom, growl and the whole apartment seemed to warp under the pressure of the noise. In the time it took to be wrenched from deep sleep to sitting, dazed, on the bed, a range of possibilities flashed through my mind but only one seemed to fit: a bomb. What else could make such a noise?

'Fuck!' said Matthew, bolt upright beside me. 'That was a fighter jet breaking the sound barrier.'

We listened and yes, the sound of a plane rumbling through the night sky, in the distance now, was unmistakable. It was the first time I had heard a sonic boom and the sound tore at something deep and internal and private. For an instant I had felt a kind of pure fear that made me feel physically sick, and for a long time afterwards I could recall the sound and my physical reaction to it with enough clarity to make it feel as if it was happening all over again.

CHAPTER 3
DISCOVERY

The fighter jet incident made for good conversation as Matthew and I sat around the bar at Chez André the next evening, trading experiences with everyone else who had heard it too.

'The windows in our apartment shook so much it felt as though they were being sucked in,' I said, and the others nodded, understanding.

This was Israel's way of letting Beirut know it was not amused by Hezbollah's habit of sending sporadic rounds of Katyusha rockets into Israel across Lebanon's southern border. Several months earlier, in May 2000, the IDF had withdrawn troops from a wide arc of land in southern Lebanon. After the siege of Beirut in 1982 that ended with the eviction of the PLO from Lebanon, the IDF had retreated to the south of the country and created a buffer zone that could be patrolled by Israeli troops and its Lebanese proxy, the South Lebanon Army.

The PLO had gone but Israel had a new enemy: Hezbollah had been created in the wake of the Israeli invasion of Lebanon and over the next 18 years Hezbollah's guerrilla tactics and intimate knowledge of the terrain, its suicide bombers and passion for the cause, had worn down the IDF. Israeli casualties became too great. Public opinion in Israel swelled against the occupation of southern Lebanon. When the Israelis left in 2000, the Islamic Resistance, Hezbollah's military wing, took credit as the only Arab army to defeat the mighty US-backed IDF, and Hezbollah was admired across the Middle East. For a while, most Lebanese were united in their appreciation.

But when the Israelis left they didn't vacate a small plot of land at the junction of Israel, Syria and Lebanon known as the Shebaa Farms. The UN had classified the region as Syrian, and Israel continued to occupy parts of Syria, so the IDF stayed in the Shebaa region. But Syria and Hezbollah agreed that the land was Lebanese and this gave Hezbollah a pretext to maintain its status as a resistance movement and to continue sporadic rocket attacks into northern Israel. Israel replied with hundreds and sometimes thousands of violations of Lebanese airspace every year, and with its own attacks on Lebanon. The sonic boom I had heard the night before was a part of it.

In spite of my jumpiness at this world of military presence, fighting on the border with Israel and threatening noises in the middle of the night, most of the time I felt very safe in Beirut. Whatever was going on always seemed to be related to politics and so, I reasoned, had very little chance of affecting me. I never heard of muggings or random attacks and I began to feel more at ease about my personal safety than I did in Australia. I thought almost nothing of walking alone anywhere in Beirut, and would even walk home by myself late at night.

Yet it didn't take long for the buzz of walking around Beirut to wane. The distances were small, but it was a city where the car ruled. I saw a road accident at least once a day. Tempers boiled over. Occasionally someone pulled out a gun and threatened to use it. Being on foot was dramatically worse. Making it through the traffic and across the road was often heart-stopping. Footpaths were cracked and broken or in the process of being dug up and repaired, and I spent most of the time scurrying along in the gutter, breathing in lungfuls of exhaust fumes and cursing.

As I began to gather a group of friends and my social life became more interesting, the need to work out how to get around the city became more urgent. The answer was *service taxis*: a system of sharing the cab with others going the same way. The problem was learning how to use them. For a start, there was the pronunciation. 'Service' was said as an exaggerated *servees* that made me feel ridiculous every time I said it. But more important was the fact that to successfully use a *service*, a degree of inbuilt knowledge of the city was required and Beirut was not easy to negotiate. No one used addresses, at least not the kind I was used to with street names and numbers. Getting around required familiarity with local landmarks, which, as a newcomer to the city, I was almost completely without. Comments like 'It's in the Saroulla building' were common when I asked for directions, which were, of course, useless to me. Everyone said it was a post-war hangover: street signs were blown away, populations moved to escape violence and didn't know the names of the roads in their new neighbourhoods. Using landmarks was easier.

One night Courtney, a photographer and a New Yorker who had been based in Beirut for the past two years, invited me to join her and some friends for a drink. 'Have you been to Rue Monot?' she had asked me over coffee at Modca that afternoon, where we had met to discuss working together on magazine features. 'This and Chez André are pretty much my locals at the moment,' I said, gesturing through the swirls of cigarette smoke to the clattering café around us. 'Oh, no, no, no!' said Courtney. She frowned, mock-stern, and took me under her wing. 'All the new bars are in Achrafieh now.' The past months had seen an explosion of nightlife in the area, Courtney explained, as bars and restaurants began to take over the damaged and abandoned buildings that butted up against the old frontline. She suggested we meet at her apartment later that night and she would take me on to a bar she had in mind. 'A few friends will be there too. You should meet them,' she said.

She turned to a blank page in my notebook and began to write down her address in her tiny, precise handwriting. I knew not to expect a straightforward street name and number, but the details were so complicated and bewildering that she included a little map.

Her apartment was near a hospital and I spent the afternoon feverishly practising the word in Arabic: *mous*tachfa, mous*ta*chfa, *mous-tach-fa*, moustach*fa*. But even with the word learned pat, I was about to find out that catching a *service* was just as difficult as making it to the correct destination.

The technique for hailing one was to stand on the side of the road, just beyond the line of parked cars. The taxis were easy to spot because they had red number plates and were virtually all mid-80s Mercedes-Benz sedans in such bad shape that many let the light in through the rust and were followed by a cloud of exhaust fumes. They roamed the scrum of city traffic and veered wildly from kerb to kerb, swaying on their suspension as they took a corner. When a potential customer was spotted the driver rested his hand on the horn to attract attention and slid alongside, leaning out the window, eyebrows raised.

So I stood on the road, peering expectantly into the traffic, when the taxis started coming for me. '*Moustachfa Roum*,' I yelled. Each time the driver jerked his chin upwards – Lebanese sign language for 'You've got to be kidding' – fixed his gaze on the road ahead and drove off. This happened again and again. The drivers weren't going my way and so I was being ignored. It seemed brash; no, more than that: rude. I started to lose my nerve. My tone became less strident, almost pleading. I felt stupid standing there copping rejection after rejection and so I almost missed it when at last a cab was willing to take me. The upwards jerk of the chin was replaced by a sideways jerk of the head towards the back seat. Almost imperceptible and yet it was the signal to jump in.

Each *service* was its own little world. Each driver displayed his political and religious affiliations prominently – Muslim prayer beads or a Christian cross wrapped around the rear-vision mirror; stickers of political leaders lined up along the windscreen. Sometimes the call to prayer was played loudly on the radio. Other times it was a station playing Arabic hits, or Western ones. But I fell in love with the *service* experience. I loved the craziness of the ride. I loved the contact it brought with all sorts of different Lebanese people. I loved the way that catching one helped me feel part of the city.

This driver had a cassette of anthems from the Islamic Resistance – Hezbollah's military wing – and a sticker of Nasrallah on the windscreen. A baritone chanted the lyrics against a solemn musical accompaniment.

The driver leaned on his horn and lurched into a swirl of traffic. He kept his eyes focused on the road ahead, studiously ignoring the swarm of cars that seemed to be coming at us from all sides. I recognised the technique from the years

I spent living in Vietnam – responsibility is allocated the moment you acknowledge another driver. So, best to put on imaginary blinkers and continue with a steady and unyielding progress towards your destination. The result was a white-knuckle ride. The driver laughed. 'Don't worry. *Insha'allah*, we will make it,' he said, and put his foot to the floor.

In the front passenger seat was Karim, a 60-something businessman dressed in a blue-and-white-striped seersucker suit, puffing importantly on a large cigar. 'I was a millionaire before the war,' he said, swivelling around to face me. 'I had a textile and ready-to-wear fashion business and a . . .' He paused, searching for the word for department store in English before resorting to French. '. . . a *grand magasin* in Martyrs' Square. During the war I left it and spent fifteen years in New York. When I came back it was gone, destroyed by fighting.'

He took a puff of his cigar. 'So tell me,' he continued. 'Why do you like Beirut?'

I considered the question. It was difficult to answer, not just because of the short time I had spent in the city but also because my opinions were based on the luxury of one seeking adventure. 'The people are very friendly,' I answered at last, and it was an honest answer.

He sighed, raised his eyes to the sky. 'Well, that's the Lebanese. They love everyone but each other.'

The cab finally pulled up nearby the hospital and Courtney came striding out of a narrow street nearby – six feet tall in heels, statuesque, unmissably American – and jumped in the front seat. She directed the driver in mixed-up sentences of

English and Arabic and we whizzed the wrong way down one-way streets and spun around blind corners and passed charmingly dilapidated apartment blocks with paint peeled back to expose soft weathered stone. After five minutes or so we emerged in another world. The same buildings, but restored: elaborate carved stone balconies and wooden shutters painted in candy colours – pale pink and blue, buttercup yellow – with brass plaques at the entrance and the names of the occupants engraved in French.

We turned another corner and were just a block away from the old frontline. 'This is Monot,' Courtney said, and waved towards the decaying blocks and almost-ruins. We began to drive down this narrow street, stuck behind BMWs and 4WDs and SUVs pumping music from big expensive stereos. A trickle of young Lebanese dressed up in silk or leather, arm in arm, was negotiating the broken footpath on the way to some bar or other. After a while there was an alley going off to the left where Courtney asked the cabbie to stop and we got out. Ahead of us were lights and there was the dull thump of a sound system. We walked up a couple of steps, pushed through a thick black cloth curtain and we had arrived. The scene could have been any bar in any city anywhere in the world, but it was in Beirut and it felt exhilarating, like a secret discovery. Two barmen were serving cocktails behind a long bar, blenders whirring, ice jangling inside cocktail shakers and the smell of freshly chopped mint. Behind them was a wall of bottles of coloured alcohol, lit up. The place was packed. One side was a restaurant and the other was full of people drinking and smoking and talking. Courtney spied a table of friends and we went over, squeezing through the crush of bodies in designer jeans and high heels and little tops that were slit to expose smooth tanned shoulders.

Courtney introduced me to Leila, a Lebanese architect

and Ramzi, a Lebanese filmmaker. Cigarettes were handed around, cocktails ordered.

Leila had spent most of the past ten years in Paris, studying architecture and working in a small practice. She had left a good job and a good life there to come back to Beirut because she had a dream of taking part in the city's reconstruction. Something wonderful was happening here: expat Lebanese were returning from adopted homes in America, Canada, Australia, France. Despite the uncertainty about how long this peace would last, despite instability on the border with Israel, and despite all of Lebanon's frustrating 'isms' – sectarianism, confessionalism, nepotism, favouritism – there was a burgeoning sense of real hope for the future.

Lebanon had always been an outward-looking place and had always welcomed travellers and traders from far-off places. Its population was bewilderingly diverse: so many religions and ethnicities and scales of economic advantage or disadvantage packed into a country only a fraction of the size of Tasmania. The Lebanese were actually remarkably tolerant when you thought about it. The returned expats were bringing with them yet another layer to that diversity: ideas and outlooks honed in Europe and elsewhere and then given their own uniquely Lebanese spin. The result was a frisson of activity – emotional, political, social. Lebanon was changing again and it felt good to be a part of it.

I liked Leila immediately. Like a lot of Lebanese she could shift seamlessly into a detailed discussion of Middle Eastern politics, before doubling back via the Gucci boots she saw at Pointure – everyone's favourite glam shoe store – the week before and the new restaurant that we absolutely, definitely, *had* to try, before ending with an explanation of the first chapter of her PhD dissertation that was almost finished. She had spent long enough away to be able to look fondly but critically at Lebanon, and as we got to know each other she'd fill me in on the latest gossip involving her circle of old school friends. I'd learn who had a new nose job or boob job. How much someone had spent on her wedding. Who was cheating on her husband. She gently chided her old chums as she told her stories, but she was affectionate. Leila said infidelity was surprisingly common in Lebanon (so *that* was why there were so many sexy lingerie shops in Beirut!) and she blamed the fact that too many people married young, to someone considered suitable by their family rather than for love.

But marriage wasn't straightforward in Lebanon. There was no civil marriage, only religious services, which made it very difficult for couples from different religious sects to tie the knot unless one of them converted. Lots of Lebanese who did marry for love circumvented the problem by getting hitched in Cyprus, where they could have a civil union. But you can imagine how the situation complicated the courting ritual. It was essential to know what religion someone was, but dreadfully rude to ask or even appear to be asking. Instead, most Lebanese adopted one of two techniques: some socialised almost exclusively within their sect; others became adept interrogators with the intention hidden underneath layers and layers of vague questioning. Often just asking a person's name could fairly accurately identify their religion: Ali or Joseph, it was obvious who was Christian and who was Muslim. If that didn't work then the family name often did, or for a third attempt you could ask what village the family came from – most had been settled by a particular sect.

Then there were Lebanese like Leila, whose forward-thinking family came from almost every part of Lebanon and could claim links to almost every religion. Technically she was a Sunni, as her father was Sunni and, apart from the few remaining Lebanese Jews (who inherited their religion down a matriarchal line) most religions were transferred from the father. But Leila had grown up learning about the Druze religion from her mother and the Shi'ite from her grandmother. Her brother married a Maronite Christian and her elder sister married an Armenian Orthodox. She would laugh about it good-naturedly. 'In our house there is a religious festival almost every weekend. Once November comes we are on holiday almost continuously until the end of April!'

All of this mixed-up experience of Lebanon and the world made Leila extremely open-minded and easygoing. She easily brushed off the Beiruti obsession with fashion and grooming and complained that the first thing other Lebanese women did when she walked into a room was look at her feet to check her shoes (style, designer, approximate value) and her pedicure (the French polish was *de rigueur* in Beirut).

'Take notice,' she counselled. 'You'll be amazed. They start at your feet and then check you out slowly and obviously all the way to the last strand of hair on your head.'

I did take notice and she was right. I was never sure whether the glances were admiring or dismissive, but they certainly made me feel uncomfortable. I was thrown. I'd expected to feel uncomfortable under the gaze of Arab men. Instead, one look from a Lebanese woman could make me cower.

Matthew joked that the Lebanese were the Italians of the Middle East: same focus on big, extended families, same love of good food and especially Mama's home cooking, same mix of modern and traditional values. But the biggest similarity of all was an obsession with the *bella figura*. Lebanese women were high-maintenance. Big hair was in. Look-but-don't-touch cleavage was in. Nails were manicured regularly and often decorated with diamantés set into the lacquer. Beirut was the only place I knew of where skin-tight top-to-toe leopard print turned heads, for all the right reasons. Matching was in: bags that matched shoes that matched the cover of your mobile phone or the colour of your earrings (which must be big and glittery). Too much make-up was never really *too* much. Suntans, fake tans and snow tans were all to die for. The look was French attention to detail crossed with Las Vegas showgirl; the goal was to look *rrrrrich*. And if your boyfriend owned anything less than a black Mercedes or BMW then *dump him immediately*.

The attitude was pure Beirut society. I began to realise it had nothing to do with religion and I was forced to quickly recast my stereotypes. The way women dressed in Beirut provided my first lesson in Islam: just as Christianity was widely interpreted and practised in the West, so it was with Islam in Lebanon. Many Lebanese turned to their religion for the big events of life: birth, death and marriage. And religion almost always guided their political affiliations. But in daily life? Forget it. I began to feel that a Lebanese woman's most important religion was fashion and grooming.

It was hopeless to even attempt to keep up. I came from Australia. We practically invented laidback style and self-deprecation. If someone complimented me on an item of clothing or an accessory I fell instantly into the ingrained patter of my homeland. 'Oh, you mean this old thing?' I'd reply. 'Had it for years!' I could see the faces in front of me fall and it took a long time to realise that I'd committed far more than just social suicide. This was not even just bad taste. It was bad manners. The appropriate Lebanese response would have been something like 'Oh, isn't it fabulous. It cost me US$500 at Aishti' (a *très chic* and *très, très* expensive boutique in Beirut that featured European designer brands). In Australia my comment would have been viewed as charmingly humble or self-effacing. In Lebanon it meant I had failed to make an effort and in doing so had unintentionally insulted those around me and raised a list of unpleasant questions: Was I *poor*? Did I lack *status*? And most horrific of all, *did this mean I wasn't even worth knowing*?

I decided that if I was to live with dignity in Beirut I needed a makeover. My hair hadn't been cut for ages – months, probably – so I made an appointment at a hip-looking new salon close to where I lived for a cut and highlights. I wasn't usually one to take along pictures of the style I wanted, but this time I did, in case language barriers meant I couldn't accurately convey my meaning. It was a straightforward style – a bob with a bit of a twist. I decided it was just the thing to take me seamlessly from restaurant to refugee camp.

'*T' fadaleh, t'fadaleh*, madam.' I was welcomed inside. A cup of coffee arrived and my hairdresser, whose name I missed, began speaking in French. I struggled to keep up, smiling, nodding, proffering my ragged magazine image, pointing to coloured strands of synthetic hair in a L'Oréal catalogue. Confident we understood each other I sat back, pleased to have begun my self-improvement drive.

I was buried in a magazine and when I looked up I was alarmed to see rather more hair than I had expected tumbling to the floor. 'Excuse me, ah, *excusez-moi*,' I began. I wanted to say 'What the *fuck* are you *doing*?' but something more polite came out. The hairdresser looked at me with a sharp expression and held a hand in my face with the thumb and fingers pinched together in a sign that meant 'Patience!' 'Madam, be quiet. I am the stylist,' he added.

Chastened, I returned to the magazine. How bad can it be? I reasoned. I'd had plenty of haircuts in my time, some good, some bad, and in fact some of the best had been when I left the stylist to his or her own inspiration.

The cut and colour done, I was anxious to see my new style dry and street-ready. The blow dry I was used to in Sydney was called *brushing* in Beirut, the French term. This one began with a liberal application of some sort of hair balm, then mousse, then curlers, then 15 minutes under a hairdryer, then back-combing and then hairspray. And more, and more hairspray. I was horrified. I looked like an extra from a 1960s sitcom. The indignity was complete when the stylist asked for US$150, which, with the appalling value of the Australian dollar at that time, meant that I had just paid a fortune for a cut I couldn't wait to grow out.

I complained feebly about the cost, about the fact that the style bore absolutely no resemblance to the image I had given the hairdresser. The salon manager beamed at me and said, 'Yes, but of course you love it!' There was really nothing to do. I walked home and felt everyone's eyes on me. I didn't even want to imagine what they were thinking.

For my next trip to the hairdresser a few weeks later I decided to go for something cheap and pay close attention to what happened. At the end of my street was a salon called Antonio's, with a sign in the window advertising hair colour for 25,000LL – about A$30. I decided it was worth the risk.

The salon had an authentic retro look, and that was because it hadn't been redecorated for years. There was a white vinyl couch along one wall, where the manicurist sat reading bodice-rippers in Arabic while she waited for clients. On a shelf above the couch was a cluster of Christian religious icons, but Antonio boasted that he maintained good relations with all his Muslim neighbours and the militias and so had been able to stay put in his little salon throughout the war. Along the other wall was a collection of certificates and awards from the 1960s and 70s when Antonio was a regular, and successful, competitor at hair shows in France. The framed certificates were dwarfed by a portrait of Antonio dressed in his Freemason's uniform, medals pinned to his breast, gavel held at a jaunty angle.

The man himself was larger than life: always dressed carefully in brightly coloured wide-collared shirts and trousers in a matching tone. Around his neck was a heavy gold chain, and chunky gold rings decorated his fingers. He often puffed on a cigar as he strode around the salon he'd opened 40 years earlier, aged just 18.

His clients were a mixed lot: older women who smoked cigarettes while their hair was stained bright colours or jet black and then rolled and sprayed into a puffed-up 'do'; younger women who wanted *brushing* for a night out. Women in *hejab* who were bustled to a small room at the back so they could have their hair cut out of sight of Antonio and other passing men. A Saudi Arabian princess booked an appointment every time she was in Beirut. Her servants waited on the white couch and she sat in the main area of the salon having her hair blow-dried dead straight into a long, silky black mane.

And there was me. As I waited for my colour to develop I flipped through an old photo album filled with advertising tear sheets that Antonio had collected from his wartime heyday. To an outsider like me, unfamiliar with the rhythms of conflict, it seemed ludicrous that at the height of war a Lebanese woman could possibly prioritise trips to a hairdresser for highlights and a trim and *brushing*. But Antonio had devised a devious marketing strategy that tapped the heart of the Lebanese psyche: 'Antoine – The Beauty Maker' the ad read. 'Be beautiful. A beautiful woman takes a man's mind off the mess the country is in.'

'We used to put boards around the salon to stop bullets coming inside,' he told me matter-of-factly as my haircut began to take on a pleasing new shape.

This was the Lebanese way. It showed either remarkable resilience, or a wilful disregard for reality – 'collective amnesia' the sociologists called it. Psychologists argued that those who survived the civil war emotionally intact were those who had focused on things they could control rather than obsessing over whether their apartment would be blown up or a loved one would be caught up in a street battle. And it occurred to me that although the fighting was over, a similar thing was still happening in Beirut.

That spring, restaurants, cafés and bars opened almost weekly around the city. Hundreds of thousands of dollars and more were being spent on interior design, and the old places like Chez André and Modca were being pushed aside – although they still kept their faithful and sentimental clientele, of which I had become a loyal member. With every cocktail drunk or *chocolat fondant* ordered the Lebanese were carefully, methodically, rubbing out the past.

The next evening I settled in for yet another candlelit bath. I sank into the hot water, rested my feet on the tiles that covered the wall at the end of the tub and watched the flame make black shadows dance on the walls. Beirut had its own black shadows and I was learning to live with them; accepting but never complacent. As I lay there making the most of the womblike peace of the warm water and the darkness, I figured I was doing pretty well at being like the Lebanese, adapting to life lived in the moment. I was still struggling to put all of Lebanon's puzzle pieces together, but that night I thought I knew one thing for certain: to worry about the past, or the future, was quite simply exhausting.

CHAPTER 4
THE RIGHT PATH

Living in Lebanon was like negotiating a matrix of clashing worlds, each challenging me to draw some conclusion or other about the place. But the country would humble anyone who had the nerve to make assumptions. Indeed, the moment I felt I had the place figured out, it would prove me wrong by throwing up some new contradiction. Just as I began to settle into my new life of glam bars and restaurants, salon makeovers and war in the background, Courtney was on the phone again, this time with an invitation to join her on a trip to Nabatiyeh.

'It's Ashura,' she said. 'I'm taking pictures for Getty Images. Why don't you come?' Nabatiyeh is a Shi'ite town in the mountains of southern Lebanon that hosts one of the largest Ashura gatherings in the country. The event remembers Hussein, the Prophet Mohammed's grandson, who was killed in a battle over who should lead the Muslims. His death in Karbala in modern Iraq around AD 680 marked Islam's split into Shi'ite and Sunni sects. Those who supported Hussein became known as the Shi'ites.

We drove south from Beirut with Hadi, one of my first

friends in Beirut, in his carefully kept vintage Mercedes. He kicked the car into high gear and we sped down the coast road. There was no speed limit and no seatbelts and I jiggled around on the big leather seat with its soft patina of years of use. I cast aside obvious fears, exhilarated by the careless freedom of it, and watched the slideshow through my window. There were banana plantations to our right that stretched down an almost imperceptible slope to the sea. To our left was the usual horror-scape of shops and half-built apartment blocks. This pollution and mess had been allowed to accumulate and swell during the war and was now so out of control it was impossible to return the coast to what it once must have been: a pristine world of empty, rock-strewn shoreline fringed by narrow sandy beaches that stretched into blue, blue sea.

We passed the site of a wartime massacre at Damour, and a little further on the turn-off to a see-and-be-seen strip of glitzy private beach clubs, with sunken bars in their resort-style swimming pools that stretched down landscaped slopes to a little arc of sand. The mess of the highway was left behind and the area was almost idyllic, as long as you ignored the fact that it overlooked an oil storage facility. We turned left and began our ascent into the mountains just before we reached Sidon. The old Phoenician port town had a labyrinthine covered *souk*, Crusader sea castle – with fallen columns still visible in the water – pastry shops strung out along the main street and the best *falafel* sandwiches I'd ever tasted.

The Mediterranean sparkled deep blue below us. We climbed rapidly, twisting along mountain roads, up and down. The air became almost instantly cooler. I put on a black cotton sweater, wound down the window and stuck my arm out, hand flat, surfing the clean-air breeze.

Ashura is a sombre occasion. Shi'ites flagellate themselves with a club made from several pieces of heavy metal chain attached to a wooden handle; or they cut their foreheads with knives and let the blood flow. Both are a symbolic suffering designed to remember the anguish of Hussein and to alleviate Shia guilt for failing to support him.

I had expected that Ashura would unite the Shia but every year Lebanon's two main Shi'ite political parties, Amal and Hezbollah, argued over how that flagellation should be carried out. Amal supporters preferred to cut their heads with swords in a ritual spilling of blood, and Nabatiyeh had become well known as the place in Lebanon where this tradition took place. Hezbollah followed the religious line issued from Iran and insisted cutting was *haram*, forbidden; only chains and the rhythmic beating of fists on chests and the slapping of palms on backs should be allowed. Sometimes the two groups came to blows over their different interpretations and there were street fights and even gun battles.

There had been no news of that this year. We entered Nabatiyeh via the main roundabout. The streets fluttered with posters of the *shahids*: young, moist-eyed, long-lashed martyrs, fighters from Hezbollah's Islamic Resistance who had died in the guerrilla war against Israel.

Hadi parked the car and we walked down the hill towards to the town's main mosque, where the commemoration was taking place. The mountain air was brisk and I was glad I'd brought the black sweater. Opposite the mosque was a sports field and a passion play was under way, retelling the Ashura story. Nearby, a crowd of men swarmed on the steps of the mosque and marshalled themselves into a line at the bottom that snaked around the sports field. The men wore simple white cotton shifts over their clothes and were slapping the heels of their palms into small cuts in their forehead, made just above the hairline. The idea was to prevent the blood from coagulating, to keep it flowing, and with each slap they chanted '*Haider, Haider, Haider*'.

'What are they saying?' I asked Hadi as we shuffled past a group of these bloodied men.

'It is a title for our Imam Hussein. In Arabic the word means "lion".'

The blood fell from the cuts in fat red lines. It covered their faces, clogged their hair, ran down their necks and soaked the white cotton shifts. The air filled with the metallic stench of fresh blood and I stifled the urge to retch.

There was so much blood that volunteers hosed the steps of the mosque and the streets in an attempt to disperse it. But as the blood mixed with the much greater volume of water the streets gushed red. Ambulance crews were on standby as the men dropped in numbers, from loss of blood, from religious excitement, from exhaustion.

Courtney disappeared into the crowd to take pictures and Hadi joined a line at the local hospital to donate his blood rather than take part in the bloodletting ritual. He supported the Hezbollah view and believed the cutting was backward and unnecessary. I walked through the bleeding crowds alone. I could hear the chanting inside the mosque and saw the heads of the men bobbing as they jumped rhythmically on the spot, slapping their foreheads and swinging their arms across each other at the elbow to beat their breast. Then, using the momentum of their own movement, they crossed their arms in front of their chests and swung them over their shoulders to slap their backs just above the shoulder blades.

I wanted to get inside the mosque to see the ritual up close, but I had forgotten to bring a headscarf. I wouldn't be welcome without something covering my head.

I stood at the bottom of the steps and hesitated for a

moment, wondering what to do. Then I remembered the sweater. I took it off – I was wearing a long-sleeved shirt underneath – and threw the sweater over my hair. I tied the arms under my chin, smoothed it around my ears and neck, and began to climb the steps of the mosque. I was looking left and right, waiting for someone to stop me, to question me about my strange outfit, but no one said a word, too absorbed in the ritual to notice or to care. I continued up the steps, sloshing through the blood and the water that was cascading down in a great rush. By the time I had reached the entrance to the prayer hall the bloody mixture was starting to seep through my leather boots and soak my socks.

In front of me was a large crowd of men split into two groups. Towards the back of the mosque, partly obscured behind a carved wooden screen, male friends and family took turns making a little nick in each other's forehead. Some used penknives or kitchen knives and others had huge ceremonial swords. I saw a father bend tenderly towards his son, maybe six or seven years old, and with a long knife he tapped the blade on the child's forehead. A little bead of red oozed to the surface. It dripped slowly down the boy's brow bone and began to collect in a ridge above his eyebrows, thickening, until it spilled down the curve of his cheek and fell in soft, fat droplets from his chin.

I was sucked into the crowd. Lines of men flowed around me, drops of red just beginning to stain their white coverings as they made their way from the back of the mosque to the steps and down to join the giant snaking line of followers outside. They held their swords above their heads, huge silver blades slicing through the air, flashing in the sunlight, and all around the trance-like mantra: *Haider, Haider, Haider*. The roof of the mosque soared above me and I felt very small as I stood inside this swirling, bleeding, chanting mass.

From time to time I'd lock eyes with one of the men and they would nod, almost imperceptibly, a kind of acceptance that reduced some of the pure strangeness. My notebook was cradled in the crook of my elbow but I was too transfixed to write down impressions, almost hypnotised. Instead, I just stayed there, watching quietly, for a long time.

Hadi was a member of Hezbollah. I had met him through a friend who knew his sister, and an unlikely but warm and open friendship had grown between us. He became someone with whom I could easily discuss the prejudices, misconceptions and differences that existed between his world and mine.

He gave the impression of being a small man, almost delicate, although he wasn't especially short. He had large dark eyes and a kind of nervous enthusiasm that was infectious and awkward at the same time. He was extremely polite and at first we curled ourselves into knots, outdoing each other in efforts not to inconvenience the other, tiptoeing around potential misunderstandings. It was a very Arab thing, the unwillingness to be direct, to state a preference. But it was also a way of feeling out the other and looking to find bridges between two very different worlds.

Hadi managed a small shop not far from where I lived – it was his uncle's shop but he was ill and Hadi had offered to look after it during what everyone said would be a long recovery. Hadi had studied politics at university and it remained his passion. The television was always on adjacent to the shop counter and when there were no customers to serve he'd sit reading books and newspapers. This was where our lives converged and we found common ground. Although his shop was a little out of my way I'd often take a detour to pick up things like milk and bread or rice and eggs. Sometimes, when he'd closed for the day, I'd linger for a chat, pull up a chair next to the counter and we would debate the day's news. And when we had finished, Hadi would close up and head back to his home in Haret Hreik, a Shi'ite suburb in the south of the city.

Hadi always attended the mosque for midday prayers on Fridays. He kept a small prayer mat folded up in a drawer underneath the cash register and he'd stop regularly throughout each day to pray the required five times. Slowly our political debates began to turn towards religion, and one day I asked if he would help me to understand something about the Qur'an.

We met at the shop after closing time. I'd brought some nuts and pumpkin seeds with me, and a packet of cigarettes, and Hadi disappeared into a little room with a kitchenette that was adjacent to the shop floor and brewed coffee in a silver pot with a long handle. I followed him and we stood together watching the coffee froth and rise to the rim of the pot. Just before it was about to spill over, Hadi lifted it, waited for the froth to settle, and then returned the pot to the flame. He did that three times so the powdered coffee separated from the liquid. When it was ready, the aroma of coffee and cardamom filled the kitchen. He put the silver pot on a tray with two small ceramic cups, no bigger than egg cups, and placed a saucer over the top of the pot to keep the coffee hot.

We relaxed into armchairs. On one wall there was a framed piece of black velvet with gold letters marking out a passage from the Qur'an. It was a typical thing to find in a Muslim home, mixed in amongst photographs of family: weddings and babies and ancestors with serious expressions.

'Can I ask you something?' he said with a kind of complicity as we took our first sip of coffee. 'Have you ever drunk alcohol?'

I answered that yes, I had. He wanted to know what it was like and I said it was nothing in particular, just a drink, another kind of drink. 'It doesn't really taste of anything.'

He leapt on this admission. 'This is what I have heard. It tastes of nothing. So I don't understand why you must drink it?'

I told him alcohol had social meaning, it was relaxing, pleasant in its way. I was trying to play it down, to demystify it.

'When I go to a café I don't like to sit at a table where they are drinking alcohol,' he said. 'If I am with friends and they are drinking, I move to another table until they are finished.'

I nodded. He wanted to know if it made me lose control and I teased him. 'Come on, Hadi! It's not like one sip and you're out of control. No, it's not like that.' I could see he was confused. 'In my religion,' I added, trying to give the drinking of alcohol a cultural and religious context, to make it deeper than just the disobedience of infidels, 'it has a sacred meaning. We say that red wine is the blood of Christ. Wine is part of one of our most important religious rituals, the Holy Communion. And the Bible tells us that Jesus turned water into wine. In fact, some people believe that miracle happened in Lebanon, at Qana.' I smiled and asked him, rhetorically, 'So, what do you think of that?'

He was quiet and looked down at his feet. 'Have you ever been drunk?'

I knew this was a kind of test and I lied, kindly. 'Once, maybe,' I told him vaguely, waving away his questions. He was silent again for a long time.

'But tell me, Catherine, when you wake up in the morning, do you feel guilty?'

We were pushing boundaries, meeting alone like this, and it only worked because I was a foreign woman and therefore, to a large extent, exempt from any stain on my reputation. And because Hadi was very religious, and proud of his morals yet also open-minded about the need to respect and understand difference. We talked a lot about this: the idea of acceptance. One of the first things he taught me about Islam was *ishtihad*, the concept of interpretation, which allowed the Qur'an to be analysed by senior religious scholars and new understandings made to help solve contemporary problems. I liked this idea. It made Islam, as Hadi practised it, seem less monolithic, less dogmatic than the stereotype that surrounds it in the West. I felt there was room to argue and debate with Hadi and, conversely, he felt less threatened by my questions and criticisms.

'You'd better watch out,' he joked with Matthew when he dropped by the shop to walk home with me one evening. 'I am teaching Catherine about the Right Path. You never know, she might want to convert to Islam.'

He was serious about that too – after all, the name Hadi meant to 'guide towards the light'. He told me that once a person has been informed of the story of the Qur'an there is an obligation to embrace it. His little explanations about the Qur'an were steadily building up my knowledge, he said, and I could no longer plead ignorance. 'Buddhists will not be judged,' he said. 'But, Catherine, I am convinced that after death Allah will ask you: "Why are you not a Muslim? You talked to Hadi." You will be judged. But, please, don't think

I am now putting myself in his place.' And he laughed to lighten the weight of his words.

I understood what he was saying; it was the same in Christianity: the ignorant could go to heaven, but those who had knowingly rejected the teachings of the Bible were doomed to hell. But I liked the fact that Hadi said he wouldn't judge my infidel status. And if Hadi was doing his best not to judge me, then I must be honest: I was also trying hard not to judge him.

At that time, early in 2001 and several months before the fallout from 9/11 would overwhelm everything, Hezbollah, or a front for Hezbollah, was still widely blamed as the organisation that had killed more Americans in a single attack than any other, although the group always denied it. American marines had been deployed to Lebanon as part of a multinational peacekeeping force during the civil war and 241 of them had died in the 1983 truck bombing that blew apart the US Marine Barracks in Beirut, payback for a perception Washington was pro-Christian and not an honest broker in the conflict.

But when you were in Lebanon, reading the local press, talking to the local people, it was impossible to see Hezbollah as a one-dimensional terrorist group. And the Islamic Resistance was only a part of what the organisation meant to Lebanon. It also had a political wing, with democratically elected politicians in the Lebanese parliament. It had a social welfare arm that did the work Lebanon's government was too cash-strapped or weak to provide: funding schools and hospitals, new roads and repairs to villages that had been destroyed during the Israeli occupation. It wasn't hard to understand why Lebanon's poor Shi'ites worshipped Hezbollah: it had defended them when Israeli soldiers occupied their villages; it had supported them in the depths of the homelessness and grinding poverty that followed. It had given them back their dignity.

I was thinking about this, absorbed in my own thoughts, when Hadi dropped something extraordinary into our discussion: '. . . when I was a fighter . . .' I looked up, startled, but the conversation rushed on and there was no chance to return to this unexpected revelation. Hadi was a fighter? I didn't know why but it had never occurred to me. The more I thought about it, the more sense it made. He was the right age to have been recruited to the Islamic Resistance during the Israeli occupation of the south of Lebanon. He had a pale scar running down part of his right hand and another on one side of his face and I had often wondered how they got there, but felt it was impolite to ask. Now the answer seemed obvious. The thought of hearing his story began to consume me.

No one in Lebanon talked about what they did during the war, or after, when the Israeli occupation persisted, and there was an unspoken understanding that these questions should not be asked.

A few days later I called to arrange our regular get-together. I was worried that Hadi had picked up on my plan to question him about his past and would come up with an excuse to avoid our meeting. When I saw him again I could barely contain my eagerness to hear his story. I dispensed with the usual chit-chat and lurched straight for my subject.

'So,' I began, and paused momentarily, hoping to make myself sound more casual than I felt, 'I didn't know you were a fighter?'

'Did I tell you that?' he answered, throwing the question back at me, and I knew this was the moment we would either progress with the conversation and be honest, or he would retreat from it and close the subject forever.

'Well, last week, you know, you mentioned it,' I said. And

then, softening my interrogation, I added, 'Maybe I misunderstood you?'

He laughed. 'Catherine, yes!' He sounded almost exasperated with my apprehension. 'I was a fighter for six years.'

'Really? I mean, why didn't I know before?'

I sensed a kind of relief – a wall of secrecy between friends had at last come down. Slowly, Hadi began to tell me about his life. I asked him to start from the beginning; to fill in all the gaps from his past. I wanted to hear the story in order, to build up a sense of all the parts of him I hadn't known about before. That way, I hoped, I would understand the progression of his decisions step by step.

Hadi was born in the south of Lebanon into a religious family. His uncle was an imam, and as a child his family home was always full of clerics and wives of clerics and the conversation was always of religion. For outings, the family would walk to the plaza of the local mosque and Hadi would play there with his friends in the quiet of the evening.

At that time, the 1970s, Lebanon's Shi'ites were the country's most downtrodden sect. They were the poorest, the least influential. It was the same all around the Middle East, where Sunni Islam dominated. But in Lebanon, the Shi'ites had it even worse. The country's complex mix of religions – Sunnis, Druze, Maronite Christians and Greek Orthodox Christians, Catholics and more – had all managed to salvage greater political and economic power than the Shi'ites. The community lacked both the political and financial clout to change its circumstances.

'There is something within the hearts of the Shia, all the Shia feel it,' Hadi said, and his face twisted in an effort to convey the community's pain. 'Oppression is heritage. Since 1400 years ago and the killing of Imam Hussein, to this day, we have been oppressed.'

And so when Hadi was a boy, he and all of the families he grew up with joined Amal, the Lebanese political movement that supported the Shia and defended their rights. It was the beginning of Shia self-determination that reached its peak with the 1979 Islamic Revolution in Iran – the only country in the world to have a Shi'ite leadership.

'We were all with Amal, everyone in the south and in the Bekaa Valley,' Hadi said, and his posture shifted and he sat up straight in his chair.

When war broke out in Lebanon in 1975, Amal members took up arms and became one of the most active militias in the war. But for years their main opponent was not the other Lebanese militias or even the Israelis. It was the Palestinians who had taken over large tracts of south Lebanon, from where they were launching attacks into northern Israel. They entered the Shia villages and demanded control so they could fight their campaign against Israel. Hadi said his small village community grew to hate the Palestinians.

'I still remember the tough days and what Arafat did to us,' he said. I was unprepared for the emotion he still felt. 'They raped the women, they killed randomly.' He turned his face to the floor and sighed loudly. 'Really tough days. I used to pray to God: "Oh God, please, when are we going to get rid of the Palestinians"?' He looked up at me and shrugged and his face said, 'Can you believe it?'

It was hard to believe. I knew that the Palestinians had caused deep rifts in Lebanese society but the Hezbollah I knew had become avidly pro-Palestinian and a lot of Western condemnation of the organisation these days was framed by its support for Palestinian groups like Hamas.

Hadi was too young to take part in combat against the Palestinians. Instead, aged just 14, he carried a gun and guarded checkpoints around the village. 'We called it to be

On Alert.' He gave a wan smile for the memory of the idealistic young man he once was. 'My friends and I would choose places to go at night and we'd protect the village. We had older fighters with us but even so, of course, my mother didn't like the idea. She cared about me, worried about me. But a young person of that age is hard to control. I was so revolutionary and I wanted to do what I believed in.'

Israel's invasion of Lebanon to kick out the Palestinians had created a new enemy of the Lebanese Shi'ites, who saw Israel's presence as an occupation, and began to fight against it.

'We didn't even breathe,' Hadi said, and he inhaled sharply, trying to convey to me the shock of it. 'So imagine, we were tired, we were forced to form a resistance. Israel destroyed our country. It's true they kicked the Palestinians out, but we got rid of one occupation only to receive another.'

It was around this time, 1982, that some members of Amal became disillusioned with its increasingly secular path and decided to break away. These more religious Shi'ites were looking for a way to contribute to the *jihad* against Israel. Their cause was ridding Lebanon of the Israeli occupation. Their inspiration was the success of the Islamic Revolution in Iran three years earlier and the ideology it espoused. This breakaway group went on to form Hezbollah, and held tightly to religious rather than secular principles. The fledgling Hezbollah was a perfect proxy for Iran and helped Tehran to pursue two important goals of its foreign policy: to find a way to fight Israel, and to strength the position of Shi'ites inside Lebanon.

A few years later, in February 1985, Hezbollah formally announced its existence and released a manifesto declaring its intent: the destruction of the State of Israel and establishment of Islamic rule over Jerusalem; the installation of an Islamic state in Lebanon; and the withdrawal of US and French troops, who were stationed in Lebanon at the time as part of a peacekeeping mission.

But in Hadi's mind, the cause was far simpler than that: he wanted Israel to withdraw from Lebanon. He was yearning to join the new resistance against Israel, but he had a problem. The group's activities were so new and so secret that he didn't know how to get in touch with them. He decided the best way to get their attention, and their trust, was to launch his own operation against the Israelis: that way his loyalty, his ability, could not be doubted.

'One day I spoke with my friends. There were four of us. I suggested we should do something,' he said. 'I had a Kalashnikov in my house and I brought that and my friends were able to get three others. We decided the attack should be against an Israeli patrol and we planned how it would take place.'

There are moments in friendships that you fear (or hope) will change everything and Hadi and I had reached one of those moments. I didn't think I could bear it if he had attacked Israeli civilians. Soldiers? Okay, it was a war, they were in uniform, it wasn't very hard to rationalise that. I could feel my skin prickling with anxiety for what he was about to reveal.

The plan was to break into an orchard that ran through the Occupation Zone and to wait until a military convoy passed. The boys would then use the Kalashnikovs to shoot at the convoy with the goal of killing as many Israeli soldiers as possible.

'One of my friends brought his father's car. We put the Kalashnikovs in the car.' Hadi looked into the space above my head, like he was staring into the distance. 'I remember it very well,' he said. 'We parked a little way from the orchard and infiltrated it. We hid behind a wall and just waited. All of a sudden we saw two Israeli jeeps coming towards us and as they got close to us we began to fire at them. This was our first operation. It was 1983. I was 16 years old.'

It was also the first time Hadi had fired at a real target. 'We were beginners,' he said, and shrugged his shoulders. 'We didn't really know what we were doing. We just fired and ran. We didn't know if we had killed. It was the first serious action in my life. Afterwards I heard the attack reported on the radio and it had been credited to Hezbollah. At that time the Israelis didn't admit losses, but Lebanon was small and people talked and I knew we had been successful.'

Hadi was only one year older than me and I felt compelled by an urge I could not control to lay the blueprint of our parallel lives on top of each other; to compare our experiences of life. I felt compassion for his 16-year-old self well up – too young to be grappling with these life and death issues. I couldn't find it in me to judge him for his choices because the problems he faced were so far outside my own peaceful and happy adolescence. I felt somewhat ashamed of my innocence and ignorance at the same age and the way fate had dealt me such good fortune.

The night after the attack, Hadi couldn't sleep. He was full of adrenaline and nerves. 'It is an action of killing, even if it is an enemy. It's not easy for a person, a 16-year-old guy, to fire on someone like that. You feel something is kind of wrong. It's an action of killing. You are young. You are not used to such a thing. It's not an easy thing at all.'

He shook his head and absently rubbed his hands together and I tried to imagine what he was thinking: these normal hands were the hands of a killer, and it was as if the knowledge haunted him somehow. But Hadi had no doubt that what he did was right. He did the predictable thing, the only thing that would give him sanity. He began to justify it: 'In the end it's an enemy. You get so nervous when you see the Israelis killing people, you know, for nothing. The feeling gets stronger and stronger against them. You just need to fight them.'

After the attack Hadi visited a man he suspected of being somehow involved with the resistance. He asked him, 'Did you hear about the operation in the orchard?' The man nodded and Hadi said, 'We made it.'

'I said to him, "I want you to put me in contact with the resistance," and the next day he put me in touch with the Hezbollah resistance.'

And from that moment Hadi began to live a double life. During the day he was a schoolboy, struggling to piece together a life amid war and occupation and poverty. At night he was a member of the Islamic Resistance, launching guerrilla raids on Israeli military targets. The declared goal was to force Israel's defence forces from Lebanese soil.

When he left school two years later, Hadi joined the resistance full-time. He lived in the mountains in the south of Lebanon, subsisting on rations provided by Hezbollah, planning and carrying out attacks.

'We were not like other teenagers who enjoyed themselves at the cinema. We were living in tough places. All our movements were secret. So, for example, we'd go to a village near their security zone and take a house, we'd live there secretly and at night infiltrate into the security zone and carry out surveillance and come back. Don't think it's easy.' He looked at me sharply and raised his hand as if about to wag his finger at me. 'It was a very, very tough life. You never know when you will die. Do you think that's an easy feeling?'

But Hadi and his comrades were never afraid of death.

'We were careful, but not afraid,' he said. 'We believed that this life pleases God and we knew that our reward will be paradise. We had strong faith and determination. We were young and we had nothing to care about. No kids. No wife. Nothing. We believed we were doing something good for our country and for our people.'

As Hadi watched his friends die in battle around him it made his faith stronger. 'It's a big reward if we become martyrs. It's not our hobby to die, of course not. But if you die in the line of a just cause you are a martyr and God promised the martyrs a special welcome. That's what we believe.'

'All we hear about in the West are the virgins,' I said, referring to the promise of virgins waiting for the martyrs in paradise. But I instantly regretted my flippancy. Hadi's face crumpled in what seemed to be real anguish. He put his head in his hands.

'No. No. This is done to discredit the sacred meaning of martyrdom,' he said, and sat there for what felt like a long time.

'Hadi, I'm sorry,' I said. 'Really, I'm sorry, it was just a comment, a joke. I didn't mean to offend you.'

After a while he sat up and looked at me, but he was so hurt and angry I couldn't meet his gaze. He spoke anyway. 'Do you really think we sacrifice ourselves and suffer the pain and the cold and the heat for such a silly thing? We are real believers. We are defending a sacred and just cause, a noble cause. If I want, you know, what you just said, then there are places I can go to please myself. I get hurt when I hear that word. It's not easy to abandon this life. Who on earth would go and die . . . for that?'

I could feel Hadi's emotion but I could not truly understand the willingness to die – for God, for country, for anyone. He sensed my confusion and tried to turn the conversation back to something I might be able to relate to more strongly.

'To understand the meaning of martyrdom, remember that Jesus Christ was the first one to sacrifice himself for the human being,' he said, searching my face for understanding. 'The meaning of sacrifice originally came from Jesus Christ. It is from there that *we* found the meaning of sacrifice. We understood.'

The desire for martyrdom was so strong that Hadi and his friends used to compete with each other to prepare for the honour. 'When we saw one of our friends die we would say, "Why didn't God choose me? Maybe it's because he doesn't like me?" That was the feeling at the time.'

I told him I didn't understand, however strong his belief, how he could get rid of the human fear of death.

'It's a feeling', he said. 'You find yourself to be just, you know, wanting this thing. You go to death not because you like death but because you love Allah. When you get close to the frontline, you get close to Allah. No longer are you living in fear. When you are on the front you expect death at any time and you just get closer and closer to God. Closer and closer. The feeling becomes so strong that there becomes a love relationship between you and God, and once you love God with a real love then what I am describing cannot be explained in words. It is a feeling. When you see God you have to go to him.'

And then Hadi smiled and there was some sort of light in his eyes. He knew what he was talking about because he came as close as you could come to being a martyr while still being alive to tell the story.

One day he and two others were on a mission to plant a roadside bomb. They were sneaking through the Occupation

Zone in a triangle configuration, one leading and two flanking behind. But the group was ambushed: Israeli soldiers surrounded them and opened fire. Bullets came from all directions. Hadi's two comrades died instantly and Hadi fell to the ground, wounded badly.

'The bullets were coming like this – de, de, de, de.' He moved his arms around and hit his fists randomly into different parts of his body. 'I thought, I am going to die in seconds. I am breathing like this,' and he demonstrated for me, struggling for breath, gurgling to mimic the sound of the blood in his lungs. 'I thought, okay, I'm going to die. I am just waiting for my soul to leave my body. I am just waiting, looking at the sky. I am not scared, and I thought, I'm going, I'm going, *yalla*, when can I go.'

But after a few minutes death had not claimed him. Hadi fell silent, remembering. 'What did you do?' I prompted after a while.

'I felt I had a chance to live again and so I began to walk. You can imagine how tough it was. I was bleeding and bleeding. It was a long way to go.'

Hadi left his dead comrades where they had fallen and began to crawl up the mountain to where he knew there was a village on the Lebanese side of the Occupation Zone. He stopped periodically to rest, hiding under the foliage of trees and shrubs with the sound of Israeli helicopter gunships above. He could hardly walk, hardly breathe. Time was a blur; hours passed but he has no memory of how many.

It was about 3 a.m. when he reached the village. He crawled to the door of the first house he saw and knocked. A man opened the door and he said, 'Who are you?'

'I told him, "Please, help me, I'm dying. I'm a fighter. I'm a resistance man." '

Hadi was bundled inside and help came. His life was saved.

~

As the *service* taxi wound its way through Beirut that night, detouring for passengers via the shopping district of Verdun, I gazed out at the mannequins in the lit-up shop windows, and diners sitting on the terrace of the Mie Dorée café looking down their reworked noses at the *plat du jour*. I had an urge to see Leila. I called: 'What are you up to?'

'Not much,' she said. 'Shall we meet?'

I asked the taxi to drop me at Otium, a sleek new bar and restaurant just up the road from my apartment. It had an almost all-white décor and projectors beaming slides onto huge screens that covered the windows. I found a stool at the bar, ordered a honey margarita (my favourite), and waited for my friend. How quickly I had slipped between worlds. The matrix closed around me and Beirut's extremes had never felt so stark.

CHAPTER 5
HASHISH

We were sitting in the garden of Mr J's house in Baalbek, admiring the ambience. The chill of those first winter months of life in Beirut had eased and the snow was melting on all but the highest peaks of the Mount Lebanon range. Matthew and I had just returned from a trip to Israel and the West Bank and I was drained from reporting on protracted, intractable Israeli and Palestinian politics, and being lectured on the integrity of each side's position. I had leapt at an invitation to join my neighbour George, a Dutch journalist, and another Lebanese friend, Malik, who had the right connections to open doors, on a visit to the Bekaa Valley. The story was still politics but it promised the thrill of something illicit: with Malik's help, we planned to investigate a resurgence in Lebanon's drug trade, which had been mostly dormant since the end of the civil war.

After the twisting journey over the mountains and then the dusty ride north and east through the Bekaa, Mr J's garden felt like coming across a sort of oasis. It had an almost tropical lushness to it: a soft green lawn, fleshy shrubs and a stand of ageing trees, tall, with wide canopies that shaded us from the sun. I leaned back in my plastic chair and spread my arms wide, tipped my head back and breathed in the countryside. Mr J's wife handed around glasses of sweet tea and we sat together – George, Malik, Mr J, his wife and two of his friends, and me. We were switching back and forth between English and Arabic, chatting in translation. Malik took out his crumpled packet of Marlboros and Mr J smoked a cigar.

In front of us, almost in the middle of the lawn, grew a cannabis plant. Its biggest leaves were larger than an open hand, and the imposing shrub quivered and shook in the breeze. The presence of the plant was a kind of provocation. Even the way we were seated was designed so that we couldn't help but notice it. The chairs were arranged like a sitting room with the plant positioned where you might expect to find a television set. Mr J was one of the most successful drug barons in the Bekaa Valley and the plant, so healthy, so prominent, came with a message for whoever cared to decipher it: I am above authority.

He certainly didn't seem bothered by the prospect of detailing his illegal business to two foreign journalists. But Mr J was not alone in his relaxed approach. That summer, 2001, was the first time in nearly a decade that large tracts of Bekaa farmland had been planted out with cannabis. There was scant attempt to hide it. Some farmers planted the cannabis between tall, dazzling sunflowers. A lame disguise? A bid to earn the subsidies offered for crop substitution? Or a nod to the Fairouz song: 'I'm being persecuted by the government. I planted sunflowers, which grew into cannabis.' Who knew? The only sure thing was that as we drove through the valley entire fields of it were there, by the side of the road, just a few months away from harvest.

'What you see this year is nothing compared with

production during the war,' Mr J said, speaking with nostalgia and bravado, chest large, chin up.

'I have read that Lebanon earned $10 billion dollars from hashish and opium poppies between 1970 and the end of the war,' I said.

'You are right. During the war we had 700,000 to 900,000 dunums planted with hashish,' said Mr J. 'Lebanon could earn half a billion dollars a year from it! We are not there yet but we are already doing well this year. Last year this area was filled with potatoes,' he waved airily in the direction of farmland on the other side of the town. 'Now we have 350,000 dunums. It is 1000 times more than last year.'

I did a bit of mental maths; about 35,000 hectares of the Bekaa was growing hashish. I had read a bit before leaving for the trip and quickly estimated that the crop would be valued at around $150 million.

In 1992, when the war and its aftershocks had finally petered out, the new Lebanese government caved in to pressure from the United States and Syria and cracked down on the drug business: tanks and tractors were sent in to destroy the crops. It was an effective deterrent (not only was the cannabis crop worthless but it was too late to plant a legal replacement and the farmers were left without any income). In 1994 Lebanon's farmlands were declared drug free.

The war years had left Lebanon with a big reputation as a producer of quality hashish: Red Leb, Bekaa Gold, the connoisseurs called it. As one of the few Middle Eastern countries not to have oil reserves, hashish was the oil of Lebanon. It helped to fund the country's myriad factions and militias and money flowed from an eager market in the West. The story went that private planes would land loaded with guns and leave full of hashish. The value of the crop meant the valley quickly became a crucible for a kind of uber-mafia, deep into the lucrative businesses of drugs, weapons, kidnapping and militia training. Militias from Japan, Iran, Libya as well as radical Palestinian factions and even European revolutionaries flooded the Bekaa's lawless isolation to milk what they could of Lebanon's chaos.

And when the war ended, the local farmers – who had been useful pawns in this network of crime – were just left behind to make the best of it. After eight years of battling with failed crop substitution schemes, the farmers had decided they had nothing left to lose. Programs to replace hashish with high-value crops like walnuts, saffron and capers had not worked, they said (they were labour-intensive, expensive to grow and took a long time to reach peak production). The farmers were impatient, they were poor, they could not afford to send their children to school or heat their homes. Cannabis was a perfect crop: it required almost no labour, grew anywhere and delivered instant, guaranteed large returns. And the drug barons were on the sidelines, ready to get back to work.

Drugs had a long history in the Bekaa. Cultivation of cannabis was rife as far back as Roman times. So modern-day farmers didn't feel like criminals. Far from it, growing drugs almost felt like a Bekaa Valley tradition. For Mr J, hashish farming was as natural as growing potatoes. It had been a family business for three generations and he had slipped seamlessly, guiltlessly, back to old tricks.

He held up a finger and told us to wait and then he walked inside the house – a single-storey bungalow painted white – and returned with a lump of hashish the size of a tennis ball. He tore off a chunk and rolled and pressed it into a golf-ball-sized piece and handed it to me. He gave another to George and dropped the rest into the pocket of his jacket.

'Feel it,' he said, with passion. 'What do you think? It's like butter, no?'

'So how much of this stuff do you have inside?' I asked him, more mental mathematics, this time trying to calculate its street value. 'I thought this was the first real year of a return to production?'

Mr J smiled indulgently. 'This is like any business. It's important to keep a stockpile ready to help us through the bad years. I see my hashish as like a bank and we protect it like any treasure.'

What this meant was that Mr J kept his hashish pressed into bars, like gold. Each bar was stamped with his personal seal and the lot was stored in boxes hidden in a vault under his bed. To keep it safe, Mr J (like the other drug lords in the valley) had hired small private militias to guard his store of hash as well as the plots cultivated by 20 or so former potato farmers he had on commission. It was too late in the season to risk losing the crop now.

After we'd drunk our tea and admired Mr J's product, we left his garden in Baalbek and drove north towards Hermel. On both sides mountains rose steeply from the flat valley floor and the sun shone out of a blue sky. As we drove, Malik told stories about being a kid in Beirut during the war and how when he was 15 he set up his own checkpoint at the entrance to his street and manned it with friends and automatic weapons. He chuckled as he recalled it, ludicrous to imagine it now with the wisdom of years, and George and I were the perfect wide-eyed audience. But it was better to remember the war like this – a boy's own adventure; it helped to mask the horror of what it must have been. This was

Lebanon, the unthinkable could become normal, and as we turned off the main road another version of Lebanon's twilight zone of B-movie strangeness appeared in front of me: private guards armed with Kalashnikovs patrolling fields of illegal crops of cannabis.

As we made our way down a dirt track the cannabis plants grew on both sides, on plots the size of football fields. When one field ended, another began. It was everywhere. We were buried in it and the crisp, grassy smell of the plants hung in the stillness of the dry valley air.

'Wow,' said George.

'Oh . . . my . . . God!' I said.

'Guess what I'm doing tonight,' he added, fingering the ball of hashish in his pocket.

We stopped the car and got out but there was nothing to do but look. A man paced the perimeter of the field with a Kalashnikov slung over his shoulder, and black-and-white-checked headgear, the *keffiyeh*, draped over his head to protect him from the sun. We stood around like this, taking in the boldness of the way this illegal activity had been once again embraced. After a while we heard the crack, crack of gunfire in the distance – probably a guard from a neighbouring field. Mr J bristled and we decided to get going. We were acutely aware that a week or so before a television crew had been shot at, at close range, while trying to film hashish fields not far from where we stood.

Back at the house Mr J's wife was preparing a lunch of *chiche barak*, tiny fried chicken dumplings smothered in a yoghurt sauce. She was chopping fresh coriander leaves to add to the ground chicken mixture. She scooped tiny lumps of spiced ground meat into squares of pastry and then pinched the pastry together to form the dumpling.

I felt that perhaps I should have joined her in the kitchen – I was the only other woman after all – but hashish was more interesting than cooking and anyway, I felt more comfortable with the men. So I sat in the living room with the others. It was a typical family home with snapshots of smiling faces in frames set around the room and little ornaments, a plaque with a quote from the Qur'an. The coffee table was decorated with a white crocheted doily and on top of it was placed a slender crystal vase, with a plastic flower in it.

While we waited for lunch Mr J gave a detailed and very enthusiastic run-down of the steps involved in illegal hashish production and sale. This is what I learned:

There are three grades. When the plants are harvested (by Syrian seasonal workers paid $10 a day) they are left for two days to dry in the sun before being transferred for processing into sheds. Just a year ago these sheds were used to house battery hens.

The flowering heads of the plant are sieved to shake out the beads of resin that make the hashish. This is done three times; each time the quality drops and the product receives a lower grading and is sold more cheaply.

The hashish is bundled into one-kilogram blocks that sell for between $500 and $1000 each and each producer marks the blocks of hash with his own stamp. The hash is then transferred to a port somewhere along the Lebanese coast (it changed regularly and Mr J was wary about giving examples). From there it went direct to Rotterdam.

'Of course we have guys who work with us at the European customs. They take about 25 per cent of the value of the shipment, either in cash or in product. It's a set price, like a tax. There's no need to negotiate.' Mr J was pleased with this analogy and waved his cigar in the air and took another puff.

Mr J's cell phone rang and he answered, stood up and strolled around the living room as he spoke, laughing and gesticulating in animated English conversation. 'Yes, yes. Very good. Okay and we will see you soon, *insha'allah. Yalla*, bye.' He hung up.

'That was a call from Holland,' he said, pleased. 'Hashish is like wine. My contacts in Amsterdam like to send out one of their men to oversee the final stages of production. They will come next week and stay until we harvest in October.'

He pulled out the piece of hashish that was left over from the ball he had shown me earlier. He began to pinch off little pieces and dried them with the flame from one of the long matches he used to light his cigar. When they had cooled he crumbled the hashish into granules and mixed them with a small amount of tobacco. He rolled two or three hashish cigarettes, kept one for himself and handed the others around the room.

As we each lit our spliffs Mr J's eldest son, about 18, walked into the room, and I couldn't help thinking how he must be the most popular boy in school.

'Do you let your son smoke?' I asked him.

He bristled, his eyes narrowed. 'Absolutely *not*!' he said, and turned to his son. 'Don't you *ever* let me catch you smoking this stuff.'

With no apparent sense of irony, he exhaled a vast lungful of fragrant smoke, stubbed out the burning end of the cigarette, and laid the rest in the ashtray for later. And then Mr J stood up, smoothed his trousers, and motioned for us to sit down to lunch.

CHAPTER 6
A SECRET LIFE

Summer progressed and the humidity was rising. The air was thick with it. The city was starting to empty of Beirutis and fill with summer visitors from the Gulf, on the run from the restrictions of life in Riyadh or Jeddah and into Beirut's warm and easygoing embrace. Most residents of Beirut had fled to the coolness of the mountains, to the north around Beit Mery or the Qadisha Valley, or to the mountain villages of the south that stretched out towards the Israeli border – or to holiday in Europe. For about six weeks in July and August the weather was so unbearable that escape was the only answer. 'It's like walking around with a wet towel on your face,' George said, struggling to find an analogy for the suffocating dampness of the air.

Matthew and I decided to abandon Beirut for a couple of nights and hunkered down at our favourite mountain getaway: a stylishly old-fashioned hotel in Laqlouq, built into barren rocky peaks high above the winter snowline. Our room had a creaky bed and delightfully worn-out rugs on the floor, and a huge 1950s-style bathroom with views over the ski runs and down, down the mountain to the alpine resort below. We filled the days playing ping-pong and horse riding, hiking and lunching for hours at the hotel's outdoor restaurant, listening to the chatter of French-speaking Lebanese families at adjacent tables, and overdosing on air so fresh and clean it was intoxicating.

When we had stored up a few days of cool we gingerly made our way back down the mountain. It was essential to take it easy. As well as coping with the heat, we were recovering from weeks of summer parties: a night at Ahmad's place drinking cocktails on the terrace; a night at the Baalbek International Festival, an annual music event held in the ruins of Baalbek's gracious Roman temples of Jupiter and Bacchus, with a coach trip through the Bekaa Valley and back to Beirut at 3 a.m. We had passed on tickets to Sting and missed out on coveted seats to see Fairouz perform at another festival nearer to Beirut, and so instead booked to see a version of the opera Carmina Burana at Baalbek. As the overture began we had heard the sound of gunfire and looked up to see a volley of tracer bullets fired, who knows why and by who knows who (members of Hezbollah? Palestinians from the nearby refugee camp? Local hooligans?), making an arc of little points of light through the blue-black twilight. The conductor stopped, the gunmen finished making their statement (whatever it was) and then the music started up again.

One morning Matthew and I joined Leila, Ramzi and our journalist crowd and headed north to Batroun to have lunch at Restaurant Jamal, where the tables were set up in the shallow water and we could eat under umbrellas with our feet wet to the ankles. There were plans for some hair of the dog once we got to the restaurant, or maybe a few hairs: bottles and bottles of *blanc de blanc* and rosé fermented from grapes grown in Lebanon's gnarled old Bekaa Valley vineyards. Grapes had been grown and wine fermented in the

Bekaa since at least the time of the Romans, who carved bunches of grapes on the grey-gold stone of the Temple of Bacchus. The Romans had held their own wild parties inside the temple, featuring sexual sacrifice and possibly human sacrifice, giving rise to the term Bacchanalia.

We were planning a bit of Bacchanalia of our own – well, the drunken part anyway – and no one was game to drive. Lebanon's roads were deadly enough when you were sober. We hired a taxi, and took the highway north out of Beirut. We passed Bouj Hammoud where the descendants of Armenian families who had survived genocide by the Turks at the beginning of last century still lived, and on to the Christian port town of Jounieh, past the casino (where I once lost all my money playing roulette), and the Super Nightclubs, where women from places like Moldova performed 'cabaret' for a male audience. There were dramatic views back down the coast. We kept driving, past the ruins of the sprawling Crusader castle at Byblos and to Batroun.

Restaurant Jamal was the kind of place you had to be introduced to; I would never have found it alone. As you drove along the coast road a little cluster of drab buildings appeared more or less out of the blue, and the entrance was nothing more than a plain door in the middle of the row. From the sea, the restaurant was obscured at the end of a channel of water cut into the rocky coastline. For Beirut day-trippers, the most popular, glamorous thing to do was travel from Beirut in cigarette boats and expensive cruisers with one's coterie and then to drop anchor at the end of the channel. A quick mobile phone call to the restaurant and a little motorboat would putt out to collect them and they would strut into the restaurant – the women in bikinis and pedicures, the men with bare, bronzed chests and glossy black hair slicked flat with handfuls of seawater.

We walked across the dining terrace that looked out over the water, down a wooden staircase and then over some rocks and across the narrow stony shoreline to our table in the water. (Leila had booked a week in advance to reserve it.) We wriggled around in our seats, driving the legs of the chairs into stable places in the sandy bottom, and then swung our feet through the cool, clear water. The sun danced on the water as it was pulled slowly back and forth by the tide and little shards of light sparkled around us. Bliss.

Leila ordered for everyone – freshly made *moutabal*, Lebanon's (superior) alternative to *baba ghanoush*, with a perfect smoky flavour and shiny red pomegranate seeds on the top; plates full of little fried fish; a fresh thyme salad and other things. While we waited for the food to arrive we snacked on tart green olives and seeds and filled our glasses with rosé from the Ksara vineyard in the Bekaa Valley, and then again with rosé from Kfraya vineyard, also in the Bekaa but much further south. There, the valley became more lush and began to close in on itself, before rising again into the Chouf mountain range, where narrow twisting roads spiralled past a forest of cedar trees and pretty Druze villages. As we drank, we compared each wine and argued over which was better.

Ramzi dismissed both. 'Château Musar is the best winery in Lebanon,' he said, quoting the accepted wisdom. Château Musar had won too many international awards to count and was famous for missing barely a single vintage throughout the long civil war.

'What about Massaya?' Leila said, waving to the brothers who owned the vineyard and happened to be lunching at an adjacent table. Massaya was one of the newest Lebanese wine labels and had quickly gathered an excellent reputation.

When I look back on it now that summer seemed so full of innocence. September 11 was unimaginable. The Palestinians and Israelis continued their tragic conflict but I had not been in the Middle East for long enough to become cynical. I actually believed there could soon be an end to it. And a war in Iraq? Well, after the bungled attempts in 1991 to overthrow Saddam Hussein, the Kurdish refugee crisis that ensued, and the threat of involving Iraq's neighbours, especially Iran, no one believed it was possible the world would go there again. Even Lebanon, for all its instability and unresolved tensions, its teetering economy and extremes of wealth and poverty, seemed to be almost back on its feet.

At least, that was how it seemed to me as I rubbed more sunscreen into my shoulders and adjusted my sunglasses and tucked into my third (fourth?) glass of wine. I had helped to empty the bottle of Ksara's rosé and we were now almost done with our bottle of Kfraya. But I had long ago lost interest in the Ksara versus Kfraya debate. They both tasted fine to me and I was drunk, but happy to be drunk, and was feeling sentimental. I had been hopelessly charmed and beguiled by Lebanon and the Lebanese. With so few other foreigners in the country, being there felt like a magical secret that Matthew and I had discovered. Living in that war-torn, rebuilding place was a wondrous surprise.

I was almost disappointed that on Monday I had plans to fly to Egypt to cover the first ever Africa-wide boxing championship for women. I had only been in Beirut for six months but, against all my expectations, Lebanon already felt like home.

I stayed in a dingy hotel in Cairo. Men from the Gulf loitered in the corridors and local women – clothes just a little too tight, lipstick just a little too obvious – rode the elevator alone. I drew conclusions.

The reception desk was wedged into an alcove of dark panelled wood next to the lift. It was staffed by two men whom I could never tell apart: same snarling, miserable faces, same oily hair, same bland shirts stretched over fat bellies. They sat together smoking and drinking coffee and monitoring who came and went. They were unlike any Arabs I had ever met – doggedly unfriendly and dismissive.

The breakfast was inedible – rancid butter, stale bread rolls, off cheese. And the dining room (a converted guest bedroom) was indescribably filthy. I was not surprised when I began to hear a mouse skittering around my room at night. There was also a hole in the bathroom wall.

I had a corner room with a large balcony. From one side I could look into the garden of the Algerian Embassy and from the other I had a view of the Nile's dun-coloured tide, framed by two adjacent apartment blocks. Best of all, I could see directly into the living rooms of these apartments, with their elegant Art Deco curves and thunking ceiling fans and painted floor tiles. I enjoyed the voyeurism. It seemed appropriate to live packed together in this gigantic city and I felt somehow at ease there.

Each morning I would ride one of the battered black and white taxis that were everywhere in Cairo to the Olympic Center at Maadi, a suburb about 30 minutes from the hotel, to watch Egypt's first national boxing team for women in training.

When you got inside these little vehicles with their unnaturally low-slung seats, in which the springs had given up the ghost, once you got over the feeling of vulnerability (eye-level with the wheels of giant trucks with bad brakes and exhausts belching black clouds), they offered a rare and powerful perspective on Cairo.

From this angle, the details seemed to jump forward and it

felt like being immersed under the skin of the city, with its kaleidoscope of history and heartbreak. As we drove past the Egyptian Museum, stocked with magnificent dug-up pieces of the past, I saw a man pushing a cart piled with watermelon. He lost control of it as it rounded a corner and the melons fell to the road, smashed. He sat in the gutter with his head in his hands; a day's livelihood (a week's?), gone. I saw lovers standing beside the Nile and I could see him gently reposition her headscarf, an excuse just to touch her.

It had taken many days of negotiations, long sessions drinking tea and ingratiating myself, to be allowed open access to the boxers as they trained. They were preparing to fight in the First African Boxing Championship for Women. Teams from across Africa were expected. The Egyptian team had been hastily put together a few months earlier after a country-wide search, region by region: if Egypt was to host the first championship then it needed its own team.

This was the first time there had been an Africa-wide women's boxing tournament, and it was important to remember that even in the West women's boxing was relatively new. It was banned until 1993 in the US and until 1996 in Britain. In sub-Saharan countries, like Nigeria, Ghana, Uganda, women's boxing was reasonably well established. But for a society like Egypt, which seemed to have become progressively more conservative since the heady days of the 1950s and 1960s when it was rare to see a woman in *hejab*, official support for what was traditionally a male sport seemed almost revolutionary.

I could see the 13 women in the boxing team training on the grass in a corner of the main sports ground, shadow-boxing, stretching and punching at paddles held up by the coach. I began to walk towards them, across the loop of running track that fringed an oval grass field, zigzagging past sprinters and high jumpers. Apart from the spire of a mosque in the distance, the scene could have been any elite sporting institution anywhere in the world. As I drew closer to the women I realised that I didn't really know what I was expecting. A lot of clichés probably: butch girls, outcasts who had turned to boxing as a way to rebel against a society that had restricted and rejected them.

'This is the team,' the coach said when I introduced myself, and pointed with his hand towards the women. 'We are doing basic training. You are welcome to sit there and watch if you like.' His hand swept back in the opposite direction towards a stand of bleachers a few metres away. I took this as a command, non-negotiable, and so moved off to find a place to sit. I pulled out my notebook and a pen and jotted things down.

The women were a clashing mixture of heights and physiques and they fought in weight categories ranging from 45 kilograms to 81 kilograms. Most wore baggy tracksuits, even though the weather was scorching. A few also wore headscarves. One of the women took her turn for individual training with the coach. She attacked him, smashing her gloved hands into the boxing paddles he held in front of her, but he shouted at her. 'Why are you on the back foot? I swear to God I will slap you. You're laughing, huh! Stand straight, girl, and hit until I'm squeezed into the corner. That's it. I'm cornered now. Finish!'

She collapsed into giggles and I couldn't tell if it was to deflect her embarrassment at being shouted at in front of her team, or because she wasn't taking it seriously. She ripped the gloves from her hands and pulled a mouth guard from her teeth, but left her padded helmet on, the straps swinging around her neck as she walked away. I was curious to know more. I caught her eye, smiled and beckoned her towards me.

'You were great,' I began.

She shrugged and began unwinding the white binding that was wrapped around her hands to protect them from the force of the blows. 'Yeah, well, my coach wasn't happy.'

'My name is Catherine,' I said, and Maiada introduced herself and sat beside me on the bleachers. She was about 20, with unusual green-grey eyes and clear brown skin stretched over high cheekbones. She had a little beauty spot above her lip. I was struck by how attractive she was, with an appealing impish energy lit by a spectacular smile. I imagined a life for her – the adored youngest daughter of a middle-class family, indulged, with the freedom to pursue her dreams free of the judgement and restrictions that affect so many Egyptian women. I noted that she did not wear a scarf over her head.

We snatched our conversation quietly between bouts. Maiada had not been a boxer for long. She had a black belt in karate and had switched to boxing more recently. She thought, why not? She was like that: always craving adventure, new experiences. She won the 54-kilo title in her district.

'Your family must be proud of you,' I said, and for the first time the smile disappeared and she was silent. After a while, she spoke.

'My village is a stupid village, a very stupid village,' she said, looking down, almost as if she was talking to herself. 'My family don't agree with this play,' she added, and gestured widely to the other girls shadow-boxing in front of us. 'It's because,' she paused again, grasping for the English translation, 'they are narrow-minded.'

It turned out that I had Maiada pegged all wrong. The only thing I'd guessed correctly was that she was the youngest daughter. But her family was not middle class, nor liberal. She came from one of the poorest regions of Egypt, from a village known for its conservatism. Her father had died when she was two, and her mother worked as a nurse to support her five daughters. The family was already pitied for producing not one son. And then to lose a husband! Well, a family like that struggled for influence and respect. They relied on kindness. The only way out was for Maiada's mother to ensure her girls married well. A good husband could provide for them and give them a place in society.

Boxing wasn't really a part of that plan. It brought the wrong kind of attention to Maiada's family and threw her reputation into question. Many of the villagers, including one of Maiada's older sisters, labelled her sporting ambitions as heresy. It was not the sport itself they objected to. It was working so closely with a male coach: the touching, handling, legs spread apart and poses that were uncontrolled, breasts bouncing with each punch. No, it was impossible that Maiada could be encouraged to disrespect herself, and the Qur'an, in that way.

Maiada said she felt angry when people accused her of disobeying her religion. She had not rejected Islam, she said. She was devout. She prayed regularly and always before each match. She told me about the Prophet's wives, how they were strong women – in business, in sport. 'Aisha, the Prophet's daughter, was a famous horsewoman and his first wife, Khadija, ran many businesses. Any man's sport should also be for women too. The world demands that women and men be alike, in everything.'

But Maiada wanted to be sure that what she was doing would not disappoint God. She had a ritual that she carried out before each match to help satisfy herself that boxing was not *haram*. She counted her prayer beads three times, and chanted *suras*, asking God to guide her. 'I asked God to let me win if it was good for me, and if it was not, and I don't win, then I would be satisfied.'

The afternoon sun was searing. We moved from the rows of stadium seating and stood together in a little shady space. It was out of the direct sun, but the air was heavy with heat. I lifted my shirt away from my body and flapped it about, hoping to generate some cool air. Maiada wiped beads of perspiration from her upper lip.

'If everyone disagrees, how do you manage to keep boxing?' I asked.

'I used to train in secret,' she said, her chin jutting almost imperceptibly in defiance. 'I told my family that I was doing extra study after college and instead I went to the club.'

Deception is hard the first time. But once you start, and it works, and you feel the relief of freedom to do what you want, then it becomes easy. It was like that for Maiada. At first she felt guilty telling her mother that she was staying back at college to study. But after a while it felt as natural as breathing, and this secret time to pursue something that she loved doing became as essential to her as oxygen.

I had heard of something similar from another Egyptian woman, who kept an apartment of her own, secret from her husband, her sister, her mother. It was her private place where she could go and do whatever she wanted without fear of judgement, rules, expectations. 'When my daughter grows up,' she told me, 'I am going to teach her how to have a secret life.'

Maiada kept her secret life from everyone but her coach and team mates for three years. Then, one day, someone saw her going to the club. Her secret was out. Maiada's mother was devastated: what would happen when the other villagers found out? Her reputation would be ruined and the consequences could be dire. The most extreme scenario was that she could become a victim of an honour crime – maimed or killed for bringing shame to her family and village.

Maiada was defiant. She refused to give up something she loved and something she believed sincerely was not wrong. She told her mother about how she prayed before each match. 'If I continue to win, then how can you say Allah is against me?' she reasoned. Slowly her mother began to soften. But Maiada's older sister and others in the village remained opposed to her. Maiada refused to be cowed. She went further underground.

'I don't stay there much, in the village,' she said. 'My village is against me and so I wake up at seven in the morning and go to college, then to the club, and when I return at nine at night people are already asleep.'

We had been talking for ages and the shadows were growing long. I said goodbye to Maiada, to the team, to the coach. There were two weeks to go until the team was due to fight.

I loved Cairo just before dusk, when the streets started to fill with pedestrians again after the heat of the day. Shops were open late, street food vendors slid back the metal doors to their stalls and started business, selling *sharwarma* sandwiches (shaved, spiced meat stuffed into bread rolls and frankly not as good as I was used to in Beirut) and a dish I'd never seen anywhere but Cairo, made from rice, pasta, lentils and tomato. The promenade along the edges of the Nile was lined with families who stood there enjoying the evening with the dirty water on one side and a highway full of cars on the other.

When I got back to the hotel I dragged my room's only chair outside and positioned it so that I saw a strip of muddy Nile water and the living room of my neighbour opposite.

I put my feet on the railing and let my mind drift, sipped a beer straight from the bottle, and listened to Cairo wake up for the night.

For the next week, it was the same: back and forth between my strange hotel and the Olympic Center at Maadi. The other girls began to open up and I got to know a little more about them. Jihan, her dark Nubian skin stretched over a lean-muscled body, her tracksuit topped with a headscarf, was fighting in the memory of her brother Mustafa. Mustafa had been a champion boxer himself before he was killed in a car accident a few years earlier. Unlike Maiada, Jihan's family was always with her, urging her on, encouraging. Jihan's boxing was a way to bring Mustafa back into their lives.

The day of the championship drew closer but the African teams had not arrived. The Egyptian organising committee began to ring around. 'Are you coming? The championship begins in a few days.' The news wasn't good: no one had money. Even if there were talented boxers to send, how could the African countries afford to fly them to Cairo, to provide uniforms and equipment? And then, just as the Egyptians were about to give up hope, the Olympic Center began to fill with long-limbed black girls with athletic loping strides from Uganda, Ghana, Morocco, Tunisia.

The mood changed. It was clear that some of these women were going to provide tough competition for the Egyptians.

The teams retreated into separate corners of the dormitory common room. The rivalry was palpable, but Maiada was too curious to go along with it. The next morning she arrived for training with her hair in corn-rows, African style.

The day of the championship was chaos. The fighters were shadow-boxing in the corridors. The dressing rooms were overcrowded with family and friends packed in to give last-minute tips and confidence to the fighters. The Egyptian coach was tense and stalked the halls with a stony expression. Two of the fighters began cat-fighting. Nadia, a serious Moroccan fighter with big ambitions, sat quietly with her coach, her eyebrows raised.

I was anxious for Maiada. None of her family was there to see her box in the biggest match of her life. She was resigned, but I knew her well enough to see the disappointment. She did a good job of hiding it, but the spark was missing and I hoped it wouldn't affect her strength of mind in the ring.

I had been at training sessions for two weeks but I still found it hard to assess how points were scored. When Maiada fought all I could see was step, punch, swing, punch, sway, hit, over and over until a bell rang. Her opponent in the championship was another Egyptian girl – the low turnout of African nations meant that dreams of heats and semi-finals were abandoned. Every fight was a grand final. Maiada's opponent came at her like a machine. The referee screamed for her to stop and she was cautioned. The crowd screamed back, deafening. They chanted, and I couldn't catch the words, and the first round was over.

Maiada sat in the corner, the coach spoke urgently into her ear, and she nodded her head, paused, listened, nodded again. Someone swabbed the sweat from her face with a towel and held a cup to her lips. She tilted her head back and let the liquid run over her face, used her hand to spread it around, shook her head and droplets of water fanned out around her. Three bells: ding, ding, ding. The next round. She went back to the fight, danced on the spot, then step, punch, swing, punch, sway, hit.

The bell rang again. The two women stood in the centre of the ring, separated by one of the officials. Someone shouted through a microphone, the voice distorted by feedback, but suddenly Maiada's hand was in the air. She had won. A gold medal was hung around her neck. She drew her gloved hands together and dropped to her knees and prayed.

The day after the championships Maiada invited me to her village. It was the first time she had been back for almost a month and she was excited, but also nervous because she knew there would be a kind of confrontation with her family and the villagers, and that her acceptance or rejection would ride on this reunion.

During the journey she began remaking herself in a way she hoped would meet with approval. She wrapped a pale blue scarf around her head. 'I'm doing this because, you know, my mother wants it,' she said. She added a pair of sunglasses and rested her chin in her palm and stared out of the window.

It was the first time I had seen her in *hejab* and I was charmed by the fashionable care she had taken putting together her outfit. 'You look like Jackie O,' I told her and she made a little face, a little pose. She didn't understand the reference but she could tell it was a kind of compliment.

We left Cairo behind us, streaking past a landscape that was flat and dry. A haze of smog hung above the horizon. And then the fields were full of cotton plants, and we passed lumbering trucks and donkey-drawn carts, people walking along the side of the road. Maiada had promised the journey would take about 90 minutes. After almost four hours the taxi slowed and she directed the driver into a small road that veered off to the right. We followed it for 15 or 20 minutes, past small, rough vegetable plots. The road got narrower, and when the bitumen ended it got bumpier and the vegetable plots disappeared into barren fields choked with rubbish. We were driving on little more than a dirt track that weaved between simple breeze-block homes, two storeys high and packed together so closely they looked like terraces. Mangy dogs stood cowed and trembling on corners or slumped in scraps of shade. A crowd was gathering around the car, faces peered inside: grubby children with cheeky grins, jumping and pulling faces, and black-toothed crones squinting at us. People came out of their houses and stood in their doorways and watched our rocking old car – a jalopy but impossibly luxurious here – lumber past. God, it was poor.

As we pulled up outside Maiada's house the villagers recognised her and someone shouted for her mother to come. Come! Arms were in the air, waving for Maiada's attention. As soon as she stepped from the car it was apparent something had shifted. This reception wasn't wary or judgemental; it was elated, excited. Then someone came forward waving a torn piece of newspaper and it became clear: the whole village had read of Maiada's win in the newspaper. Quite simply, they were proud.

When she made it out of the taxi, hands appeared, grabbing at her medal, and she passed it around and began to tell her story: of the fight, of the big city, of the girls from Africa, of her new foreign friend.

At the back of the crowd stood a woman, simple and quiet. Maiada went to her. 'Mama, I missed you,' she said. The two embraced. 'I got you the gold.' Maiada gestured to the crowd and someone passed the medal forward and handed it to Maiada's mother.

'How are you, honey?' her mother asked softly.

'Thanks to God, I am fine,' Maiada answered her. '*Hamdi-lallah.*'

Maiada took my hand and led me into her home. We walked this way together from room to room and Maiada explained who lived in each, what it was used for. The house was worn and in need of repair. Clouds of flies moved through the place and it smelled of sewage. I fixed a smile on my face, wanting to show neither pity nor disgust.

There was very little furniture or decoration, but the house was cared for, swept, with little lace doilies on the coffee table and a vase of plastic flowers. The home stretched over two floors. There was a small sitting room, a dining room and a kitchen downstairs. The bathroom had a pit toilet, a single tap and a bucket for washing. Upstairs were three bedrooms, with a mirror and washbasin on the landing between them. Maiada had stuck posters of Egyptian pop stars and film stars all over the bedroom she shared with a sister and her bed was covered with soft toys.

We climbed further, through a door at the top of a staircase and onto the roof. Here was the source of the smell and the flies: the roof had been turned into a chicken coop. There was quite a flock of them, shitting and scratching and squawking, their little beaks pecking at crusted-over skin where the feathers had been rubbed away. There were also two turkeys, moving through the crowd of agitated hens with their grotesque jerky movements and folds of scabby skin. And above them all, the hideous cloud of flies hovered in a black haze. The birds' feet crunched over dozens of empty vials of hormones and I felt the smile slip.

After the tour of the house, Maiada dragged an elegant veiled woman holding a baby from the crowd. 'This is my sister,' she said. 'You know, the one I told you about?' Then, turning to her sister, she goaded, 'Come on, tell her how you disapprove of me.'

The sister was uncomfortable. 'It's just that, well, Islam says that women should . . .' She turned to Maiada, full of fondness and concern. 'Oh, you say it.'

'Relax. No problem,' Maiada said.

'You won't be angry?'

'No.'

'Okay. Well then, Islam told us that women should stay inside their homes where men will not look at them,' the sister said. 'Islam states that a woman should not show her hair or parts of her body and that she should not move her body like that.' Maiada's sister looked at her with love. 'But, sister, I am satisfied that you prayed before the match and asked God that if winning is right, then to win. But if it would turn to evil, then to let you lose.'

She turned to me. 'I hope God has answered Maiada's prayers.'

While we talked, Maiada's best friend stood beside her, her hands around Maiada's waist, looking wistful. 'I wish I could play boxing but my parents do not allow me,' she said.

Another of Maiada's sisters called from the kitchen. 'Come on, eat! Eat! The food is ready.'

Maiada's mother fluttered around her daughters, proud of them and excited to have a foreigner in her home. 'I'm happy, by God. I'm very happy. And I'm also happy that you came here,' she said to me, holding my hands in hers.

Maiada hit her mother playfully on the arm to tease her for carrying on. '*Yalla*, it is time for lunch,' she said, and shooed me inside. A turkey had been killed and another sister was struggling with a giant pot suspended over a wood fire.

The family squeezed together on the couch and I sat with Maiada at a small table, set carefully with a white cloth, in the centre of the room. The turkey was brought from the kitchen – a huge bird, pale from being boiled in water, its skin white and gelatinous. It was an extravagant gesture of welcome, to Maiada and to me.

With the family smiling, watching, expectant, I tore a piece of turkey from the breast and began to eat.

CHAPTER 7
LOVE, DEATH AND PARADISE

Back in Beirut, I was struggling to dress for a meeting. What do you wear for a visit to the Party of God? One hour and four outfits later I was dressed in a long-sleeved black shirt buttoned to the neck and hanging loosely over long black trousers; minimal make-up. I stuffed a black scarf into my bag – in case I needed to cover my head – and hurried downstairs to meet my taxi driver, Khaled.

'How do I look?' I twirled theatrically in the street.

Khaled nodded encouragingly. 'A good choice for a visit to Hezbollah,' he said, and I was relieved.

I had met Khaled a few days after arriving in Beirut because he was often hanging around outside the Mayflower Hotel where I was staying. He gave me his mobile telephone number and he became 'my' taxi driver. I would call him whenever I needed to go somewhere out of the way and felt unsure about negotiating a *service* ride.

Khaled drove one of those ubiquitous Mercedes-Benz 230s. His was buttercup yellow and in immaculate condition.

I climbed in the front beside him and we sat in a traffic jam, smoking Gitanes and practising the Islamic greeting, *salaam aleikum*, peace be upon you. 'Catherine, Hezbollah will be very impressed if you use this greeting,' Khaled assured me. I hoped he was right. I was nervous. This was to be my first visit to Hezbollah, and even though I had spent a lot of time with Hadi, it felt different to be visiting the organisation itself. I was imagining dour bearded cadres and radical rhetoric.

My appointment was at the organisation's Foreign Media Relations office. The fact that Hezbollah even had an office dedicated to spin doctoring its public profile to the media seemed at odds with its evil and secretive reputation. But no one could disagree that Hezbollah had an image problem, and even inside Lebanon debate was intensifying over what sort of role the organisation should play.

The Foreign Media Relations office – along with much of the rest of Hezbollah's administration – was based in the suburb of Haret Hreik in the south of Beirut and included a large network of social welfare organisations, the offices of Hezbollah MPs elected to the Lebanese parliament, and Al-Manar (the Lighthouse), a satellite-television channel backed by the group.

If you were a journalist wandering through these areas, and you pulled out a camera without Hezbollah's explicit okay, it was typical to be detained for a few hours and questioned about what you were up to. Everyone was suspected of being an Israeli spy until it was proven otherwise. Even journalists who called for an appointment at the Foreign Media Relations office were thoroughly researched: passports taken and photocopied along with press credentials, a search done of previous published work and potential biases. I couldn't decide if it was paranoia or excellent pre-emptive PR. Probably both. Either way, as Khaled drove me through

Haret Hreik's streets that day, I felt I was slipping into the dark heart of something dangerous and forbidden.

I tried to shuck off my preconceptions and mused over a conversation Courtney had told me about during one of her first visits to the organisation. The assistant press officer told her Hezbollah suffered unfairly from its reputation as a terrorist organisation. 'It is a stereotype, they think we are the terrorist,' he told her.

'Hey, I am an American woman living in the Middle East. Don't you think I know all about stereotypes?' Courtney – tall, blonde, single and voluptuous – shot back.

'Yes, yes!' the official replied. 'It is true. It is true, they think we are the terrorist and you are the sex machine.'

Haret Hreik was filled with refugee families from southern Lebanon, Shi'ites who had fled villages inside the Israeli Occupied Zone and had made new lives in Beirut. It was a poor and crowded area dominated by street after street of drab high-rise apartment blocks with thick canvas 'balcony curtains' in bright colours that allowed the women of the house to access their verandahs without risk of being seen without *hejab*. In summer the curtains shielded the apartments from blazing sun, and from a distance the different colours, some faded, some bright and new, made the buildings look like they were covered in giant patchwork quilts. Electricity wires hung in black knotted tangles above the street – the evidence of hundreds of illegal connections siphoning power to an uncountable number of apartments.

This was Beirut as I had never seen it before. It was far from the glitz of Downtown, the lazy Mediterranean atmosphere of the Corniche, the retro bustle of Hamra or the

French chic of Achrafieh. Hezbollah was everywhere. The party's yellow and green flag hung above the street, on buildings, on lamp posts. Interspersed between them were portraits of the young men who had died fighting Hezbollah's guerrilla war with Israel. These were the *shahids*, the martyrs, and they were the reason I had come to visit Hezbollah.

Khaled stopped the taxi in the middle of a small strip of shops. We were early. I opened my notebook and wrote down a few questions in preparation for my meeting and looked out at the shops: a supermarket, a kitchenware shop, and then right at the entrance to the building that housed Hezbollah's Foreign Media Relations office, the Romance Lingerie Boutique. The window display included an eye-popping collection of silk and lace. A woman walked past dressed in a black *chador* and I couldn't help a little smile at the juxtaposition of the two images.

The office was inside a residential apartment block – a security tactic to deter attacks on Hezbollah infrastructure. There was a serious-looking bearded fellow sitting on a chair outside, whom I assumed was a Hezbollah security guard. He didn't say a word as I said goodbye to Khaled and walked past him and into a concrete foyer, featureless except for a staircase and a tiny rickety-looking lift. I took the stairs, and followed a discreet arrow pointing upwards with Hezbollah's symbol beside it.

I approached the receptionist and I wanted to be polite, to make a good impression. I decided this was my big chance to use my new Islamic greeting. I felt self-conscious as I quietly stuttered out the words: '*Salaam aleikum*.'

'Ahh, *aleikum salaam*,' the receptionist replied. He broke into a smile and bowed his head slightly. 'And upon you be peace.'

I felt buoyed; I was off to a good start. I introduced myself and the receptionist showed me to a row of chairs in a small waiting room. A television set was mounted on one wall and tuned to Al-Manar. Portraits of Hezbollah's leader, Sayyad Hassan Nasrallah, and Iran's now dead former leader, Ayatollah Ruhollah Khomeini, were carefully arranged on the other.

Al-Manar was screening a station promotion in support of the Palestinians. An image of Shimon Peres flashed on the screen and underneath it the place of his birth, Poland. The next image was of an old Palestinian woman, underneath it the name of the coastal town of Haifa where she was born and which is now a part of Israel. The promo continued in the same vein, alternating pictures of prominent Israelis and their places of birth outside Israel with those of displaced Palestinian refugees.

I was watching the television distractedly when a man poked his head around the door and called my name. I had expected someone serious, middle-aged, but instead Hezbollah's foreign information officer was surely not much more than 30, smiling and energetic.

His name was Hussein Naboulsi. He had spent his childhood split between Iraq – where his father studied in the Shi'ite holy city of Najaf before moving the family to Baghdad, where he became a well-known imam – and Lebanon. Later, he had spent several years in Canada and the United States. 'You know, Catherine, I can speak Arabic with a perfect Iraqi accent,' he told me later, speaking English in a vaguely American one.

I relaxed and moved towards him, my hand extended, anticipating a firm, friendly shake. Hussein glanced at my open palm and politely took one step backwards. I stepped forwards and again he stepped backwards. I was oblivious and we continued this little dance, a step forward, a step backward, until Hussein short-circuited what was quickly becoming an awkward situation. He placed his right hand over his heart and with his left hand motioned for me to follow him. I had accidentally tripped over one of Hezbollah's fault lines. Devout Muslims believe it is *haram* for unrelated men and women to touch each other and I had very nearly caused Hussein, and myself, a serious embarrassment.

We entered an adjacent room with couches lining both walls, heavy curtains on large windows and more portraits of Nasrallah and Khomeini. Hussein called a colleague and a few minutes later coffee arrived in tiny cups.

'So, Catherine,' he began, 'how can I help you?'

I told him I wanted to interview the widows of Hezbollah's martyrs.

The families of suicide bombers were frequently portrayed as crazed fanatics, delighted to hear of the deaths of their sons, husbands, brothers, whom they believed had ascended to paradise. When news of their deaths broke, the bombers' families were quoted as saying how proud they were, how they could wish for no better death for their loved ones. This reaction comes from the Qur'an and there are several references to the rewards of martyrdom. Chapter Three, verse 169, for example, says:

> Never think that those who were slain in the cause of God are dead. They are alive, and well provided for by their Lord; pleased with His gifts and rejoicing that those they left behind, who have not yet joined them, have nothing to fear or to regret; rejoicing in God's grace and bounty. God will not deny the faithful their reward.

I was always wary of judging these families too harshly for this apparent joy. To me, it felt more like an emotional survival tactic – something to help the families of these suicide bombers negotiate the black cloud of shock and sorrow, and yes, of pride. And so I was intrigued to hear the stories of the women whose husbands went willingly, even eagerly, to their deaths. I wondered how all of that public stoicism intersected with the emotional world of private grief.

'Give me a few days,' Hussein told me. 'I will call you when I have arranged your program, *insha'allah*.'

I had quickly come to dread the words '*insha'allah*, 'God willing'. They were tacked on the end of almost every sentence. In Hussein's case it was a reflection of strong faith. But many Lebanese did it out of superstition or habit and the words often doubled as an excuse for inaction: 'Will you be able to fix the leaking pipes this afternoon?' '*Insha'allah*.' 'What time will you arrive?' 'At 9 a.m., *insha'allah*.' If these things didn't happen, the message seemed to be: 'Well, it wasn't that I didn't *intend* to be there on time, but it just wasn't God's will, you do understand.' Under these circumstances, it seemed almost blasphemous to make a fuss.

Leila tried her best to explain to me the subtleties of the term. 'The bottom line is this,' she said one day when I was struggling to read between the lines of another encounter. 'If someone tells you *insha'allah*, then for sure it isn't going to happen.'

Her assessment made me pessimistic now. I began to doubt that I'd get anywhere with my request to Hezbollah. My experience in the Middle East so far had taught me that if something was not going to happen it was unlikely I'd be told directly. It was considered rude and too confronting to be told 'no' upfront. The usual technique was to politely delay and delay, and make more and more excuses for why a thing had not happened, until I slowly, eventually, got the hint. But God was willing after all. Two days later Hussein called.

'Catherine, your program is ready. Can you come to the office tomorrow at 10 a.m.?'

'Sure, Hussein. That sounds great. I'll see you tomorrow then.'

'*Insha'allah*,' he said, and hung up.

The next morning at precisely 10 a.m. I once again climbed the scruffy staircase to Hezbollah's media office to meet Hussein. Once again I studied the portraits of Nasrallah and Khomeini, their black turbans denoting descent from the Prophet, their identical dark, penetrating gazes seeming full of menace and disdain and a strange kind of peace. Once again I watched Al-Manar while I waited. There was an advertisement for an upcoming documentary on Hitler and the Nazis. I had noticed Al-Manar screened a lot of documentaries like this, and it smacked of anti-Semitism rather than a pure love of World War II history. I sat there, watching television and waiting to talk about death.

Hussein ushered me back into the meeting room. More coffee. Chit-chat. I asked him to explain the process for recruiting martyrs. (The term 'suicide bomber' is insulting to Hezbollah and the families of those who have died, as suicide is forbidden in the Qur'an. Instead, Hezbollah refers to the technique as a martyrdom operation.) All those who die in battle are considered martyrs and revered. But fighters who volunteer for martyrdom operations, whose deaths are premeditated, are especially sacred.

The first step in Hezbollah's recruitment process happened in secret, Hussein told me. Potential martyrs were not solicited. The fighter must approach his commander privately and tell him of his wish to carry out a martyrdom operation, Hussein explained. From that moment the fighter faces annual reviews of his military skill, strength of mind and religious commitment.

When a martyrdom mission is planned, the list of volunteers is checked and a candidate chosen. His psychological state is assessed once again, and if the fighter is judged to be ready for the task he meets Sayyad Nasrallah for a final blessing and records a farewell video. The selection process was so streamlined, Hussein said, that no one had ever lost his nerve. Most, he said, were excited about the task ahead.

I had read part of a transcript of the farewell video recorded by the martyr Salah Ghandour, who had carried out one of Hezbollah's most successful martyrdom operations.

> I, Salah Mohammed Ghandour, known by my alias Malak, Angel, ask God to grant me success in meeting the master of martyrdom Imam Hussein, this great Imam who taught all the free people how to avenge themselves on their oppressors.
>
> I shall, God willing, shortly after saying these words, be meeting my God with pride, dignity and having avenged my religion and all the martyrs who preceded me on this route. In a short while I shall avenge all the martyrs and oppressed of South Lebanon as well as the children and sons of the *Intifada* in ravished Palestine.

At the end of his statement Salah said, 'We belong to God and to God we shall return.'

Salah had to debate Hezbollah to be allowed to take on the mission. He was a father of three, married and in love with his wife, and Hezbollah had an unwritten rule that such men should not be chosen for martyrdom missions: they also had a responsibility to their families. But Salah was determined. He argued that if Hezbollah avoided assigning martyrdom missions to married men, the organisation risked discouraging members from marrying, which was in itself an important Islamic order.

And so it was that on 25 May 1995, not long after he had recorded the video message, Salah drove a white Mercedes-Benz sedan packed with 450 kilograms of explosives into an Israeli military convoy as it travelled through the Occupation Zone on Lebanese land. His final journey took him along a dirt track towards the convoy, a radio link fed him continuous intelligence updates. As he approached the convoy he radioed his commander for a final time. 'The time has come,' he said. '*Salaam aleikum, Allah o akbar.*' His Hezbollah commander reported that his voice revealed no hint of uncertainty as he pressed the detonator, blowing himself and 12 Israeli soldiers into pieces. Another 35 soldiers suffered horrific injuries. Salah Ghandour was only 28 when he died and he left behind his wife, Maha, a son, Mohammed Hussein, and two daughters, Fatima and Zeinab, who was only four months old when her father died.

I asked Hussein if I could begin by interviewing Ghandour's widow. We drove to her home in the back of one of Hezbollah's office cars: a large black Mercedes sedan with curtains covering the windows. We stopped outside a block of apartments built above a row of shops. It was indistinguishable from all the others, apart from a small brass plaque on the wall outside with Hezbollah's symbol – the fist and the Kalashnikov – scored into the metal. 'Here lived the martyr Salah Ghandour,' it said.

Cilina, a Shi'ite friend and also a journalist who worked for Beirut's English-language newspaper *The Daily Star*, had come along with me to translate. Together, with a Hezbollah official in tow, we took a small lift that thunked and juddered as it made its way to one of the building's upper floors. The official knocked on the apartment's brown wooden door and it was opened by a slight, ethereal woman hidden beneath a swathe of black. She had a pale, pretty face and large soft eyes and invited us into her sitting room. Giant portraits of Salah in military fatigues hung on several walls and smaller photographs of the family, happy together, cluttered the sideboard.

We sipped glasses of sweet black tea. Maha sat with her hands folded in her lap, polite but remote. I felt she had agreed to the interview out of duty; the role of a fighter's wife was to support him in life and now in death. And, of course, when I thought about it I had to acknowledge that it couldn't have been easy or pleasant to go over and over this subject with a stranger. When she began to answer my questions it was in a mechanical fashion.

'He didn't kill the innocent,' she told me, eyes full of challenge. 'He killed soldiers who were occupying our land and killing our people and so I am proud of what he did to defend our country.'

I didn't need her lecture on the honour of Hezbollah's fight against Israel. Perhaps because of my friendship with Hadi, I felt I had a pretty good understanding of the motivations and consequences of that fight. But I was stuck for conversation. I took another sip of tea, a punctuation mark. The electricity was out and the air conditioner had gone quiet. I remarked lightly that the day was hot.

'You must be boiling under there,' I said, and gave a sympathetic smile. But she refused to be coaxed by my attempts at sisterhood. 'You are also hot, no?' she replied, nodding towards my much cooler shirt and scarfless head. I agreed, yes, I was hot. It was a hot day, inescapable. 'So we are both hot,' she concluded.

Touché, I thought, she's not going to let me get away with insinuating her *hejab* is causing discomfort.

I wanted to dig beyond this stoic, public face. 'I know this is a difficult subject,' I told her. I was anxious to be sensitive and tried to find a way to connect us, two women separated by such different experiences of life. 'I am sorry if the questions I ask are intimate or painful.' She shrugged, unconvinced by my show of empathy. I continued to probe, gently, self-consciously, and felt my face flush with the anxiety of trying to make a good impression, with the heat. Gradually she began to tell her story, to fill the silences.

'I met Salah at a friend's house when I was 17 and he was 22,' she said, softening at the memory. 'It wasn't love at first sight for me, but Salah told my friend he'd like to see me again and the next time we met I remember my heart was beating very fast.'

The two began to meet regularly at Maha's parents' home. They would sit on the couch together, she covered completely – only her hands and face were visible – and talk for hours. It didn't take long for Maha to begin to fall in love. 'I felt as if I had known him all my life. I fell in love with his thoughtfulness, humour and faith,' she remembered. 'He used to tell me he couldn't live happily while others, especially children and old people, were being killed.'

Salah told Maha he was a member of Hezbollah and that he dreamt of becoming a martyr. 'He told me that anyone who married him must understand that he might become a martyr. My brothers were activists and I admired Salah's principles,' she said. 'From a young age, it was my dream to be the wife of a Hezbollah fighter because I felt it was an important way to contribute to fighting the Israeli occupation of Lebanon.'

They were engaged within a month. For the first time Maha was able to take off her *hejab* in Salah's presence. When they were alone together at last he cupped her face in his hands and kissed her gently. 'An electric shock ran through my body,' she said.

Their married life was bliss. He was a doting, loving

husband. If Maha was sick Salah would tuck her into bed and bring her hot drinks. If she was tired he'd banish her to the couch and clean the house while she rested. 'Sometimes I'd try to provoke him but he'd just laugh and say, "I could never be angry with you," ' and she brightened as she recalled it.

As their life together progressed, these happy moments became haunted by the possibility of what lay in the future. 'I always knew that Salah might die young, but I never asked him to reconsider. He'd asked me never to talk about it and I knew he'd made up his mind. Most of the time I tried to lead a normal life. But when I heard of attacks against the Israelis I would get nervous. I knew Salah took part in operations like these, but he always returned safely to me and I learned to adapt.'

She sat very still as she spoke. Her hands were still folded, her knees pressed together and her feet placed neatly side by side. She had a serenity about her that made me feel bumbling and gauche.

For two weeks before Salah was martyred, Maha said she began to feel his death was imminent. It felt as if she had received a prophecy and she couldn't shake it. Then one night he came to her and said, 'Maha, my love, take care of yourself and the children.' They were simple words, tender, but she could read the subtext. Her fears were confirmed and she couldn't stay silent. She begged him to reconsider. 'I pleaded with him not to leave us. I said our baby daughter is only four months old and we still need you. But he was short with me and I closed the subject.' Salah told his wife he loved her but she had always known this would be his fate. He told her the children would be well brought up and she would always be well cared for. Hezbollah had a system of volunteers – women who were assigned to help the families of martyrs. In the early weeks that support was practical:

organising the endless well-wishers, making sure they were comfortable and catered for, the house was cleaned. As the weeks passed the support of the volunteer became more emotional, helping the widow to confront and accept her husband's death. Over time, the relationship often deepened into friendship.

But at that time, before Salah's martyrdom mission, there was no one to help Maha, and because the attack had not yet been carried out she could not confide in anyone for fear of compromising it. 'I felt as if my heart had been ripped from my body,' she said simply. 'But I knew I could not stand in Salah's way. I had no choice but to accept it. I tried to convince myself that for him to die a martyr was better than being killed in a car accident, because at least this would encourage the Israelis to pull their troops out of Lebanon. I should feel proud.'

The last time Maha saw her husband she couldn't take her eyes from him, she wanted to burn his image into her memory. They kissed goodbye and she watched from the balcony as he crossed the car park at the back of their apartment block. Her son, Mohammed Hussein, too young to know the significance of the moment, called out a farewell. Salah heard him and he turned and came back to the apartment. He kissed everyone again. When Mohammed Hussein called out a second time Salah kept walking. 'I think that he was crying,' Maha said.

Waiting for Cilina's translations made this a strange way to talk. I would ask my questions and then there would be long gaps in my understanding while Cilina translated them to Maha and I waited for her to answer. I could tell from Maha's voice and her movements, or the look in her eyes, or from Cilina's sighs and gasps, how the story was unfolding, but I understood little of what she was saying. She would look over at me meaningfully, but it was hard to know how to react. I gave her soft smiles and looked down at my notebook and drew spiralling doodles in the margins.

The next days were an agonising private wait for word of Salah's death. News of a successful martyrdom operation travelled quickly through the large community of Hezbollah supporters. Maha was visiting Salah's family when the buzz of rumour began: at least 10 Israeli soldiers had been killed and many wounded. The family was upbeat and began trying to guess who the martyr may be. Maha could not share their excitement. She felt heavy inside. She left the group and went to pray.

'I always used to end my prayer by asking God to bring Salah home safely to me,' Maha said. 'Now there was no point.' She collapsed into tears. The pressure of her secret was too much and she confided the truth to Salah's family.

Soon after, a Hezbollah official came to the house to formally announce Salah's martyrdom to his family. The apartment quickly filled with guests who came to pay their respects. A cassette tape of a recitation of the Qur'an played loudly.

Hezbollah's Martyrs' Association swung into action. At last Maha was assigned her volunteer. Islam's laws of inheritance under the *sharia* were dealt with – Hezbollah bought out anyone eligible for a stake in Salah's estate so that Maha and the children could remain in the apartment they had shared with him. The goal was to cause as little added upheaval as possible to their lives. Her children were sponsored by Hezbollah supporters who donated US$30 a month to help her pay for clothes and other necessities. Hezbollah opened a fund to pay for their medical care and schooling.

'I started to feel proud rather than sad,' Maha said. 'Salah had told me never to cry for him in public and I tried to do as he had wanted.'

One month later, when the house at last emptied of guests, and when Maha was really alone for the first time since her husband's death, she sat and watched the farewell video he had recorded before he died.

Maha took Cilina and me into another room where there was a television and video recorder. We sat on the floor on mattresses that were spread out around the walls. Her children were home from school. Fatima, now six, clutched a plastic doll as the video began to play. The three children lounged on the floor beside their mother with their heads lolling back and watched the video with familiarity on their faces. In the months after Salah's death, and then in the years that followed, it had become regular family viewing.

Salah was wearing his fighter's uniform; Hezbollah's flag was behind him. He began with the political messages I had already read explaining the motivation for what he was about to do, exalting Hezbollah. And then his demeanour shifted and he stared lovingly into the lens. 'To my dear wife and the tender mother of my children,' Salah said. 'You know where I am going and why I must do this to the enemy. Look after yourself and don't forget to raise my children in the path of [Islam].'

The video then switched to a scene from the south of Lebanon. It was very grainy and hard to make out. The original tape, captured by a Hezbollah combat cameraman, had been copied many times and so as Maha explained what was going on she used her finger to trace the path of the white Mercedes as it picked its way along a dirt road. And then an explosion mushroomed into the air.

'At last I could allow the tears to come,' Maha said of that first private viewing. 'I cried for hours. I missed Salah but I knew I had to be strong. I wanted the children to feel proud, not sad. Now my eldest son says he wants to be a martyr like his father, but I am trying to encourage him to go to university. I don't know if I can stand to lose a son as well as a husband. I am trying to teach him that education can also be used as a weapon.'

Maha had remarried. She wed Salah's brother, Khaled, after some prompting from her family, who told her she needed someone to support her and to take care of her and her children. 'I live happily now but my first husband will always be my true love,' she said, and tilted her face and raised her eyebrows as if to say 'surely that must be obvious'. She continued: 'People view our family as special, even sacred, and I receive great respect. But I am just the same. The only difference now is that I am missing someone.'

Khaled and Maha have a son of their own. They named him Salah. He was nine months old and, when the Hezbollah official left the room, Maha sat breastfeeding him in line with the Qur'an's recommendation that children be breastfed until two years old. Apart from her exposed breast she remained covered entirely in black. There was no need to keep her *hejab* on, since now we were all women together, but Maha admitted that she preferred it because she hadn't had time to change out of her pyjamas or fix her hair before we arrived.

Over the next weeks I visited many more martyrs' widows. It was Sanaa who lingered longest with me.

Her husband, Ali al-Zein, was dispatched to the south to carry out an attack on an Israeli military installation. It wasn't a martyrdom operation like Salah's attack, but it was so extremely dangerous that Ali must have known it was unlikely he would survive it. The operation was successful, but as he drove away Israeli helicopter gunships retaliated, firing a rocket at his car that killed him instantly.

There was a blackout in Sanaa's apartment block so the lift wasn't working. We walked up nine flights of stairs. As Sanaa welcomed us inside, her two-year-old triplets gathered around the folds of her long black coat. Her eldest son – all of six years old and now the man of the house – stood quietly behind her.

This is Sanaa's story:

We met at high school, in the Baccalauréat class. I knew Ali was a member of Hezbollah and although I was a veiled woman, an observant Muslim, I didn't know a lot about Hezbollah. At that time Hezbollah was growing stronger and we would talk about it at home. My family were not members but we supported them as a resistance group.

Ali was new to the school. His family had been living in Kuwait and my first impression was that he was a very complex man. I knew he was religious. He was always spending time with his sister.

I was one of the top students in the class and so a lot of my classmates would come to me to ask for help with their schoolwork. Because he had been in Kuwait it was not easy for him to catch up and so I began to help him. We used to sit together often in class. I never felt embarrassed. Our relationship was full of respect.

Over time he became my best friend. He would come to me for help with his schoolwork and I would go to him for help with my own problems.

When we graduated from high school we both went to study mathematics at university. I loved it and that's why I enrolled, but Ali didn't like maths. He enrolled just to be with me. After our friendship through high school and university I began to fall in love with him. Sometimes a person needs a moment to discover what they really feel for someone else. I knew that what I felt for him was love, not only friendship.

I saw him in many different situations and I could see how much he cared for others. His family were well off, but he always insisted on working to earn his own money. I liked these things about him. Everyone who knew him liked him.

In the summer after school and before university he first told me he wanted to marry me. Another man proposed to me around the same time but I said no. I explained to my mother why I had refused the other proposal and she understood and supported my decision. But I lived in the kind of society that made it difficult for me to spend time with Ali without being married. He was very conscious of that and was never inappropriate.

He was honest from the beginning, in high school, about his desire to be a martyr. He used to talk a lot about it, how he appreciated the martyrs and wished to be one of them. I was convinced that the martyrs were good and important, but still, because I loved him, I didn't want to lose him. I wanted him to stay with me because I loved him.

Because of the strength of my feelings for him I used to sometimes be afraid he would die a normal death. It was his dream to become a martyr. My love for him went beyond thinking about the possibility that he might die. Whatever the risks, I wanted to be with him. I used to try to rationalise it by thinking that if I loved someone else, not a fighter, he might die for another reason. In the end my love for Ali was so great that the idea he might die was not enough to dissuade me from being with him.

We had a language between us so I would know he was going to fight without him having to tell me directly. He would say things like 'I'm going to spend three or four days with the guys' and I would know that meant he had a mission. I was always afraid for him. But the last time I remember being distracted and thinking, I'm busy with the children. He smiled at me in the same way he smiled when I delivered our first son. I didn't feel scared. I didn't feel I would lose him.

After he left I began to feel that I needed to talk to him. I phoned him all day on Sunday and again on Monday, and on Tuesday I rang someone from Hezbollah to ask where he was. They told me not to worry but I was really nervous. His mobile phone was off and he never turned it off; even in the most difficult times he would take my call. I kept redialling and redialling and my hands were shaking.

On Tuesday night I was dialling constantly and nothing. I rang one of his Hezbollah friends, crying, and he told me, 'There's nothing to worry about, he's okay.'

I remember screaming at him, 'No one can tell me where he is and you think he's safe!' I couldn't eat or sleep. On Wednesday morning a relative called and said maybe he's in Palestine. It was the only explanation for why his phone was not answering.

I couldn't conceive of the fact that he might be dead. I kept thinking he was wounded somewhere and that I had to find someone to sit with the children so I could look for him. I never let the idea of him being dead enter my mind.

My sister was due to come to visit me and while I waited Ali's brother arrived. The electricity was off and he had walked up the stairs to reach the apartment. He was not a very fit man and I'd never known him climb all the stairs, not for any reason, and so when I saw him I knew that something was very wrong.

He was trying to act normally. He sat down and we spoke and I just couldn't contain myself. I told him, 'Okay, tell me, what's happened.' He stood up and just told me, 'Sanaa, be patient.' This is always said when someone has died and I just collapsed on the floor.

For the first few days I was in very bad shape. I was screaming. I knew I would never see him again but the thing that made it slightly easier for me was knowing that he had wanted to be a martyr. This pulled me through. Even though I used to think I could never live without him I kept telling myself he was in a place he wanted to be.

As it all began to sink in I spent a lot of time just walking. I needed answers to things I could never know, like, 'What were his last thoughts?'

I have never asked about his injuries. Although there is so much I want to know that I can never know, there are also things I will probably never be ready to know.

I have kept everything he owned. There are even clothes he wore before he went away that I have not washed because they have his smell on them. It is difficult to see these things, but at the same time it brings me relief. When I open his cupboard I feel as if he's just gone abroad for a while and he's coming back.

I feel Ali is still with me. We are linked together in so many, many ways. We have children together and these are the fruits of our togetherness. We created them and through them he is with me forever. I chose that my life would be with him. And it is still with him. Even now, if I feel bad, I will go and speak to him in a loud voice. I have even written him letters.

> What I went through losing Ali makes me feel I can go through other things in my life and survive.

It was late. I slipped my pen into the centre of the notebook, like a bookmark, and slowly closed it. I could sense that Sanaa wanted the interview to be over. I wanted it to be over too: there had been many hours of back-and-forth conversation, translation, earnest attempts to convey truths to each other, dredging up the past, going over it and over it, talking about violent death and the fight for rights and what sort of compromises you can accept for love. There was an awkward moment as we attempted to return to the conventions of normal polite social interaction. But it was impossible to cast aside the afternoon's discussion so easily. I held out my hand and we shook a goodbye. I thanked Sanaa, and she opened the big heavy door again, and we began the dizzying spiral walk down to the street.

A few weeks later, when my mind was still full of these stories of suicide, something cataclysmic happened that would shadow the rest of my time in the Middle East.

On 11 September 2001 I was interviewing Mustapha Barghouthi at his office in Ramallah in the West Bank. Mustapha was a doctor by profession and a politician by persuasion, and at around 40 he had become an influential member of a younger generation of Palestinian leaders. Fair, open, honest elections would be a start, he argued. He was a refined man, educated and articulate; a godsend for Western reporters looking for measured, sophisticated Palestinian voices. I never had a chance to ask him his opinion of what happened in the US that day because, although the attacks must have taken place as we were sitting together in his office, news of them was yet to reach us.

After our interview I walked into my favourite internet café in the main street of Ramallah. The place was always packed with students from the Bir Zeit University – some finishing assignments, others fervently checking their email and Yahoo or Hotmail messenger accounts, writing phonetically in Arabic, using Roman letters, or often in English. There was a palpable need to communicate with the world 'outside' the West Bank's claustrophobic uncertainty.

While I waited for a computer to become free I smoked a filthy Cleopatra cigarette that I'd bought in Jerusalem's Old City when I could find nothing else. I was tired and preoccupied with what Mustapha and I had just discussed, and so when I saw a picture of a burning building on Yahoo's homepage I didn't even register it with enough clarity to recognise the tower as the World Trade Center. I remember thinking, why is some fire in America front-page news and not this sad and endless conflict?

I checked my emails, bought a *sharwarma* from my preferred little takeaway stand, and caught a minivan back to Jerusalem. I walked up the Nablus Road past the US Consulate (and I remember now, there were a few bunches of flowers leaning against the gate) and to my guesthouse in the grounds of the St George's Cathedral. I had just reached the gate when the guesthouse concierge, who lived in a small room built into the stone arched entrance to the compound, ran out to meet me.

He was agitated, alarmed. 'Ma'am, see what has happened to the Americans. Television, television.' He was almost running as he headed back into his room, beckoning wildly for me to follow, which I did.

He had the TV tuned to CNN and now I recognised the

World Trade Center. It was still burning. By the time I got back to my room the entire thing was collapsing. I stayed up watching television until 5 a.m. It was clear that this horrific, colossal event had changed everything.

Almost instantly the US declared it was at war. And while it seemed almost certain that Osama bin Laden and al-Qaeda were responsible for the 9/11 attacks, Washington quickly made it clear that the enemy was not just Afghanistan (which had welcomed bin Laden and his supporters) but any nation that harboured America's violent opponents. Not long afterwards, hawks in the Pentagon began talking about Saddam Hussein and his Iraqi regime as a potential target in this new War on Terror.

Most of the journalists headed to Afghanistan to watch the US Army defeat the Taliban: payback for allowing al-Qaeda to flourish unchecked in the remote mountains and tribe-run villages. The US troops brought carpet bombs and cluster bombs and daisy-cutter technology that ate into the earth and destroyed al-Qaeda's underground bunkers and munitions stores. They were helped by the Northern Alliance, a band of west-leaning Afghan rebels who opposed the Taliban and had years of experience fighting in Afghanistan's remote and freezing mountain terrain.

But Matthew and I didn't go to Afghanistan. Instead we prepared to travel to Iraqi Kurdistan in northern Iraq to see if, like Afghanistan's Northern Alliance, the Iraqi Kurds would help the US to overthrow Saddam Hussein.

CHAPTER 8

AN IMAGINARY PLACE

One day in mid-November, not long after dawn, Matthew and I left Beirut for Iraqi Kurdistan. It was two months since the attacks on America and just a few days before Ramadan began. The journey took three days and it felt epic.

We crossed two mountain ranges (snow-capped), a valley, a desert and two of the world's oldest rivers: the Euphrates and the Tigris. We travelled by taxi (a huge old American vintage car, painted yellow), by Syrian bus (sharing pistachio nuts with our fellow travellers and watching Egyptian movies), by dinghy and by four-wheel-drive. We passed the remains of the ancient Roman city of Palmyra rising out of an oasis in the Syrian desert. We were heading for the far eastern corner of Syria, to the border town of Qamishle, which lay at the borders of Syria, Turkey and Iraq. From there we planned to sneak, undercover, into northern Iraq.

We arrived in Qamishle after midnight. All we wanted in

the world was a hot shower and a comfortable place to sleep. Our hotel room had two sunken single beds covered with scratchy brown woollen blankets and a hole in the wall that had been covered over with cardboard in the space where an air-conditioning unit was once installed. The bathroom was a sort of detachable plastic bubble mounted in the corner of the room. But the truly overwhelming thing was that the whole room was vibrating with noise from a nightclub directly below us. As the chorus surged above the doof, doof of the bass I could hear the sound of women ululating. Despite the late hour, it was clear there would be no sleep for a long time. We ordered bottles of local beer – vile-tasting but better than nothing under the circumstances – and dragged a small table into the space between the two beds, sat on our scratchy blankets and played a game of cards.

In the morning light we saw Qamishle for the first time: sprawled, flat and dusty, nondescript. It was a true border town, its population a mixture of ethnicities (Arabs, Turks, Kurds) branded by their different costumes.

After breakfast (bowls of a kind of clotted cream, flat bread, honey oozing from lumps of honeycomb, sweet tea), a representative from the Kurdish political party that had helped to organise our passage from Syria into northern Iraq collected us in his car and we set off for the border. It had taken months of negotiation to get this far. Matthew had arranged invitations for us to visit northern Iraq from the presidents of its three largest universities – in the towns of Dohuk, Erbil and Suleymanieh. The invitations stated that we were to lecture the students in journalism. We presented them to the branches of Kurdish political groups based in Damascus and they worked on our behalf to acquire permission from Syria to cross its northern border with Iraq. The political situation – sanctions on Iraq, a frosty but slowly warming relationship between Damascus and Baghdad – meant that the border was not open to just anyone and getting permission to cross it was excruciating. If we made it we would be among only a handful of journalists who had visited Iraqi Kurdistan in the past decade.

As we drove along narrow, winding country roads towards the border, the late autumn sun was shining sweetly, softly, on small tumbledown villages and farmers tending vegetable gardens. But I couldn't enjoy the view because my mind was racing with schemes to save us from being turned back if our carefully laid plans to cross the border began to unravel.

When we reached the frontier, not far from the banks of the mighty Tigris River, flowing fast, murky and thick, we faced our first test: we were sent to drink tea in friendly silence with the boss of the Syrian border post. He directed his lackeys to serve us while he sat behind a large desk picking fluff from his epaulettes. We smiled a lot and he smiled back, and when he was sure we had drunk enough, and he had spent long enough being seen to assert his authority, he stood and waved us graciously towards a fly-screened door. We stepped outside onto a covered wooden verandah that felt oddly Australian at this axis of Oriental nations. We were on our way.

The car took us down a steep and muddy track to the river. Our belongings were stacked into a dinghy and we squelched over the riverbank to the boat. The sky was huge above us; drifts of silt sat like an obstacle course in the river. A small outboard motor throbbed against the force of the tide. When the dinghy reached the other side it was pulled onto a pebbly shore. Matthew jumped from the boat. Someone brought a plank of wood to bridge the distance between the bow of the boat and the dry part of the pebble beach and I was helped down.

We were in Iraqi Kurdistan, and it felt like stepping through the looking glass.

Kurdistan stretches in an arc the size of Switzerland from the east of Turkey to western Iran, via northeast Syria and northern Iraq. In this crescent of land about 20 million Kurds live, an ethnic group distinct linguistically and culturally from the Turks, Persians, Arabs and Assyrians around them. But politically, Kurdistan is an imaginary place. The Kurds have never had their own state and have been forced to assimilate into whatever country or dominant culture they found themselves in.

In Iraq the Kurds fought persecution violently and had attracted occasional conciliation from the Iraqi government, usually followed by brutal repression. If you had read a newspaper or switched on the television in 1988 it would have been impossible to forget the images of dead bodies in the streets of the Kurdish town of Halabja, bloated, discoloured, dead from toxic bombs that filled the air with the scent of onions and garlic or chewing gum and apples, before caustic fumes turned their victims mad and then shredded their flesh from the inside out. Halabja was just the best-known of dozens of villages bombed with chemical weapons during the Iraqi regime's Anfal Campaign to exterminate the Kurds, and for a few years this onslaught terrified the Kurds into silence.

Now, as the US promoted its case for war against Saddam Hussein, that horrific history was frequently held up as evidence of the Iraqi regime's brutality, its threat: look what Saddam is capable of. But this ugly piece of history was almost two decades old and said very little about what the Iraqi Army really had left in its arsenal.

The Iraqi Kurdistan we encountered on our visit that spring was a strange, landlocked otherworld. It was technically a part of Iraq, but since 1991 a No Fly Zone, patrolled by American and British fighter jets, had been set up to protect the Kurds from attacks by the Iraqi Army. This had left the Iraqi Kurds free to build a quasi state using their share of money from the UN Oil for Food program (and a bit of extra cash from taxing oil smuggled across its territory in violation of sanctions). In one short decade the Kurds had built an unlikely and yet inspiring little democratic enclave. They had a parliament and elected politicians. They even had a Kurdish 'national' flag that hung in the parliament building in Erbil: horizontal bands of red, white and green, with a bright yellow sun shining out from its centre.

True, Iraqi Kurdistan's two rival leaders claimed their positions from pasts as warlords or tribal leaders and fought each other for dominance. True, both of them had at one time or another demonstrated the ultimate hypocrisy and done business with the Baath Party or cosied up to its cadres as a way to get back at each other. But apart from intermittent civil war between Jalal Talabani's Patriotic Union of Kurdistan (PUK) and Massoud Barzani's Kurdistan Democratic Party (KDP), the two leaders more or less served their people.

By the late 1990s, Iraqi Kurdistan was in many ways a far more pleasant place to live than the Republic of Iraq. The horror of the past was finding its place in history. Money was being ploughed into hospitals and roads and universities. The KDP and PUK had overturned censorship and satellite television reception and internet connections were everywhere. The Kurds even had their own currency (the old Iraqi dinar without Saddam's picture) with its own (more favourable) exchange rate.

It was the closest any Kurd had ever come to nationhood, and it was all because of the No Fly Zone. As a result the Kurds were the most openly pro-Western, pro-American, pro-democracy citizens in the Middle East. So when the US began to scout around the region for support for its plan to overthrow Saddam Hussein, the Kurds could barely contain their eagerness to join in and Washington knew it was on to a winner. The Kurds offered more than just a flagrantly pro-Western and anti-Saddam agenda. Kurdish guerrillas, the *peshmerga*, had years of experience fighting the Iraqi Army and a generation's worth of reasons to hate. It was early days yet, but the Kurds of northern Iraq were up there with the Northern Alliance as the A-team of allies in the new War on Terror.

We spent our first night in the northern town of Dohuk and stayed in a large hotel built on a low hill that looked over the rickety, rundown old part of town and a former Iraqi interrogation centre that was in the process of being rebuilt to house a School of Law and Political Science.

'See how we have buried the past,' said Dr Asmat from Dohuk University, one of the three university presidents who had helped to secure our invitation to Iraqi Kurdistan, as he showed us around town that first afternoon. 'We have taken a brutal past and transformed it into hope for the future.'

After a few days we travelled south to Erbil, Iraqi Kurdistan's unofficial capital, to interview Massoud Barzani at his presidential compound in the mountains nearby. The fact that Iraqi Kurdistan was not a real state didn't faze its leader, who came with all the trappings of statehood. Barzani was surrounded by advisors and assistants, bodyguards, and met with us in a stateroom decorated with the equally stately Kurdish flag, hung prominently beside formal portraits, and overtly ornate furniture upholstered in embossed chintz with gold leaf on the woodwork. Barzani arrived for the interview dressed in traditional Kurdish costume – he was rarely seen without it. On his head was a *jamadani*, a red-and-white cotton cloth rolled into a kind of turban. He wore the *kurtaku sharwal* and *bishden*, traditional baggy pants with cummerbund, in military olive green with a matching shirt.

He was a small man, nuggety and short, a sort of Kurdish Napoleon. But his face had an unexpected gentleness about it and his expression seemed too mild for a revolutionary leader, even though he was born to it – the son of Mustafa Barzani, the Kurds' most famous nationalist. Barzani left school in 1962, aged just 16, to join the armed struggle for Kurdish rights that his father had founded the year before. He was very serious, not particularly chatty or charming, and I got the feeling he was submitting to the interview under duress: foreign journalists were a rarity in northern Iraq and he must have known that the opportunity to discuss the Kurdish situation was too good to miss, no matter how distasteful the routine of cameras and notebooks and questions and answers. When he spoke his voice was almost inaudible, but Falah, his favourite interpreter, who had travelled with us from Erbil just to translate the interview, was practised in deciphering the president's whispered insights and he relayed them with deferential care. We listened closely.

'In what circumstances would Iraqi Kurdistan support the United States in a strike on Iraq?' Matthew asked.

'Our view is that we don't want more suffering to be added to the Iraqi people,' Barzani began and then fell silent, weighing up his answer. 'But if there is a plan to improve the position of the Iraqi people, we will not follow any plan in blindfolds. Of course, we need guarantees for the future of the Kurdish people and what would be the alternative for Iraq.'

In truth, the Kurds were thrilled at the prospect of war in Iraq. If all went well, it could be the answer to their prayers. The outcome of the fight for Kurdish rights that Barzani and his father had waged for four decades was within sight and the Kurds had a powerful bargaining chip to ensure it went their way: they would provide ground troops to help the US fight the Iraqi Army. In return, they expected the US to promote Kurdish interests in post-Saddam Iraq.

Barzani was careful not to be so explicit. But at the end of the interview his son, Masrour, met with us and we sat together drinking tea while we waited for our car. Masrour was typical of the sons of Middle Eastern leaders: educated in the West, urbane, worldly, charming, and not nearly so guarded. The Iraqis had begun to reinforce their frontline into Iraqi Kurdistan, he said, estimating an extra 18,000 troops had been redeployed to the border. 'So far we have not seen an offensive position, but let's not forget that this is an army on demarcation lines, minutes away from our cities. In seconds they can change from a defensive army to an offensive one.'

'Do you think a war is likely?' I asked him.

Masrour raised his shoulders helplessly and made dovish pronouncements: 'The last thing we need is another war, but if this is the policy of the US to attack Iraq, we are not in any position to change that.' He stirred his tea thoughtfully. 'If the US is to attack Iraq we need to be sure that Kurdistan will have its fair share of the future of Iraq. We have been living freely for ten years and we want to stabilise this. We certainly hope that the US will keep an eye on the Kurds.'

The Barzanis may have been looking after their own interests but their reasoning was sound. The great flaw in the rise and rise of Iraqi Kurdistan was the lack of long-term security and decision-making independence. The region could only flourish for as long as the No Fly Zone remained in place, and how long that was so depended on the political interests of the US and Britain, who implemented it. But for now, at least, it suited them to nurture this pro-Western enclave in the heart of the Middle East.

A few days later Matthew and I began the journey south from Barzani's KDP fiefdom to Jalal Talabani's PUK alternative. We had organised to interview Talabani at Dukan, a resort in the hills above Suleymanieh. Prior to 1991 Dukan had been a holiday spot for the Iraqi regime's favoured cadres. But these days it was Talabani's patch. The PUK leader was born not far away, and had taken over a large complex at the edge of a dam with a sweeping outlook across a man-made lake that had submerged tracts of the hilly countryside.

We drove from Suleymanieh with Ala, our PUK translator and guide, in our 'good car' as she called it (a sturdy but worn four-wheel-drive), past the remains of villages destroyed in the Anfal Campaign and peasant farmers who looked tired and old. I wondered if they cared about democracy and internet connections when they couldn't afford new clothes and there was never enough food on the table.

We stopped to look at a cemetery full of Anfal victims. Someone had scavenged the shell of a very large bomb and buried it tip-down in the dirt at the centre of the graveyard as a kind of memorial. The fins stuck out over the top of the headstones, forming a grim sculpture that could be seen for miles around.

The village was nearby: small flat-roofed houses made of

cement and stones, clustered on the dome of a low hill and separated from each other by muddy pens with a few sheep or a donkey inside. We saw a family – a woman, a man and two small, tattered children – sitting in chairs on a concrete platform adjacent to their house. It was probably the foundation for a new home that was never built or the ruins of an old one, and it now served as a sort of terrace. We asked if we could speak with the family, and they told us about the day of the attack.

'It was late in the evening when they started bombing,' said the man. He told us his name was Taha, and as he recalled the memory he wrinkled up his face and squinted as if looking into the distance. The skin around his eyes had been forged into deep creases and his cheeks were worn shiny rough and red by the weather. He said he was born in 1976, which made him about 25. 'I was very young that day and so I don't remember a lot, but I remember the smell, it was like chewing gum. We were just about to pray and to have our dinner when we heard the planes and the sound of the bombs falling. Our house wasn't hit directly and we felt lucky to have escaped. We didn't know it was a chemical bomb until some of our relatives began to choke, to fall unconscious. And then they began to die. My mother, two sisters, two brothers. They all died.'

Taha spoke almost without emotion. These were events lived with for so long he had become heartbreakingly matter of fact. We sat quietly, in a kind of reverent silence, and a neighbour wandered up from the road and joined us all on the concrete platform. The sky was low and grey and it was cold. The two children burrowed further into their mother's dress.

'How can you live here?' I asked. 'With memories like that?'

He thought about the question for a long time. 'Our life here is hard,' he agreed finally, and nodded, looking over at his wife. 'We have no running water. No one buys our agricultural products. But it is expensive in the city and we can't afford to live there. We have come back to our village to try to reconstruct our lives. What else is there to do?'

He looked out at the piles of rubble where homes had once stood, and then looked at me, as though I might have an answer.

We continued our journey to Dukan and for a long time we travelled in silence. I was thinking about Taha and his story, his family, and looking out of the car window at winding roads and pretty countryside that, paradoxically when you thought about its history, became more and more beautiful. High in the distance, I could see jagged mountains covered in snow. Lower down, the landscape was almost European: rolling green hills and valleys.

After a while we arrived at security boom gates and entered a landscaped holiday compound dotted with cabins that had once provided the accommodation for Baathist families. They were empty now, but a large hotel nearby was being renovated with plans to turn the area into a getaway for wealthy Kurdish families. The spot was quite idyllic – that magical Kurdish light, spectacular scenery, cool, fresh air. Its appeal was obvious.

Talabani had just finished a meeting and was farewelling his guests – important-looking men in suits – as we drove up. It was immediately obvious that the two Kurdish chiefs had very different leadership styles. Where Barzani had dressed traditionally, Talabani was a bear of a man and his

Western-style suit and tie sat awkwardly over his bulk. His hair was ruffled and he wore wire-framed glasses at an angle. The effect was a slightly ragged charm. Nonetheless, like Barzani, Talabani had all the trappings of leadership: he too rallied behind the Kurdish flag, he had boardrooms and lackeys and a parliament with ministers. Most importantly, he had a vision: to protect his people and to turn Iraq into a federation with Kurdistan as an independent state within it.

He took my hand in an exuberant shake, rested the other hand on my elbow and smiled winningly as a photographer from the PUK-run newspaper snapped pictures and a cameraman from the PUK-run television station filmed the greeting. Kurdish journalists were always following Talabani around, just like any head of state, reporting on his movements, his meetings and, therefore, on us.

Talabani had always known how to reshape himself. He'd been a law student and a pro-Kurdish student activist in Baghdad, a journalist, a guerrilla fighter and an exile. He'd urged an uprising against Saddam Hussein, and then, sensing opportunity, he'd switched tack and travelled to Baghdad to schmooze with the man who had tried to exterminate his people. He'd allied himself with Massoud Barzani, then gone to war with him, and then allied himself once more. Yet I doubted that even he, the great survivor, the master reinventor, would have predicted that in just over four years time he would have succeeded Saddam Hussein as the president of Iraq.

Talabani knew that war was on Washington's mind and so war was on his mind too. 'I think we are stronger than the Northern Alliance,' he said, squeezed behind his desk, hands clasped in front of him. 'We are stronger than them. The Kurds are not alone too. Arab forces in the south are waiting for any force to liberate their area. Turkey, Syria, Iran have their own policies, but the US is the country that is deciding, and if they want to attack Iraq then no one can prevent them.'

'But aren't you suspicious of the Americans?' I asked him. 'Surely you haven't forgotten 1991 when the US promised to support your uprising against Saddam and then left you to his mercy?'

'Of course we must be certain that we understand each other,' he said. We spoke in English, one of several languages Talabani knew well. 'But the Americans have a goal this time. They know we can help them.'

In our hotel room that night Matthew and I drank from our stash of Ramadan-friendly non-alcoholic beer. We kept the balcony doors open and a freezing wind billowed into the room. This was the only way to make the temperature tolerable: our air conditioner was on an unalterable setting, so high that with the doors closed it was like living in the Sahara.

'It's a bit dangerous to be featuring on television and in newspapers, don't you think?' I said to Matthew. 'We're supposed to be keeping a low profile.'

Although the No Fly Zone had forced Saddam to leave the Kurds alone, it was well known that some of his *mukabarat*, secret police, had infiltrated the enclave. We were told to be vigilant: we were in Iraq illegally and there were rumours that the price of a foreign head was US$10,000. At the very least, if caught, we could be forced to travel to Baghdad to explain ourselves. It may have been just rumour and hysteria, but it was enough to make me anxious.

There was something else too. Matthew and I had spent a day in the mountains that stretched towards the Iranian border, travelling with the Kurdish *peshmerga* who were fighting a radical Islamist group they said was affiliated with al-Qaeda. We'd followed the *peshmerga* as they marched single file over the ridge of mountains, dressed in their tattered uniforms, on their feet boots with flapping, broken soles or sandshoes with the tread worn to nothing, rocket launchers over their shoulders and grenades in their pockets. We sat behind them as they rested their weapons on sandbags and pointed them into the valley below where they said Arab fighters from this group of radicals were hiding out. The threat was real and horrifying. The group had already captured several villages and imposed a Taliban-style regime – schooling for girls was banned, music was banned, women were forced to wear a kind of *burqa* covering. Fighters from the group – which was known as Jund al-Islam and, later, Ansar al-Islam – had already sneaked down into the Kurdish town of Halabja and slit the throats of 26 *peshmerga*. No one knew where its orders came from (Osama bin Laden? Saddam Hussein?) but Jund al-Islam was trying to eradicate northern Iraq's democratic West-leaning enclave and, as Westerners in the area, we had been told to be careful. The PUK had provided us with armed guards for some of our trips into the mountains and they'd sat in the front seat of our 'good car' with their Kalashnikovs resting between their knees and followed us like shadows when we walked around.

But it was too late to do anything about the press coverage now. The next day, Ala gave me a copy of the story. It was a full-page spread. There was a picture of Matthew in mid-conversation, and another of me caught in a demure pose, gazing downwards with a shy smile. Something in the picture caught my eye: my hair seemed unnaturally lush and dark. At first I couldn't tell if it was bad printing or if the back of my head had been caught in shadow. I looked more closely and it became clear. This had been done deliberately: my head had been artfully drawn over in black, so it appeared that I was wearing an Islamic headscarf.

'Hey, take a look at this,' I said, handing the newspaper to Matthew. It was an unexpected encounter with *hejab*.

On my last night in Kurdistan, Matthew and I met a couple of European expatriates, faces flushed red from cigarettes, whisky and cold, who worked as engineers, stitched somehow into the huge and cumbersome machinery that administered the United Nations' Oil for Food program. We bought takeaway beer from a bar in the Christian quarter and smuggled it into the hotel under our coats and sat in the room of an Australian UN engineer who had spent 18 months in Kurdistan, to drink it from the bottle. He played Beatles songs on his guitar and sang with a soft and faraway look in his eyes. After a while we joined in, singing those over-familiar melodies in this odd made-up land. It was a strange and strangely pleasant way to spend our last night in Kurdistan, Iraqi Kurdistan, northern Iraq, or whatever the hell it was supposed to be called.

CHAPTER 9
EXTREMISTS

At the end of our first year in Beirut we flew home to Sydney for Christmas. Everything was summer, bright, crisp, electric. We woke that first morning to the sound of birds in the trees around my parents' house and Matthew cursed in mock fury. 'I can't sleep in! It's like waking up in a bloody wildlife sanctuary,' he said, and we laughed about how quickly we'd become lulled by Beirut's soundtrack of car horns and construction and street hawkers.

Being home again felt like swimming underwater. Compared with the way senses were heightened in Beirut (the sheer noise and clatter of it, the way life was thrown in your face, unavoidable), everything in Sydney seemed to be in slow motion, muffled, trapped inside crystal light. We went to barbeques and dinner parties and picnics at the beach and told stories. The responses were always extreme: 'When can we visit?'; 'Enough! Surely you're not going *back*?' In truth, I couldn't wait to get back to the Middle East. Despite Sydney's overwhelming beauty, the lightness of life and the warm feeling of being with old friends and family again, my head was in another place. Matthew and I applied for visas to

Iran, and as soon as our passports returned from the embassy in Canberra with the green visas stamped inside we boarded the plane home to Beirut.

Whatever else was going on in the Middle East, the one relentless, intractable, endless problem was the conflict between Israelis and Palestinians. There was no shortage of efforts (most of them depressingly useless or insane) to find them a future. But while we waited for a result, Palestinian suicide bombers continued to blow themselves up and kill innocent Israelis, believing they were effectively resisting Israeli occupation and progressing the fight for a Palestinian state. Israeli settlements and checkpoints around the West Bank and Gaza multiplied, and tanks and helicopter gunships continued to kill innocent Palestinians, thinking they were effectively providing security for Israel.

In March 2002 there was another attempt to find a route to peace. It was Lebanon's turn to host the Arab League Summit, with 22 member nations from across the Arab world invited to attend, and the main talking point this year was to be the Israeli–Palestinian crisis. The *intifada* was now 18 months old and the Saudis were bringing a peace plan to the negotiating table in Beirut.

But in an irony so painful it seemed to exemplify the hopelessness of the Middle East peace process, on 28 March, the same day that summit delegates in Beirut were busy inking their Beirut Declaration, Israel launched Operation Defensive Shield, the most extensive military operation into the West Bank and Gaza since Israel was created.

People continued to die. The situation seemed sadder than ever.

And then it got sadder still.

On 3 April the Israel Defence Forces invaded the Palestinian refugee camp at Jenin with shocking force. It was from there – in the poverty of the camp's narrow lanes and hopelessness – that many of the suicide bombers had been recruited, trained and dispatched. Helicopter gunships were followed up with supersized bulldozers that razed block after block of homes. Anything or anyone in the path of these armour-plated dozers was simply flattened. The Palestinians were calling it a massacre. The Israelis, an operation to cleanse the camp of terrorists.

The first I heard of it was when Leila called, grave. 'Something has happened at Jenin. They are calling it a second Shatila,' she said, referring to the massacre of Palestinians at a Beirut refugee camp under instruction of Israel in 1982. Two days later I was in Jerusalem.

Our small group of journalists – Niels, Alexandra, Kai and myself – gathered in my hotel room to discuss how to get into the Jenin refugee camp. No one yet knew the details of what had gone on.

The route into Jenin from Jerusalem was not assured. For the previous three days journalists and aid workers had been returning unsuccessful, with stories of being turned back at checkpoints by IDF soldiers, of roads made impassable by ditches and roadblocks, of driving into gun battles.

'I think this will work,' said Niels, taking charge. He traced a line with his finger on a map of Israel, moving north from Jerusalem along the Jordan Valley, and then west, deep into the West Bank via a spider's web of back roads, and to Jenin.

Niels was a Danish journalist who had lived in Jerusalem for several years and spoke Hebrew well. His Arabic was okay too. This alone impressed us. He was angelic-looking with a pale, unlined face, thick blond hair, always neat and somehow without the layer of dust that covered everyone else's clothes. But he had a substance about him and we trusted him.

He took a sip of coffee and launched into an elaborate argument designed to cement our confidence. It was based on a contact inside the Jenin camp and a process of elimination. What he had in mind was one of the only routes not yet tried. We agreed. A few journalists were starting to trickle inside, or emerge from hiding places inside the camp, and file reports. We didn't want to be left behind. There was nothing else for it.

I borrowed a flak jacket and helmet from an acquaintance who worked for a Dutch television station. We had been introduced through another friend at the bar of the American Colony Hotel. This was how it worked: favours, instant friendships, trading information. The Colony's subterranean bar had become the crucible in which all of these deals were devised and distilled – and then toasted with a beer.

I returned to my room and taped the letters 'T' and 'V' on the front and back of the jacket with black gaffer tape. I did the same on the helmet. This had become the common method of identifying media. I tried it all on. It was ludicrously large, with gaping spaces around the neck and armpits that shrapnel or any decent sniper would have no trouble penetrating. It felt like half my body weight and I wondered how long I could realistically wear the thing without collapsing. But despite the weight, despite the size, I felt safer to have it with me.

I had spent several months that past year on trips back and forth to the West Bank and Gaza, listening to stories of Palestinians caught up in the conflict: the young man, 15, jailed without charge and tortured for three months because he'd been walking home after curfew from a day working in his father's carpentry shop; the young woman, 21, who had died because she wasn't allowed across a checkpoint to hospital for her regular dialysis sessions. There were stories of schools razed to the ground and students who lost months and months of their education; of a father so stressed by the presence of a tank at the end of his street that one day when a soldier demanded his car be searched he collapsed with a heart attack and died; the students at a school for the blind that was peppered with bullets and the terror of those children, sightless, in the panic.

No one was above suspicion. Checkpoints were everywhere. Curfews were in place. Palestinians were used as human shields to protect the Israeli soldiers as they conducted house-to-house searches. While there could be no argument over the right of Israelis to look for ways to stop suicide bombers entering Israel with the intent of killing and maiming innocent people, the tactics they employed punished all Palestinians. The horror was everywhere. Anger grew.

Early the next morning we met to drink more coffee, smoke more cigarettes. Niels had a car and we did the same trick to it with the gaffer tape.

We drove up the Jordan Valley, talking the whole way about whether we would get through, what we would do if we didn't, rating our chances, back and forth. Niels kept calling his Jenin contact. 'He insists this is the best way. Two journalists got through this morning.' Our confidence in Niels had been endorsed. We drove on, debating the validity of the latest rumours and conspiracy theories: how the IDF had trucked bodies in refrigerated vans from Jenin to secret land along the Jordanian border to hide evidence of a massacre.

After a while we turned off the main highway and onto a narrow road flanked by low mountains, groves of olive trees and rocks and scrub. The countryside was silent. It would have been almost peaceful except for an unmistakable impression of dread that hung over the place. It took about 30 minutes to reach the checkpoint: a single-roomed hut built to the left of the road, protected by concrete barricades that stood in a line out front and then veered a part of the way across the road. There were two soldiers at the checkpoint. Niels spoke to them in Hebrew. They agreed to let us cross, but warned it would be dangerous to drive our own car because it had black and yellow Israeli licence plates, not the green Palestinian ones. It was sensible advice.

We discussed a change of plan. A Palestinian taxi driver was standing next to his car, no more than 100 metres away on the other side. It was unbelievable luck. We were in the middle of nowhere, the nearest village at least 20 minutes away by car, and then no guarantee we'd find someone with a vehicle willing to drive us. It seemed the most sensible choice.

We emptied Niels's car of our bags, flak jackets, helmets, and walked through the checkpoint. We put on all our bulletproof gear and squashed into the back of the orange-yellow taxi with its green plates. We were twice our size in flak jackets, reinforced with ceramic plates front and back, and helmets that scraped the grubby roof of the cab, and we rode this way, hunched and mostly silent.

The landscape closed in on itself. We were driving through little gullies and tiny abandoned hamlets of just one or two homes, quiet. Our driver's name was Mohammed and he provided a steady commentary, pointing out the blackened homes of dead Hamas leaders, describing the battle that had killed them just the day before. He was angry. He said he wanted to join the militias. His goal was to 'put bombs in my car and drive to Tel Aviv'. He told us he would do anything, even give up food for his family, if it meant he could afford explosives. 'Two weeks ago I was just a normal man. Do you believe me? Now I can't wait to join Hamas, Islamic Jihad or Fatah.' We nodded grimly.

As we drove, the quiet road became quieter still. It felt as if the entire area was holding its breath. Mohammed slowed the car and we stopped at an intersection. A building on one corner was burnt out but the rest of the area was empty farmland. He looked frightened. 'I cannot go further,' he told us. 'It is too dangerous. Jenin is ahead of you. There.' He pointed along the road to our right.

We were too close to give up now. We all agreed: we would walk. We heaved ourselves from the car, counted our possessions, loaded up like donkeys and began to walk with our hands held out slightly from our sides, our palms facing forwards. It was supposed to be a show of surrender. We didn't want to look suspicious, as though we were reaching for something.

The road ran along a ravine that rose steeply on both sides. There were homes built sporadically along the ridges. It was a perfect hiding place for snipers. We were deeply, intensely aware of our vulnerability, but we held onto the hope that if we presented ourselves clearly as journalists then Palestinians would aid our passage – wanting more coverage of Jenin – and Israeli soldiers would not be so careless as to fire on foreign reporters. Perhaps they too wanted the story of the camp to reach the outside.

We walked for 15 or 20 minutes and then heard the unmistakable growl of a tank, the crunch of the caterpillar wheels as they tore up the asphalt. We froze. There was a corner ahead and we didn't want to startle whoever was driving that tank. We debated what to do and decided to continue with the plan, walking slowly, hands out.

As we rounded the corner an Israeli tank was right there in front of us, perhaps 20 metres away. We could see the soldier buried inside it, peering through a narrow window, his helmet pulled low over his forehead so it just met his eyebrows. He swung the barrel of the cannon in our direction; all I could hear was the mechanical whir of the machinery and the crunch of the asphalt being frayed by those giant wheels. Everything else faded to black. There was nothing to do but wait.

We waited. There was no sound of cannon fire. The tank driver's colleagues, whom I could now see standing behind him at the checkpoint and patrolling the roofs of adjacent buildings, beckoned for us to proceed. We were timid. We didn't move. They called again: 'Who are you?'

'Journalists,' we replied. 'We are journalists.'

They asked us to drop our bags and walk forward with identifying documents. We had each been issued with little plastic cards from the Israeli Media Department, which included our photograph and various details about the newspapers we wrote for. We showed these, our passports, our business cards.

We were instructed to return and pick up our bags and hand them over to be searched. As we did, I noticed a white pick-up truck idling beside us. A Palestinian family was on board: two children, a husband and wife, an elderly man. The tray of the truck was piled high with household goods, clothes, furniture. They seemed to have fled the city during the fighting and now wished to return. They were frightened of the soldiers and were using us for cover, advancing when we advanced, stopping when we stopped, retreating when we did.

The soldiers were busy processing our passage through

the checkpoint and the Palestinian family was being ignored. They were still there, waiting for the truck to be searched, when the soldiers told us to walk on.

This was Jenin. We were on the outskirts and the place was abandoned. There were no taxis. We had no map. We stood there on the street, alone, once again vulnerable. A Palestinian man appeared. We sat with him and drank coffee. It seemed a ridiculous thing to do given the fact that the street was tense and empty, waiting, and no one knew if the fighting was over. But every transaction in the Arab world began with tea or coffee, a chat. It was unthinkable to do it any other way, even during the anxious uncertainty of conflict. When we had finished he said he could help us; he could find us a taxi to take us the final leg into town.

We were driven through Jenin's scarred streets – past posters of martyrs, old and new; past evidence of recent gunbattles and holes in buildings where rockets had been fired – to the Jenin Hospital, which was on the edge of the camp. There were two cars parked out the front belonging to aid workers from Médecins Sans Frontières and Human Rights Watch. A small shop opposite was open, trading coffee, snacks, cigarettes. It seemed there was nothing stopping us from entering the camp. We asked around for information. The way was clear; there had been occasional sounds of gunfire, nothing extreme.

We entered the camp from the south. The walls that contained it had been bulldozed flat and ahead of us was a wide pathway on a slight incline. It took a moment to piece together the view in front of me. But then I could see that the swathe of cleared land on which I was walking was in fact dozens and dozens of crushed homes. To the left and right were the remains of partly demolished buildings, their sides sheared away, lying half-destroyed on the 'roadway'. Partly demolished rooms were in full view. It was tragic and bizarre. Families were carrying on daily life, brewing tea, hanging washing, with half their homes missing.

I walked on, past a group of three women standing on a small hill of rubble, pulling at bits of metal and kicking at the ground. When they saw me they raised their hands and one of them shouted, 'Allah, Allah, what has happened to our home?' and gestured towards the rubble. 'Eleven people were inside – me, my children, my husband. We saw the bulldozer coming towards us and we started screaming but it didn't stop.'

'What did you do?' I asked her, as she turned and sat in front of me, her hands white with dust and her face ruddy from wind and sun. I took a step forward and sat on a lump of concrete next to her and took out my notebook.

'When they started to destroy the house we began to take the children out of the windows, but when we got outside there was shooting from every direction.' She lifted the scarf from the front of her head and slipped her hand inside, smoothing hair streaked with grey. 'To be honest, we feel very lucky to be alive.'

Behind the women a group was digging earnestly and I stopped to watch them. They were scraping carefully around a dark mass and after 10 or 15 minutes two of the group began pulling it free. I couldn't make it out – a tangle of dark shapes and angles – and then it was laid carefully on a hot-pink sheet. As my eyes adjusted there was a terrible moment of knowing. At the centre of this thing, a woman's hand, black with death and decomposition, pointing upwards, almost elegant. I could even make out the manicured nails carefully filed into points. A few moments later, another ghastly find: the woman's hair. I can still picture the perfect brown plait held aloft, silhouetted against the blue April sky.

~

People crept out of their shattered homes when they saw us coming and they told stories.

I found Issa as I found most of the others, standing in front of the remnants of a home where he'd lived with his wife and two sons. 'First my eldest son was killed. He was 18 years old,' he said, speaking in the steady monotone of someone repeating facts but clearly still in too much shock to fully feel or understand his loss. 'My son was studying on his bed on the second floor of our house and a bullet came through the window and travelled through his arm and into his body.' As he spoke, Issa mimed the motion of the bullet by holding his arm out into the air above his head and then jabbing it with force into his stomach. 'The next day my wife was making bread with my nine-year-old son when another bullet came through the window and hit her in the stomach. She collapsed in front of us.'

Issa stopped talking and rubbed his face. His hands were rough from salvaging lost items in the rubble, and there was black dirt ground into his fingernails. When he pulled his hands away his eyes were blinking fast to stop the tears coming. 'The blood mixed with the dough,' he said, shaking his head as if he couldn't comprehend how these two apparently unconnected things had come together in that tragic, life-defining moment. 'My wife and son are only one story,' he added. 'What kind of peace is this?'

I stumbled around like this for a long time, collecting stories and feeling helpless as I wrote them down in my notebook. I couldn't move very well. The flak jacket was very heavy and the weight had begun to turn into pain. It hung too far past my hips, and when I tried to bend my knees to climb up the rubble I couldn't lift my leg high enough and many times I almost fell. I decided to leave the others so I could find somewhere to sit and recover.

I passed a family sitting on the step of their home – still standing and built on a slight incline overlooking the flattened area of the camp that I had taken to calling Ground Zero. They saw me watching them, curious, and they beckoned me inside. The house was plain but comfortable and I guessed the family must have been some of the camp's wealthier residents. We sat on hard chairs in a sitting room and there was an old sofa against one wall; a table in the centre covered in a plastic sheet, decorated with flowers, served as a coffee table. The walls were painted white with a patina of dark cloud smudges where countless hands had brushed past. Coffee was brought, and then tea, and we sat together, sipping, and it gave us time to feel comfortable with each other.

After a while an older man, perhaps 50, spoke up. He said his name was Jamal and explained that the building we were in had been split into two apartments: one for his own family – and he gestured towards a young woman and man, and towards his wife – and one for his brother and his brother's wife and children. Then he pointed to a large hole that had been bashed in the dividing wall so the two apartments were now awkwardly linked. I could see through to the hallway of the adjacent home, leading to a bedroom. Bits of broken brick and splintered wood and dust lay around on the floor. 'The Israelis occupied our house and they did this,' Jamal said, and I could see that he had been humiliated. 'They wanted to be able to access the two apartments without going outside.'

Jamal's wife picked up the story. 'They were here for seven

days and we were all together, in one room, there.' She pointed to the front of the house. 'There were 22 of us and most were women and children. Jamal and his brother were the only men. We were not allowed even to go to the toilet without permission. Only one woman was allowed into the kitchen to make meals. In our own house!' She set her lips in a line and shook her head.

I asked to see the room where the two families – two brothers, their wives and relatives and children – had been kept. It was the size of an average bedroom, perhaps three metres squared. There was a vanity table set against one wall, and behind it several rows of louvred windows. The windows gave a perfect view of the camp and the entire expanse of Ground Zero was in full sight.

Jamal saw me looking and must have guessed my thoughts. 'The Israelis used our house to shoot from,' he said. 'Come.'

We walked to the bedroom next door and he pointed to two holes, about the size of a loaf of bread, which had been knocked through the front of the building. It was the perfect spot for a sniper.

While I had been drinking tea and listening to Jamal and his wife, their daughter Reem, who was 15, had been watching me – still and silent – from a distance. She had a very striking face: thick, dark eyebrows that had been subtly plucked into shape, dark eyes, perfectly sculpted cheekbones and a long straight nose, beautiful soft brown skin. She wore a silver-grey headscarf wrapped tightly around her head so that not a skerrick of hair was on show. On her body she wore a coat that looked a bit like a dressing gown – olive green velour with an impressionistic flower pattern dotted here and there. Her composure was unnerving. I couldn't work out if it was delayed shock or muted acceptance of her situation, or whether she had reserves of inner strength to draw on.

I asked her what the family had done to fill in the time during the long days trapped together in the room and she told me she had written a diary and listened to the radio.

'My uncle is a writer,' she said. 'And so I decided to do like him.'

She pulled a dog-eared exercise book from a drawer in the vanity table and began to read.

> April 3: It has started. The tanks have surrounded the area of the camp and they are in the camp. There are Palestinian people here trying to defend us from the helicopters and air attacks. There is a lot of violence between the two sides. Israel has occupied many houses that are in strategic places.
>
> April 4: Fire has started in the camp. The Palestinians are trying to stop Israel from entering the camp.
>
> April 6: After one week of attacks with the tanks and fighters and Palestinians trying to defend the camp, Israel started to destroy houses. They turned the mosque into a military camp.
>
> April 7: The Israelis continue to damage the buildings and houses on the east side and took some families from the houses and destroyed them. Israelis used some Palestinian families as human shields.

The diary continues like this, a dogged, laborious recording of what she heard on the radio and saw through the louvred windows. Her last entry, on April 22, says simply: 'Israel left today.'

'What happened when they left?' I asked her. 'What did you do?'

All the while we had been speaking, Reem had held the diary in both hands, against her stomach. Now she clutched it more tightly, as if it somehow made all her memories real, validated them. She straightened her back and tipped up her chin and stared intently through the window before she answered.

'The day the soldiers left, we went outside for the first time. In the beginning we felt we had a new life again. But then we were shocked to see all this destruction. It was a terrible shock. From the windows we saw only one side. We couldn't believe what had happened. I felt like I was in a dream. Maybe you would expect they would go from house to house and take the people they wanted, but you don't expect the destruction.

'I will never forget this in my life. If I have learned one thing from the Israelis it is that I hate them more than ever.'

I travelled back to Jerusalem that night. The route we had taken to get into Jenin was now blocked because of a helicopter raid on the home of a senior Hamas member. I crept across the green line with Niels, Alexandra and Kai, and we rounded a corner to see a group of Israeli snipers pointing their guns at us. The snipers were patrolling the border and they were angry, rightly. 'How do we know you are not suicide bombers?' they said. 'We could have killed you.'

They detained us and checked our identities and corroborated our story about having to find another way out of Jenin. After darkness fell they drove us in their military jeeps to a nearby checkpoint and we were free to go. I bought a hotdog and a coffee from a fast-food cart that served the soldiers. We called a taxi and waited. When it came, we rode back to get Niels's car, then travelled down the Jordan Valley, past Jericho and on to Jerusalem.

CHAPTER 10

THE PHOTOGRAPHIC WORKSHOP

A few weeks later I spent a month in Shatila, the most notorious Palestinian refugee camp in Lebanon. It wasn't that I had planned to remain immersed in the Palestinian story, yet for whatever reason it came back to me.

There are 12 Palestinian refugee camps in Lebanon but the most famous are Sabra and Shatila. The two camps butt up against each other, forming one huge shantytown, home to 20,000 people crammed into a space only 1.4 kilometres square. The two camps were always referred to in the same breath, like this: *sabrashatila*.

I had been to Shatila only once before, in early 2001 when I interviewed the camp's residents about what they thought of the upcoming Israeli elections. At that time the *intifada* was in full swing and Israeli opinion was hardening against the Palestinians. Analysts were predicting that the Labor Party's Ehud Barak would be defeated by Ariel Sharon, the leader of the right-wing Likud Party. That turned out to be the case and Sharon became Israel's new prime minister.

There was a reason why the opinion of the Palestinian refugees of Shatila mattered so much. In the late summer and early autumn of 1982, when Sharon was Israel's defence minister, he masterminded and then carried out the invasion of Lebanon and bombardment of Beirut, including the massacre of Palestinians at Sabra and Shatila.

The Phalange and the Israelis had common enemies: the PLO had joined Lebanon's leftist Muslim militias in fighting Lebanon's Christians. When Lebanon's Maronite President Bashir Gemayel was assassinated by a bomb hidden inside a suitcase (a typical death for a man who conducted his political career mafia-style and had assassinated two of his rival Christian warlords), the IDF troops in Lebanon gave the Phalange the green light to take revenge.

While IDF officers waited nearby, Phalange militiamen entered Shatila and, over three days, massacred hundreds and perhaps thousands of camp residents. The stated goal was to kill the thousands of PLO militiamen the IDF believed were still hiding in the camp. But many of the corpses were old men, women and children.

When I visited Shatila that first time, I had sat with my notebook on my knees in a musty, dusty little shop that sold food in plastic packets – cakes, biscuits, noodles – and cigarettes, always cigarettes, and spoke to a woman who had survived that massacre. She sat behind a desk under a tube of fluorescent light recording details of items sold in a dog-eared exercise book with her large, strong hands, rough and callused. She told me about the day of the massacre, how she had lain under corpses for many hours, left for dead and then pretending to be dead in case the Phalange came back to finish the job. Later, she escaped by walking over the trembling, oozing piles of bodies that had choked Shatila's narrow alleyways, barely wider than two arms stretched out. She told how her sister had smuggled her children to safety, gathering them under her long skirts and walking with them, shuffled, hidden.

I was returning now to interview Alan, a British photographer I'd met in Iran a few months earlier who had been commissioned to take photographs in Shatila for an American newspaper. When Alan saw the camp he was shocked by the conditions in the place, then, when he had learned more about its history, he felt embarrassed by his ignorance and decided to do his bit to try to change things. He came up with the idea of teaching a photographic workshop to a group of kids who had lost one or both parents, not just from the massacre, but from fighting in the Lebanese civil war. Whatever the reason for their parents' deaths, one fact remained undisputed: Shatila's orphans were the victims of violent politics; another layer of disadvantage on already disadvantaged lives.

Alan thought photography could help these children to understand their lives by documenting them. He thought that maybe the act of capturing moments would elevate those moments somehow, make them special, and that the children would see the dignity and wonder in their existence. The possibility of transferring a skill, or even of inspiring a career, was only a minor part of his motivation. He saw photography as a kind of therapy. The plan was to find a photographic company willing to donate disposable cameras and printing facilities, and at the end of the course the kids would mount an exhibition of their work. Alan's blustering, relentless proactiveness was enormously endearing. And he seemed to be everywhere at once that summer – a bustle of sandy hair and sweat and swinging cameras, mobile phone in one hand and electronic organiser in the other. He was at the newspaper offices, spruiking his idea and hoping for coverage; at the photographic companies, arguing how a donation would be good for business; at Shatila, urging kids to join the group.

I thought Alan's project might make a story and so I'd arranged to meet him at the camp one day, planning to write about it.

'I'll meet you at Beit Atfal Assumoud,' he said, using the name of the organisation that was hosting the workshop. It offered after-school and holiday activities for camp kids of school age, as well as a kindergarten. The kids who were to take part in Alan's photographic workshop were chosen from those who attended Beit Atfal Assumoud.

'You'll find it down an alley off the main street where the market is,' Alan told me.

Shatila was in the south of Beirut, behind the huge rebuilt sports stadium, the Cité Sportif, and on the edges of the city's sprawl of southern suburbs. It was a poor place, desperately so, and as well as Palestinian refugees it had become a magnet for all of Lebanon's disaffected and displaced: illegal immigrants; African workers who had escaped from their employers but were without the documents or the funds to make the journey home; Syrians and Egyptians who had hoped to find work in Lebanon, or did find work but were paid too little to afford to live elsewhere. Even a few poor Lebanese families were drawn to the place.

At the entrance to Shatila was a memorial to those who died in the 1982 massacre. A little further on was a steaming, fetid mulch of waste right by the side of the road. The stench flowed out over the street where children played while their mothers picked over bits and pieces in the market, and people tried to get on with their lives.

The main street of the camp was crowded with stalls stuffed into alcoves at the base of broken apartment blocks, selling cheap clothes, plastic kitchenware, electronics. On the street itself, coffee sellers had set up mobile carts, the wheels dug into ruts in the asphalt; beside them, others sold fresh fruit juice that they squeezed by hand in elaborate and old-fashioned metal contraptions. There was a chicken shop that you smelled before you saw it, with cages filled with live birds out the front; and a butcher's shop with carcasses hanging in the window, bulls' scrotums swinging, glistening.

Cars and taxis, rusted out and ramshackle, jostled for space along the crumbling and muddy stretch. When I looked up I could see apartment blocks four or five storeys high, pitted by bullets and shrapnel from one of countless battles. Running in and out of windows were electricity cables, twisted together into thick black ropes and criss-crossing each other so that they formed strange black nets above the alleys and above the road, so thick they dulled the sun.

Where was the alley? I peered down one of the narrow passageways that led into the heart of the camp, but it didn't seem to be the place. A man sat on a wooden crate at its entrance, smoking a cigarette, and I could see he was wondering, 'Who is this stranger and what is she up to?' By way of introducing myself I decided to ask for directions in clumsy Arabic. 'Please, can you tell me, where do I find Beit Atfal Assumoud?'

He jumped up, his eyes bright with recognition and understanding, and began to walk. I followed him further down the road, past more stalls and people and cars, and it seemed I was a long way off the mark. We walked for several minutes until he stopped and pointed, and I could see it now – a mural painted on the far wall with the name of the centre written in Arabic: Beit Atfal Assumoud. Underneath the Arabic was an English translation and as I read it I couldn't help smiling, with resignation as much as with understanding: The House of Children's Resistance. Even here, a kindergarten, an arts and crafts centre, it was impossible to escape the grinding reality of Palestinian refugee life; the strength to survive it taught subconsciously alongside nursery rhymes and colouring in.

And yet, when you took the time to look around you Shatila revealed moments of delightful normalcy. As I was about to step inside, four boys, about eight or ten years old, came screaming around the corner, laughing, chasing a battered old football. In an instant I could see that their hero was not Arafat or some tragic Palestinian martyr. Every one of them had exactly the same haircut: cropped very close all over except for a thin fringe that was bleached yellow-white, just like kids all over the world, just like their idol, Brazilian football star Ronaldo.

It didn't take long to see that Alan was hopelessly overworked. His students shouted over one another and spoke bits of English and lots of Arabic, eager and excited and uncontrollable. I had studied photography and remained an enthusiastic amateur, and so instead of interviewing and writing that day I began to help him. I went back the next day, and the next, and by the end of the week it seemed that I'd become indispensable.

Our little gang of would-be photographers were a mixed bunch of girls and boys. Most were around 12 or 13, and my favourite was Ahmad, a precocious sweet-faced child who had lost both his parents and lived with his aunt and uncle and a younger sister. He compensated for the loss of the unconditional love of a mother and father by being utterly charming, helpful, spirited and enthusiastic. He drew people to him. It was impossible to ignore him and, even if he wasn't conscious of it, attention was precisely what he needed. Walid, who was 18, was the eldest; talented and intelligent, but he had been worn down more than the others and was old enough to know that there was no glittering future. Life was hard. Life as a Palestinian refugee in Lebanon was even harder. There were two older girls, Lina and Samar, who were both 16 and spoke excellent English. They helped me with translations and guided the little ones with the sort of practised calm that is only possible from those who have spent long hours with children. At least that was one thing Shatila couldn't take away: families were large, boisterous, and the saving grace among many final straws.

I was amazed by how scrubbed and well dressed the children were as they emerged from the squalid alleys and tiptoed down the filthy streets to attend our classes. They showed a huge hunger for information and experience beyond the oppressive sameness of the camp.

We began each lesson with a theme – portraiture or still life, or focusing and framing images – and we would talk about these subjects, miming our meaning or speaking in our mixed-up sentences of English and Arabic, with Lina or Samar or Walid chiming in with translations. After a short theory session we went outside to take pictures around the camp. Being with the children gave me access to parts of the camp I would never have seen without them. In the back alleys another world opened up. Life was lived so close that privacy was almost impossible. It would have been difficult to walk around here as an outsider; it would have felt too voyeuristic. This was not like public space. It was like being in someone's backyard. As you walked down the lanes you could look directly into bedrooms and kitchens. Women who preferred to cover were forced to wear their *hejab* almost all the time; there were few places where they could guarantee enough privacy to take it off. Some families hung bedsheets or curtains on wire or makeshift rods in an effort to add another layer of privacy.

Each day we left the kids with half a roll of film and asked them to keep shooting what they liked. When these pictures were developed they were inevitably shots of family and friends, usually standing ramrod straight and staring seriously into the lens. But after a while the novelty of posed shots wore off and the pictures that they returned became more interesting: images of family fooling around at home; a picture of a young boy's new tattoo; a sister's wedding. The children brought images from inside their lives and in doing so Alan's expectations were confirmed: they seemed to gain a new status; the minutiae of refugee life was given tender, heartfelt dignity.

'What do you feel when you see this place?' I asked Lina one day as we looked through a roll of film together – pictures of the rabbit warren of lanes, walls with murals of Al Aqsa Mosque, strangely distorted portraits of Arafat, the Palestinian flag, rubble. 'Aren't you angry that your family has been forced to live here?'

'When you see these alleys I know you see the dirt and the rubbish and the bombed buildings,' she said, looking at me almost with pity (how could I be so shallow?). 'But when I see them I remember myself as a little girl running down here after my first day of school. I remember around this corner' – she pointed to a junction in the photograph – 'the look on my mother's face when she saw me coming. I remember sneaking into that little shop and buying sweets and eating them quickly before I got home so I didn't have to share with my brother.' Lina smiled. 'I was happy, even if the situation was very bad. I am still happy. I have friends, I have family near me. When I want to go anywhere in the camp no one says to me, "Be careful, be home by a certain time". No. This place is my home.'

We talked some more. Lina admitted that it was very difficult for her at high school. She had a place at a normal Lebanese school, but to be Palestinian in Lebanon was not easy. Despite widespread hatred of Israel among the Lebanese – for the 1982 invasion and bombardment of Beirut, for 22 years of occupation of the south of the country – few had forgiven the Palestinians for their role in agitating Lebanon's already heated domestic tensions. Many blamed the Palestinians for sparking and then prolonging the civil war, and when I told some Lebanese about this month in Shatila teaching photography, I would sometimes be chastised: 'Why not help our poor Lebanese children?' The argument was fair and I didn't have an answer.

But, like so many of the Shatila refugees, Lina had been encouraged to retreat from trouble into myths about the past. 'Here I am in a Lebanese school and the others in my class always say to me, "Go back where you came from. You are not a citizen here," ' Lina said. ' "You are in our country and we don't want you." It really hurts. I try to tell them that I also have a homeland but I can't go back. I would love to go back.'

Instead, Lina dreamed of becoming an actress. 'My mother wants me to finish my study. She doesn't want me to act. But you know, Catherine, ever since I've been six or seven I've sat in front of the mirror and started to become a different girl, not Lina, not this Lina.'

She shrugged and smiled. She didn't say it, but the meaning was obvious: this was her escape, her way to survive.

I could see that the amount of energy required just to exist there was enormous. The effort needed to get ahead, to make something of your life, was extraordinary. Poverty and war and exile were just a part of it. The Lebanese police and army were forbidden entry to Shatila and as a result there were always stories about how the camp, and others around Lebanon, was harbouring criminals and terrorists and al-Qaeda sympathisers – which were, to a greater or lesser degree, true depending on the week. Many of the Western embassies, including Australia's, recommended against their citizens entering the camps. But I never felt unwelcome.

The Lebanese claimed they didn't want to give Israel any reason to avoid granting Palestinian refugees right of return. This meant they gave few rights to Palestinian refugees: no right to build or extend their homes; no social or civil rights; limited access to Lebanese government health and education services. Not only this, but because Palestinians were considered foreigners, they were prohibited from working in more than 70 trades and professions. (In fact, this discrimination against Palestinians probably had more to do with balancing Lebanon's precarious sectarian make-up.) Unemployment was high and reliance on aid agencies was routine. As a result, Shatila was its own little city. Internet cafés, pool halls, hairdressers, corner shops, dentists, doctors, accountants – all operated inside the camp, run by the Palestinians for the Palestinians, or run by foreign aid organisations.

As well as the outside pressures, a hierarchy existed within the camp: were you a refugee from 1948 after the creation of Israel, or a refugee from the Arab–Israeli wars of 1967 and 1973? Aid and other money that came to the camp was filtered through factions and alliances and political groups. All of the major Palestinian political factions had offices, presidents, members inside the camp: Fatah, Hamas, Islamic Jihad as well as independent candidates. There were elections, and from time to time there was rivalry as one faction beat out another for influence and control in the running of the camp. It was important for each family to be accepted by one of these groups if their children were to be in line for scholarships to help them study or to be given a chance to upgrade to better housing.

But family life was always more important than anything else. With great frequency Alan and I would discover one of our students missing. The reasons were always the same: they were at home helping to care for a sick brother, aunt, mother, grandfather; they were at a funeral; they were helping an uncle at work. A part of me would feel annoyed – Not again! How many aunts does this kid have? – but I grew to realise that this tight web of relationships and responsibilities was just how things worked. This unflinching ability to rely on family was the only thing that remained consistent when everything else fell apart.

The children linked themselves utterly with the Palestinian story: they spoke Arabic with Palestinian accents, and spoke of themselves as being from Haifa or Akka or other places inside Israel, even though in most cases the family had been refugees for so long that not even their parents had ever been there. It was both a mark of strength, of survival, and a mark of desperation, because these people were trapped. Technically, there wasn't even a Palestine, and they were not entitled to Lebanese citizenship. Where did they fit? There was no discernible future. The past was all they had and it was inevitable that it would be mythologised and sanctified.

'In Palestine we were very happy. We had fields, land. We were working,' Lina said, and it didn't really matter whether it was true or not, because this pride in the past was all anyone had. The longer I spent in Shatila, the more obvious it became that these families could not go on if they gave up the dream of Palestine. As refugees they could not progress with lives in Lebanon, that was clear: they had no rights. The only hope they had was of return, and to hope for that they had to believe there was something better to return to. I hadn't the heart to tell them how much the Palestinians in the West Bank and Gaza were suffering too.

Some of the Palestinian villages the children spoke of no longer existed, razed during the creation of Israel. And yet the keys and title deeds to these old family homes were often still around, kept in pots or boxes tucked away under beds and inside cupboards. Families would talk of returning to Palestine, of picking up life in their villages. They would describe the layout, how there was an olive grove behind the house, how the well was a few metres from the back door. The children knew the rest of the story by heart too, of leaving Palestine, the fear, the uncertainty. The first night their grandparents spent in a camp, in Syria, Jordan, Lebanon. How they would calm themselves: 'Oh, this will only be for a few days, a few weeks at most.' And then the day they realised they would never be going home.

Lina told me that she remembered lying in bed as a child and listening to her grandparents whispering to each other about the past. She would lie there, still, pretending to sleep, and hear the regret in their voices and the sadness as they talked over the past. 'Sometimes,' she told me, 'I would hear them cry.'

On the day of the exhibition, held just a week before the twentieth anniversary of the massacre at the camp, the children and their families filled four busloads. The show was at the UNESCO Palace – a conference and exhibition centre with lots of prestige. It was the first time most had been there and they walked into the large foyer craning their necks, excited.

We had spent hours, days, sifting through negatives and

prints and selecting a range of images. Next to each child's work was their picture, their name and age, and the village their family was from. Then we typed out a little interview with each child, reflecting on their lives, hopes and dreams. It was printed in Arabic, French and English.

Lina, 16, El Yajour, wrote:

My dream is to become an actress who will succeed very well and be loved. I would also love to study architecture at the university because as we say 'art doesn't feed'. I'm a girl from Shatila camp who stays quiet all the time in the institution where I practise lots of activities such as manual jobs and sports, art, lecture studies. Despite many things that we don't like in the camp, because it reminds us of everything we want to forget – the destroyed buildings, the holes in the street – we also find beautiful things in camp life which reminds us always of our cause and situation. Here, life is simple and the friendship between people and attachment to each other exist. They try to live traditionally as in their village in Palestine, as their ancestors lived. Those traditions we keep. In a marriage ceremony we don't use a DJ but choose traditional songs and the 'dabke' dance that shows our culture. Our dream is to go back to our country. I dream always of my return and it's sure and certain that one day this dream will be realised: the dream of being an actress in Palestine.

Ahmad, 13, Jaffa, wrote:

I live in Shatila camp. The people here are poor and they have no possibility of a decent life. I would like to have a beautiful house, a clean neighbourhood and lands to play in. I expressed in my pictures the poverty in which we live. I couldn't take beautiful pictures in our camp because of the dirtiness and the emptiness of all freedom to play. I wish the

> sewers were not overflowing and that the electricity wires were not hanging overhead and that the garbage everywhere was cleaned up. The people who live here are good people.

Samar, 16, Ramallah, wrote:

> My dream is to become a doctor to help heal my people in Palestine. This dream is impossible now, but if I won't make it one of my children will. The hope of returning to Palestine in my eyes will stay until my last breath. My parents taught me that return to my country is possible. I have grown up far from my country. But I'm not far from my people, because we are all together in one land, despite the problems that we confront. We take pictures of the camp to show the whole world that despite all the garbage and destruction our Palestinian people live hand in hand. The pictures show that 'despite' life in the camp our people are evolving. I worked to take pictures of kids and their activities. I also took pictures of the real life of the Palestinians in the camp who never forget Palestine. This is what I think but I will let the pictures tell their own story. The hope remains and is growing for us to return to our country.

Very early on in the workshop, Walid had stopped attending. I could only guess that he felt too much older than the others and had better things to do. He did not return to write up his little biography or have his picture taken to hang next to his work, and by the time the classes were over he had not taken enough shots to make a proper display. So Alan and I didn't include his work in the exhibition.

The Lebanese Minister for Culture came to open the show and people gave speeches. Samar and Lina set themselves up in a corner and gave a demonstration of Palestinian cross-stitch – beautiful, intricate combinations of colour that were usually embroidered in panels on the *abayas* worn by the women. That night, with the busloads of Shatila families arriving at UNESCO, their eyes wide with the wonder of it all the kids laughing and pulling each other from display to display, excited, proud, teasing with no mercy friends who appeared in the shots; with the Minister for Culture standing behind a lectern offering praise, I began to feel seduced by this role of the foreign volunteer.

Alan stood to give a reply to the minister's speech. Every face in the room was turned towards the lectern and I took the chance to look around. I was surprised to find two dark eyes staring back at me. It was Walid. When the speeches finished he stepped forward to greet me. I could see two little crescents of tears welling in his eyes and he was fighting them bravely. I tried to lighten the moment, to lessen his feeling of rejection, but it was useless. Suddenly I was full of guilt: what had we done?

The encounter with Walid left me feeling defeated. After everyone had gone home I hung around to look more closely at the work: this was, after all, the sour reality of life for our little photographic gang and after the night's snacks and drinks and important speeches it was the reality they would return to. I began to wonder if any lasting good had come from what we had done, and who had really benefited from our brief month of philanthropy.

Lina had taken a lot of pictures of the camp kids balancing on fallen pieces of concrete and playing hide-and-seek inside the shells of buildings, bombed years ago and never repaired. Another photograph – the one we used on our advertising poster that was stuck up all around Beirut – showed a boy on a red bike, hunched over, riding earnestly through the flat dirt expanse of an empty lot. Framing the picture in the distance were rows and rows of battered high-rises with flapping, faded laundry hanging from shrapnel-damaged concrete balconies. There was also a shot of a boy, around 13 or 14, standing in his family's living room and posing like a body builder, very serious about it, his eyes bulging as he strained to bulk up his small, sinuous muscles. An older man, perhaps a father, an uncle, lounged on a couch to the left of the frame, observing with a kind of pride on his face as he smoked a cigarette. There was another of a tea set, a stack of tiny cups, a stainless steel pot, arranged on top of a woven plastic mat.

Perhaps my favourite shot, the one I will always remember, was a picture by Samar: a child's doll, missing its legs but with wild eyes and hair, squashed into a lump of broken concrete.

As I walked around the exhibition that night, absently scavenging up photographs that had begun to peel from the display boards in the September heat, I felt overwhelmingly tired of all the hatred that ricocheted back and forth between the Palestinians and the Israelis and the Lebanese and the various lobby groups that appealed to the interests of each. The kids I met in Shatila were just kids; they were sweet and vulnerable and they needed help and encouragement and options.

Their families had suffered. It was just a fact; and they were still suffering. Failed conferences or stern warnings from the White House or massive military campaigns or rounds of suicide bombings were pointless, tragic noise. While these people waited for self-interested politicians to climb down from their moral high ground and admit that the situation was dire and the only answer was to surrender to compromise, then every day would remain a monumental struggle; a struggle to get on with life and everything that was glorious or heartbreaking about it. That was what the pictures showed: a kind of joy, mixed with sadness.

CHAPTER 11

OSAMA'S BEST FRIEND

It was 25 December 2002. In Saudi Arabia that meant Shawwal 21, 1423 on the Islamic calendar. Christmas Day was banned.

In the early afternoon – just after everything had opened up again following Dhuhr, the second of the day's five prayer times – I circled the hotel buffet, my black cloak wafting behind me, wondering what to have for lunch. One of the Pakistani waiters slid alongside me. 'We have roast turkey today,' he whispered, and then locked eyes with me and nodded hopefully. 'I think, ma'am, *you* may like to try?'

A disguised Christmas lunch. How sneaky! I thanked him, filled my plate and sloped back to the family section of the hotel dining room, which was screened off from the men-only part with bushy pot plants and wooden partitions made from tiny pieces of turned wood that fitted together in tessellating squares. Matthew was back in our room looking through tapes of interviews, so I ate alone. It wasn't very festive but I felt wicked as I bit into my Christmas turkey. Perhaps I even hummed 'Jingle Bells' to myself. For sure a little smile was playing on my lips.

Matthew and I were in Saudi Arabia to report on a fledgling group of reformers who were challenging the ruling royal family to introduce democratic change. By chance our visas had been approved in December. In this homeland of the Prophet Mohammed, all religions but Islam were banned, and yet I was still surprised by how absolutely Christmas Day was ignored. Not that I'd expected fanfare, but some acknowledgement perhaps? After all, the Muslims considered Jesus an important prophet, second only to Mohammed – although they didn't go in for the bits about being born of a virgin and rising from the dead.

It was the same on my New Year's Eve a week later: nothing. I lay in bed playing Freecell on my computer, waiting for the clock to tick over. Matthew was asleep beside me. 'I can't be bothered,' he'd groaned at 11.36 p.m. when our non-alcoholic beer ran out. At 00.08 a.m. on 1 January 2003 – or Shawwal 28, 1423 – I switched off the light.

The next morning, New Year's Day, as I handed in my key at the front desk, I noticed the Filipina receptionist was limping. 'Are you okay?' I asked. 'What happened?'

'Nothing, ma'am. I am fine,' she said. And then, quietly, as she bent towards me to take the key: 'Last night . . . ballroom dancing.' She smiled conspiratorially – such a thing would not amuse Saudi Arabia's *mutaween*, religious police, who were on the look-out for anything that would offend Saudi Arabia's ultra-conservative version of Islam. Unrelated men and women dancing close would not be approved of.

I had been in Saudi Arabia for a week but was still often caught off guard by the seemingly incomprehensible restrictions placed on interactions between men and women –

separate rooms in restaurants, separate banks so faces could be uncovered to verify identification, and on and on.

But hearing about the receptionist's night of dancing made me think everyone in Saudi Arabia must have a secret, and my clandestine Christmas lunch didn't seem so naughty after all. I felt emboldened. I decided I'd look for some other ways to challenge the system. I headed outside to find an internet café. There was one just up the road from the hotel but it was for men only. I hovered outside and convinced Matthew to go in and ask if I could quickly join him to do a few minutes of research. There was no one else in the place so surely my presence couldn't be too offensive.

The owner, bless him, looked around nervously. 'Okay. But please, tell your wife to be quick.'

I hurried to the upstairs terminals so I was less obvious and had just logged in when the manager came rushing up the stairs: 'You must leave immediately. The police are coming.'

A friend in Beirut had told me about a Saudi man named Jamal Khalifa, and given me his email address and told me to get in touch. 'He'd make a good story,' she said and lifted her eyebrows into a knowing expression. 'Put his name into Google and see what comes up.'

I did, and discovered that Mohammed Jamal Khalifa was the brother-in-law of Osama bin Laden. He was accused of links to the 1993 World Trade Center bombing and of funding Islamic extremist groups in Southeast Asia, including Abu Sayyef. Khalifa was the first suspect to be arrested and interrogated after 9/11 and is named in the court case for damages by the victims of that tragedy.

Khalifa was a free man but the suspicion around him

remained immense. In 1994 he was jailed in the United States for a visa violation – an excuse to hold him on suspicion of involvement in terrorist plots. But the Americans couldn't make anything stick and so they extradited him to Jordan, where he was facing the death penalty for allegedly masterminding a series of bomb attacks. But he was released again – a legal error made his case inadmissible, the Jordanian court said. The Americans were furious. They were looking for any excuse to take him into custody. After the September 11 attacks Washington pleaded with the Saudis to arrest him and Khalifa was the first person to be interrogated. He was jailed in Saudi Arabia for several months while he was being questioned. But there was no hard evidence and once again he was released.

I assumed Khalifa would be ultra conservative and so asked Matthew to email him, in case he was offended to receive a message from a woman. Matthew wrote that we were coming to Saudi Arabia and could we meet him. A few days later Khalifa emailed back: *I am waiting for you in Jeddah.*

We called him in secret and arranged to meet him in the late afternoon when Mohammed, our Ministry of Information minder, had gone home for the day. We were worried Mohammed would prevent us from doing the interview if he found out. The Saudi royal family, the Saud clan, already had enough trouble distancing itself from Osama bin Laden and most of the 9/11 hijackers. We could be fairly confident Mohammed wouldn't be encouraging us to interview another of the country's shady sons, so we were pretty pleased with ourselves for giving him the slip as we hired a taxi to take us to an outer suburb of Jeddah for our meeting with Khalifa. We were also nervous. Many times we asked ourselves: Are we being stupid? Are we crazy? It was difficult to know whether we were stepping across a line of safety. I didn't want to be melodramatic but the horrific story of Daniel Pearl, who was murdered chasing an interview with a senior al-Qaeda member in Pakistan, had driven home the risks of investigating links to this monstrous entity that the world had become obsessed with.

We turned up at Khalifa's office just as the afternoon's call to prayer, the Adhan, rang out: *Allah o Akbar. Allah o Akbar . . .*

God is most great
I testify that there is no god but God
I testify that Mohammed is the messenger of God
Come to prayer
Come to success
God is most great
There is none worthy of worship except God.

In Beirut, I loved the sound of the call to prayer. It had a delicate, otherworldly quality and the timbre of the muezzin's voice seemed to float above the din and crash of the city. I found it calming, a series of punctuation marks to ease me through the day, and I would often find myself woken in the pre-dawn by its soft and haunting melody drifting to me from blocks away, through the city's sleeping stillness. In Saudi, the call to prayer had a different tone. It was more forceful, strident, piercing. It sounded like a command and it put me on edge.

'Should we wait until it's over before going inside?' I asked Matthew. I was worried Khalifa would be in the middle of prayer and annoyed at being interrupted. Despite the niggling fears that I was choosing to ignore, I felt excited about this interview. I wasn't sure what Khalifa would tell us, but I didn't want to do anything to put him off.

We stood alone at the bottom of a flight of stairs that led to a modest block of apartments. The street around us was unremarkable, almost empty, tree-lined. We were wondering what to do when a young man in a white *thobe* – the long, slim shirt-dress worn by Saudi men – and a white crocheted cap on his head walked out of the building and straight towards us. He beckoned and we followed, unquestioning.

In an office several floors up, Jamal Khalifa was sitting in a high-backed black leather chair behind a large glass-topped desk. He stood up as we entered the room. He was small, wiry and looked very fit. He was almost vibrating with energy and his smile was eager. His cheeks were slightly pock-marked with scars, which I guessed were caused by teenage acne, and he had a small mole above one eyebrow. He also wore a white *thobe*, black sandals and a white crocheted cap. I was surprised to see that he was almost clean-shaven, without the long beard associated in Sunni Islam with deep religious conviction, often grown long from the chin but with the moustache shaved clean.

Khalifa shook Matthew's hand, then turned to his assistant – hovering deferentially in the background – and requested tea. When it was my turn to be greeted I placed my right hand over my heart in the gesture of respect that is universal across the Arab world and enables men and women to greet each other without touching. (I had learned that lesson from my early *faux pas* with Hussein Naboulsi on my first visit to Hezbollah.) But Khalifa thrust his hand towards me and looked at me with mock outrage. 'Let me shake your hand,' he said. 'Do you think I'm the kind of person who would not shake a woman's hand?' As I extended my hand towards his I noticed that the tip of the ring finger on his right hand was missing.

I looked around the room, trying to build a picture of the man. A copy of Thomas Friedman's book *The Lexus and the Olive Tree* sat on his desk next to a sign that said 'Cows may come and cows may go but the bull in this place goes on forever'. There was a television set against one wall with a small, roughly drawn coloured-pencil sketch of a country landscape sitting in a frame on the top. The curtains covering the windows were orange. I tried to work out what these things said about him. They were not easy to interpret: the latest book from a popular and moderate Jewish-American journalist-cum-analyst; a plaque of banal humour that you might expect to find on the desk of a going-nowhere manager in some anonymous office in middle America; the orange curtains – not an Islamic colour at all, too garish, too wild. And then there was the handshake. But the sketch was really out of the box. It was almost childlike, naïve, in its style and yet it could not have been drawn by one of Khalifa's children in Saudi Arabia, as it showed a chocolate-box farmhouse in the middle of green hills. Definitely not the Middle East.

I smiled and sat down. After the tea had been drunk, we began to talk. I asked him about his relationship with Osama bin Laden.

Khalifa met bin Laden when the two were students at the King Abdul Aziz University in Jeddah. They became close. 'More than brothers,' Khalifa said. 'We almost never separated.'

'What was he like?' I asked, full of impatient, ghoulish curiosity.

'Osama was a very normal person,' Khalifa began. He was smiling fondly. 'Very humble. Very simple. Very polite. Quiet. He forced you to respect him from his attitudes. He is not a person who's aggressive or even thinking to hate anyone, even by a word. He's selecting his words very carefully. He's a very nice guy. Really, a very nice guy.' Khalifa looked down and doodled on a piece of paper. He was lost in recollection. 'Yes, he's rich, from his family, but you never saw that. He was very simple. I never heard him say a bad word. His voice was always low, very polite.' He looked at me and repeated, 'A very nice guy.'

I wanted to go back to the beginning, to build up a picture of Khalifa, and asked him if we could start again. 'I'm sorry for all the questions,' I added.

'Oh, don't worry, I'm used to it,' Khalifa said. 'I'm very good at answering questions. Ask the police.' He said it without malice or embarassment, laughing.

Khalifa was born in Medina in 1957. His father married three women and he had 14 brothers and sisters. He studied biology at university, where he met bin Laden, and then became a high-school science teacher in Jeddah. During this time Khalifa and bin Laden were always together. Bin Laden arranged for one of his sisters, Sheikha, to marry his good friend. It was a mark of respect; a way to bind the two men together. Sheikha (who was older than Khalifa) became Khalifa's second wife.

'I had rented a very humble place and my in-laws didn't agree,' said Khalifa. It must have been hard to please the fabulously wealthy bin Ladens, who had made a fortune in the construction business. 'So Osama divided his house. He built a wall in the middle so we were sharing the same house and we lived that way for almost two years. This is how close we were.'

Khalifa and bin Laden always spoke about religion. They prayed together and studied the Qur'an together. In 1984 they joined a prayer group run by a Palestinian, Dr Abdullah Azaam. At that time Azaam was active in encouraging Saudi youth to go to Afghanistan to fight with the *mujahedeen*. Western governments encouraged it too: it was in their interests to find a force willing to fight against Russia's invading, expansionist Communist army.

'Dr Azaam told us it was our duty to go to Afghanistan to

help our brothers there, to make *jihad*,' Khalifa said. He raised his eyebrows and clasped his hands in front of him on the desk. 'And so Osama and me, we decided to go. He went ahead of me to see how it was and then came back, and on 1 January 1985 we left Jeddah together. I remember it well because they served champagne on the plane and it was the first time I had seen alcohol in my life.'

I didn't ask him if he drank it.

Instead of fighting, Khalifa said, he volunteered to run the Peshawa offices of the Muslim World League (MWL) – a huge Islamic charity with branches around the world. 'We collected money and bought things the Afghans needed. That's how it was at that time.' He shrugged, as if to say 'it was that simple'.

While Khalifa was in Peshawa, bin Laden set up a camp. It was a kind of initiation camp, where the fighters from around the Arab and Muslim world who were flooding into Afghanistan to participate in the *jihad* could be grouped and briefed, trained and assigned a role. Bin Laden called the camp al-Ma'asadah, the Lion's Den. It was right on the frontline. This is the place that analysts and experts say forged the kernel from which al-Qaeda grew, with bin Laden as its leader and Azaam as the religious and ideological inspiration. Khalifa said it was around this time that several Egyptian clerics moved into the camp. 'Zawahiri, I remember him,' he said, referring to the man who is now bin Laden's second-in-command.

Khalifa said he was against the camp. Young fighters with scant battle training, only an ingrained sense of religious and political obligation, were sent from the camp to the frontlines. Scores of them were killed fighting the well-trained Russian soldiers. Khalifa claims the Afghans were also uncomfortable with al-Ma'asadah. It felt like something they could not control. 'I was meeting regularly with the Afghans to talk about aid and education. They knew I was close to Osama. They asked me, please talk to him.'

Khalifa travelled from Peshawa to al-Ma'asadah. He watched what was happening there. He watched as, one by one, the young *jihadis* were taught basic military skills and then dispatched to the frontline to their death. After three days he sat down with bin Laden to talk about it. 'I told him, "Brother, we came here to work among the Afghans. We came to help but this is not helping. We have created a new leadership and that is not what the Afghans want from us. We are throwing Arabs into conflict and they are being killed day and night. Who is responsible?" '

Khalifa thought his friendship with bin Laden would carry weight. He thought his friend would listen to him. Instead they began to argue: their first fight, Khalifa said. He was white-hot with rage. Bin Laden was quiet, stony, resolute. 'I shouted at him. "This camp has to be closed right now! You have to close it. If you don't, our relationship with the Afghans will be destroyed." '

At the end of Khalifa's tirade, bin Laden told him: 'This is my way. If it is not your way, then go.'

Apart from family functions during the 1990s, Khalifa says he and bin Laden have not seen or spoken to each other since. 'Osama is my best friend. More than my brother. I love him very much, even now,' Khalifa said, shaking his head. 'But from that time until now we have had no relationship. I don't know what's going on with him. But I can say that this is not the Osama I knew.' He waved his hands in the air to encompass an imaginary image of bin Laden. 'Either he has changed, or everything they talk about, this al-Qaeda network, does not exist. I really have my doubts. Believe me.' He looked down at the desk and peered through the glass to his black-sandalled feet below.

As we finished the interview Khalifa fell silent for a moment. Then he said, 'You know, I saw Osama three or four days ago and I asked him, "What is al-Qaeda?" He said, "Don't listen to these things. There is nothing like that."'

I was incredulous, on the edge of my seat. 'You *saw* bin Laden? When? *Where*??'

Khalifa looked shocked and realised his mistake. 'In my dream. I tell you, this is a dream. I repeat that: *This. Is. A. Dream.*' He laughed. 'I must be careful.'

We shook hands again and Khalifa's lackey led us back outside to the taxi.

The street was in darkness. The mosque at the intersection at the end of the road was lit up and glowing like a spaceship. Our taxi driver was waiting for us, tall and elegant in his long pale grey cotton shirt and sandals. He was Pakistani and said he trained as a lawyer but couldn't find work at home. His name was Zwan and he'd been in Saudi Arabia for three years, like thousands of others from South Asia and Southeast Asia who were brought in on temporary work visas to do the jobs Saudis didn't want to do. They were an underclass, existing in a world of paid servants, apart from the elite and tightly bound Saudi society. 'I don't speak Arabic,' he said when I asked how he liked the place. 'Why would I want to speak to these crazy people? They think they are special. They think they are better than others.'

We were hungry and not keen to eat another meal in the hotel. 'Do you know a good restaurant?' I asked Zwan. He said he knew an Indian place that was popular and not expensive. 'Let's go!' we said.

It was early. We stood around in the foyer of the restaurant watching tropical fish swim back and forth in a giant tank while we waited for the family room to open. As in the hotel, I had to eat segregated from the main part of the restaurant. The problem, it seemed, was that veiled women couldn't eat comfortably if they had to keep on their *abaya* and *niqab*, the cloth flap that covered the face. I remembered seeing a woman eating French fries at a McDonald's outlet in Dubai airport. She sat hunched at the table, one hand manoeuvring fries into her mouth and the other holding the veil at an angle away from her face. This problem was overcome by having two dining rooms: one that was open plan for men only, and another that was sectioned off into small individual rooms for women to eat with their husbands and children.

The Indian waiters pointed out a table in the far corner, then moved four large screens on wheels around us so we were closed in, hidden from the view of the other tables.

'Do you think I can take the Little Black Dress off in here?' I asked Matthew and we debated the etiquette. I kept it on and held my arms high as I reached across the table for spoonfuls of curry and rice and chutney, trying to stop the sleeves of my *abaya* dangling in the food.

∾

On Thursday night we went for a walk through Jeddah's shopping district. It was the beginning of the weekend. In Saudi, like Iran and most of the Muslim world, Friday was the day off. It was winter but the weather in Jeddah was mild and the atmosphere almost festive. Young men piled into their four-wheel-drives and cruised the streets swerving and weaving through the traffic. They opened the windows and let music from their car sound systems fill the night.

We were with H, a reporter from *Arab News*, an English-language newspaper that's published in Jeddah and is a helpful source of information for visiting foreign reporters. H had offered to show us around and had already taken us to a swish outdoor restaurant that was liberal enough to let women and men eat together in the open. Tonight we were going dating, Saudi-style. 'Watch closely,' he urged, pointing to the cars. 'You will see how we court in Jeddah.'

I watched as a young man held a piece of white paper with a telephone number written on it in the window of his car. A second car slid alongside; through the dark tinted glass I could make out the silhouettes of three women in the back seat.

'Did you see that?' H said. 'The girls take down the number and if they like the look of the guy they call and arrange to meet. They go for a coffee in the family section of a restaurant and pretend to be brother and sister or husband and wife.' He paused and twisted his wedding ring thoughtfully. 'Of course, a Saudi man would never actually marry a girl like that. Saudi men want good girls that cover their faces.'

Women aren't allowed to drive in Saudi Arabia and so are driven around either by a male family member or, if the family is rich enough, by a chauffeur. It was those cars, driven by a Pakistani or Indian chauffeur, that the young men were looking for. The last thing they wanted was to flash their phone numbers to a car driven by an irate Saudi father.

Hidden behind the flashing new cars and bright lights was a subversive dating scene. It was incredibly risky and risqué behaviour – and it delighted me to see the determination of young people to negotiate ways around the restrictions of their conservative society.

The guys who didn't get dates (most of them) adjourned to the car park of a nearby shopping mall. They opened the doors and windows of their cars, opened up the roof, turned up the stereo then lounged around their vehicles, some in traditional Saudi dress, but most in American streetwear – baggy jeans and tracksuits with T-shirts advertising well-known brands or fashionable slogans. They chatted with their friends, laughed, and the Jeddah night was filled with the sound of rap music.

It was still quite early when we got back to the hotel. I logged onto the internet (I had organised a connection in my room after the internet café debacle) and did some more research on Khalifa.

Khalifa said he'd left Afghanistan after a falling-out with bin Laden. But terrorism experts believed he left with instructions to expand the fledgling al-Qaeda movement into Southeast Asia. He was accused of helping to fund and set up Abu Sayyef, the Islamic separatist organisation based in the southern Philippines, and then to extend al-Qaeda's links to groups like Jemaah Islamiyah in Indonesia. It was true that Khalifa lived in the Philippines on and off for many years, and two of his four wives (the maximum number allowed under Islam) were Filipina. So what was he doing there?

The internet revealed a picture of a man who used Islamic charities as a front to raise money for al-Qaeda and then channelled it into a network of organisations across Southeast Asia. Khalifa's work brought him into contact with men like Ramzi Yousef, the 1993 World Trade Center bomber, and a slew of others with known or suspected ties to al-Qaeda or bomb plots or attacks.

The FBI had its eye on Khalifa long before 9/11. In 1994 he was picked up in the US on the visa violation charge, allegedly carrying a suitcase full of documents on assassination training, weapons and explosives and a strategy for bombing churches and murdering Catholic priests. He was jailed for six months in California's Santa Rita prison before being extradited to Jordan to face the death penalty for an alleged plot to bomb public places including movie cinemas. But, as I already knew, he had been released.

The next morning I spoke with Jamal Khashoggi, a well-known and respected journalist from *Arab News* who had known Khalifa since childhood and had been a *jihadi* himself in Afghanistan. 'There's no way I believe he's guilty of these things,' he said. 'I've never heard a radical word come out of his mouth.'

I was thoroughly confused about Khalifa. Was this guy lucky or was he being wrongly accused? Matthew and I tried to work through all the various possibilities in his story. Maybe he was telling the truth and he had gone to Afghanistan to fight the Russians, disliked the direction his friend Osama and the group of Egyptians were going in, and left. Perhaps he had fought with Osama for dominance of this burgeoning al-Qaeda movement and lost. Had he been recruited, as the international intelligence experts said, to expand the movement in Southeast Asia? Maybe he'd been an active member of the group but his cover had been blown and he was of no more use to al-Qaeda. Whatever the answer, it was obvious that there was a lot more of Khalifa's story to tell. I decided to wait a few days, then call and ask if we could have another meeting. I was confident he would accept. I felt I understood his motivation in speaking to us: he was trying to clear his name.

'Let me take you to dinner!' Khalifa said when I called. 'Did I tell you I own a fish restaurant at Dahban? You will love it. We are famous in Saudi Arabia.'

A dinner date with Osama bin Laden's (former) best friend, the possible creator of Abu Sayyef and mastermind of the 1993 World Trade Center bombing? Weird, but, well, I accepted. 'If you are sure it's not too much trouble,' I said.

As the appointment drew closer all the old fears started to come back. We would be riding in Khalifa's car, alone, through the desert to reach Dahban, a town north of Jeddah on the Red Sea coast. Once again it seemed like a stupid thing to do.

I thought back to the story Khalifa had told us in his office. He told it with the utmost conviction. But to believe him I had to discredit the best counter-terrorism analysts the West had to offer. There was overwhelming circumstantial evidence against him. I didn't know what to think. All I knew for sure was that we would be vulnerable if he had any motivation to harm us. I wrote a note and left it on the table in our hotel room: *Dinner with Jamal Khalifa in Dahban*. I added the date and Khalifa's mobile telephone number.

Matthew looked at me as if I'd gone mad.

'Well, at least if we don't come back and someone searches for us, they'll know where to start!' I said, defensive.

We waited for Khalifa in the lobby, sitting together on a cream leather couch in a little alcove that had mirrors on one side and more of the tessellated wooden screens on the other. He arrived on time, buoyant as usual. We walked out together and I felt a sense of foreboding. I wondered if anyone recognised him. I half-expected someone to come up to me and whisper, 'That's Jamal Khalifa. He's one of the world's most wanted men. Where are you going with him? Are you crazy?'

I stepped into the back of the car, my imagination unstoppable. Every movement seemed loaded. Is this the last time I . . .? The last time we . . .? The last time . . .? We drove through Jeddah's northern suburbs, down Sharia Tahlia where I'd seen the four-wheel-drive dating scene, and past the shiny shopping malls with well-known Western fashion chains lit up like shrines. Soon we left the city behind us and were speeding along a smooth highway. Although we were close to the Red Sea coast, stony desert stretched out on both sides.

'Osama and me, we used to come here a lot to ride horses or take a four-wheel-drive jeep into the desert,' Khalifa said suddenly and my stomach flipped. 'His family had a ranch and we would ride through this desert together.'

'What did you talk about?' I asked.

'We didn't have particular things to talk about, so it's about horses or cars and the normal things youths talk about.'

After a while we turned off the highway onto a road that spiralled towards the coast. Several seafood restaurants appeared by the side of the road; I couldn't begin to describe the relief.

Khalifa pulled into the car park of his restaurant. We got out of the car and he greeted a tall, large man whom he introduced to us as his brother. The two brothers showed us through the restaurant. It had a large area for viewing the fish before it was cooked and a huge industrial kitchen for preparing it.

The restaurant itself was all outdoors. There was a large landscaped area and a man-made river that ran through it, with little arched wooden bridges built in different places. Of course, because this was Saudi Arabia the dining areas were built so that they could be closed off from view. Some were little cabins, like holiday cabins, and others were raised grass-roofed huts with walls extending part-way up, enough to hide diners at a table. The top half of the hut was left open to the air. Each had a television set and lounges so families could spend an entire day there, eating, sleeping, relaxing.

Khalifa directed his staff to create a little picnic spot for us on the grass next to the river and beside one of the little arched bridges. I was beginning to see how utterly strange it was that I should so willingly agree to dine with Khalifa so openly, without reserve. To Saudi onlookers I must have appeared without self-respect. Matthew must seem to have no dignity, to allow his wife to display herself publicly like this. But I could also see that these were not so much purely Islamic principles as cultural and traditional ones. Certainly it wasn't strange to dine in public in any other Arab or Muslim country I'd visited; the opposite – outdoor cafés and restaurants were famous across the region. Even in Iran, dining at outdoor cafés was a favourite pastime. Saudi Arabia was a special case.

Life here had been built, until very recently, on strong desert traditions. It was a harsh existence. The climate was all extremes of heat and cold; stronger tribes would think little of pillaging the women and the wealth of their neighbours. There were stories of how family groups would live together in the desert and the women would be kept inside the tents, protected from the heat and dust, and when groups from neighbouring tribes came past the women would cover their faces with cloth to hide their beauty or their youth so they were less appealing. These traditions had been woven into Islamic ones, so that now it was hard to know where tradition ended and religion began.

After our tour Khalifa guided us to the little picnic spot. We sat on a blanket, Matthew and I on one side, Khalifa on the other. He took off his sandals and positioned them neatly on the grass at the edge of the blanket.

The food came on giant silver trays, far more than we could possibly eat. Each tray was piled high with rice or fish dishes, and from time to time Khalifa called to the waiter and asked for more of this or that or a change to the way the dish was usually prepared. The food was delicious, heavily spiced, and the fish was smothered in thick fragrant sauces.

We talked as we ate. The conversation was easy. Khalifa was an enthusiastic host. He continued his story.

When he came back from Afghanistan, after the fight with Osama, Khalifa returned to teaching biology to high-school students. But he couldn't focus. He was restless. He wanted to earn more money. He now had two wives and a growing family. Life was expensive.

'A lot of people see having more than one wife as a privilege, but the Qur'an tells us that it is a duty,' he said as he bent forward to place another spoonful of rice on my plate.

He pointed out how pleasing this extra wife was a religious duty. I had assumed it must be an erotic pleasure. He explained how he compartmentalised his time to be certain that he was not favouring one wife over the other, as it insisted in the Qur'an. 'It's very important to divide time and money equally among each wife. If you cannot, then you cannot take more than one wife. This is very difficult,' he said, mulling over the dilemma as he fed himself another spoonful of fish and rice.

So he decided to go to the Philippines. 'I had visited in 1985 and I liked it,' he said, as if the decision to move there was straightforward, obvious. 'So I went there. It's a simple life, the people are very friendly, and it's cheaper than here. So I went to see what I could do there.'

Khalifa built a business exporting rattan furniture. The margins were huge and he quickly made a lot of money. In 1988 he was approached by the Muslim World League to manage its international Islamic relief work in the Philippines. 'They said it's difficult to find a Saudi to work outside the country, especially this kind of work; it needs someone prepared to work a little bit like a volunteer. I had experience from Pakistan, Afghanistan, and so they came to me and said, "Please, we want you to help us." '

Khalifa took on the charity job. It was a high-profile position and he received a lot of guests and visitors, and worked often on the Muslim-dominated island of Mindinao in the southern Philippines, where Abu Sayyef was based. He was well known, and attended many conferences and hosted many visiting Muslims who were interested in his charity work.

It was around that time that rumours began to circulate that Khalifa's furniture business and his involvement in the MWL (as well as a second charity that he set up himself) were fronts to channel money into recruiting, training and arming extremist Islamic groups.

I wanted to confront him with some of the allegations against him. I asked him about the associations with people like Ramzi Yousef, the World Trade Center bomber. For me, those connections were impossible to explain away as mere coincidence.

'They were looking for evidence against me,' Khalifa said. 'What did they find? My calling card [in Ramzi Yousef's apartment]. I am a businessman. I am head of a very big organisation. Plenty of people came and met me and I gave them my card.'

'But what about Wali Khan,' I said. Khan had assisted Yousef in the World Trade Center bombing in 1993.

'Wali Khan was a student at the high school I taught at,' Khalifa said. 'He's from Uzbekistan. When the Afghan problem happened he decided to join the Afghanis. He went there to Afghanistan and came to the Philippines in 1992–93. When he came, who do you think he contacted? Me. Of course. I was his teacher, and even if I am not his teacher I was the director of MWL. Anyone coming there would have contacted me.'

I had a list of convicted extremists with alleged contacts to Khalifa, but every time his answers were the same and I realised I was never going to get the information I sought. I didn't even know what it was I was looking for exactly. The truth? As Khalifa told it, each encounter *was* mere coincidence.

The Americans certainly didn't believe in coincidence. When Khalifa visited the US in December 1994 and was taken in for the visa violation, he was locked up inside California's maximum-security Santa Rita prison next to some of the country's most-wanted murderers, armed robbers and rapists.

'They put me in a small cell and, you know, I am a person who doesn't like to be in a room, in a house,' he said, shuffling around on the mat. 'I stand up, I open the door, I never stay in one place. Then finally I found myself in one small cell alone. From that moment I knew that if I didn't learn to control myself I would go crazy.'

The prisoners were not allowed to mingle. He was alone when he showered. He was alone when he telephoned his lawyer. But Khalifa was nervous. He was a small Arab man in a prison packed with huge muscled Americans, hardened crims, black and white. He tried to win them over. He slipped coffee and chocolates under their cell doors. The crims glared at him as he bounded past, smiling his energetic smile.

A few days later the newspapers were full of Khalifa's story. So he asked for a newspaper. He found his name all over it: he was suspected of masterminding the Oklahoma bombing – which happened while he was in prison. 'They were saying I am a trainer, a founder, a planner, a financer of terrorist groups in many countries, some of which I couldn't even find on a map.' He threw his arms in the air, laughed and opened his eyes wide, disbelieving. 'Believe me, I was shocked. My neighbour in the jail, in the cell next to mine, was this huge criminal guy and he became very small when he saw me and he said, "Wow, you are all that?" '

Khalifa was laughing about how his prison status had shifted. He had no need for coffee and chocolate bribes after that.

'What got you through it,' I asked him, expecting a line about his religion.

'I didn't surrender,' he said. 'I made use of a book, a great book. It is called *The 7 Habits of Highly Effective People*.'

I tried hard to stifle a giggle – the arch-terrorist turning to a notorious American self-help guide was just too funny. But Khalifa was very serious. 'I was helped enormously by this book. It teaches how you can control yourself and not let situations affect you. And that's what I did.'

He reminded me of the pencil sketch in his office, the one of green hills with blue sky and a little farmhouse in the centre. 'That was the view from my cell,' he said. 'I looked at that image every day and I never lost hope that one day I would be free to enjoy it again.'

It was getting late. We walked back to the car, and once again stopped to admire the rows and rows of fresh fish displayed on ice, while Khalifa spun his stories and his jokes, charming, hospitable. I wanted to believe his story, I thought as we walked back to the car. Despite myself, I liked him.

I stayed in touch with Jamal Khalifa. We emailed from time to time and I often asked for more details about his life for this book or asked him religious questions because I was curious. He always wrote back quickly in the same buoyant style I had noticed when we were face-to-face. He maintained his innocence. He was writing a book about his life. He still wanted to clear his name.

Then, on 31 January 2007, Khalifa was gunned down and killed by a group of 20 or 30 assassins. He was in Madagascar working at a gem mine he owned. Was he robbed? The assassins took papers and computer equipment but no gemstones.

Stories began to circulate on the internet, saying intelligence organisations had discussed Khalifa in the two weeks before he died. Was his death a bungled attempt at rendition? But then it happened that Madagascar had become a favoured destination for al-Qaeda members to go for R&R. Another coincidence? Only God knows what Khalifa has done.

I often tried to work out why Khalifa's story fascinated me. No doubt a part of it was simply curiosity – becoming acquainted with a man who had known bin Laden and had bits and pieces of insight to offer about him and the genesis of al-Qaeda. But when I thought about it, there was more. Khalifa interested me because he seemed to represent the failures of this War on Terror. If he was a guilty man, if he had done all that he was accused of, then how could a succession of legal encounters in several countries have failed to convict him? Why was he living more or less freely in Jeddah?

The alternative troubled me even more: if he was innocent, as he proclaimed, then the assault on his liberty, his destroyed reputation, represented a horrific injustice, and you couldn't help but wonder how many others had been wrongly accused, their lives destroyed.

Either way, Khalifa's story left me with a great sense of mistrust for what the West had planned for the Middle East. And I watched with gloom as Washington began to line up its next target.

CHAPTER 12
A WAR IN IRAQ

That February Matthew and I celebrated the end of our second year in Lebanon and the beginning of our third with a weekend at Faraya, a popular ski resort just outside Beirut. But the holiday was overshadowed by the churning, dread feeling of yet more conflict to come, which lay above Beirut like a deadweight. A war in Iraq now seemed a certainty, yet people were doing an excellent job of getting on with things. Our street was full of life.

The Hajj, the annual pilgrimage to Mecca that was considered an essential quest for those financially and physically able to fulfil it, had just finished. At the airport in Riyadh, while I was waiting for the flight back to Beirut, I had seen many pilgrims on their way to Mecca. Those taking part in the Hajj were required to enter a spiritual state known as *ihram*. They must free their bodies and minds of negativity – greed or vanity, anger, hate, arrogance. There could be no quarrelling and no sex. As a sign of their humility male pilgrims removed their jewellery and changed from their usual dress into what looked like two large white bath towels wrapped around their bodies. Women also wore white but it was not allowed to cover their faces. It was impossible to tell the poor Indonesian street sweeper from the wealthy Kuwaiti businessman. Before God, all Muslims were equal.

Two residents of our street in Clemenceau had made the trip, and although I didn't know them it was impossible to miss this milestone in their lives. As was traditional, coloured streamers were stretched from the balcony of the apartments where the new Hajjis lived and anchored to a lamp post on the street below. Large green banners – the colour of Islam – hung across the lintel into the foyers of each apartment, printed with a quote from the Qur'an. As I walked along the street the streamers fanned out above the footpath and formed a kind of victory tunnel that allowed everyone who passed to share in their achievement.

But this show of normality couldn't last for long. The newspapers were full of politics, and as February progressed Beirut's streets filled up with demonstrations against the war.

The rallies were not in support of Saddam – the Lebanese knew the history of Iraq well – but they were fed up with what they saw as Washington's arrogant grab for more influence in the Middle East, for oil; for its overt support for Israel at the expense of Palestinian rights. The looming war in Iraq felt like a humiliation for the Arabs and just seemed to confirm everyone's worst fears about America's willingness to twist the facts to suit itself, to dehumanise Iraqis so that the 'collateral damage' of its planned 'shock and awe' scarcely seemed relevant.

Matthew and I began to make plans to travel to northern Iraq. We had visas for Iran and intended to travel over the mountains and across the remote border between Iran and Iraq, to cover the war from northern Iraqi Kurdistan.

While we waited in a holding pattern between war and peace, between work and unemployment (the sad fact was, war was good for journalism), I took a lightning-fast trip to

Tel Aviv to buy two chemical weapons suits – the experts called them NBC suits because they protected against nuclear, biological and chemical weapons. Matthew and I spent a hilarious evening trying it all on: enormous pants made from clear plastic with elastic around the waist and ankles; a matching hooded jacket that could be pulled tight around the face; rubber boots; rubber gloves; and a heavy black gas mask with a little canister that you screwed on the end, near the mouth, to filter whatever God-awful poison had been detonated into the air. The whole lot folded up inside a little blue backpack. We laughed because the reality of actually needing to use this stuff was too terrifying to contemplate. This was in the days when we were told that Saddam Hussein had a large and deadly arsenal of weapons of mass destruction and I held precisely no hope that I'd get the suit and everything else on fast enough to save my life.

In early March, shortly after my birthday, I packed up my best *hejab* coverings, my satellite telephone, the NBC suit, a stash of notebooks and thousands of dollars in cash and Matthew and I flew to Tehran.

It was Ashura once again and Iran was in mourning: all around us, black, sombre grief. We interviewed some Iraqi exiles who had escaped Saddam's purges of the Shi'ites and now lived in ghettoes in Tehran, speaking Arabic, practising their religion, but missing home. Always missing home.

'Maybe next year you will be commemorating Ashura in Iraq,' I said to one of them and he gathered some enthusiasm, nodded, smiled.

As we spoke, a young girl curled herself around the man's legs and pulled self-consciously at the scarf tied around her head, staring up at me, curious and shy.

'She has only recently begun to wear the *hejab*, *hamdilillah*,' the man said. 'Thanks to God.'

I looked at the little girl. 'We are the same,' I told her. 'I have just started wearing *hejab* too.'

She grinned and buried her face deeper into her father's clothes, shy and self-conscious and delighted.

After a few days I left Matthew behind – he was putting finishing touches to a script about these Iraqi exiles in Iran – and drove the long and winding mountain roads to Kermanshah in the far west of Iran, past a backdrop of snow-covered mountains and sweeping valleys, chill winter air and pale skies.

At the border, I sat with the sun on my back and read an old copy of *Time* magazine while I waited with a little crowd of journalists, photographers, cinematographers and television reporters to cross into northern Iraq.

There were taxis waiting to drive us from the border and into the southern Kurdish town of Suleymanieh. I booked into a dreadful hotel on the edge of town, all the best rooms long ago taken by other journalists with much bigger budgets than mine, and I couldn't help comparing it to my first trip when foreign journalists were so scarce Matthew and I had featured in the local media. That night before I went to bed, I unzipped the little blue backpack and took out the NBC suit. I put the gas mask on a chair beside my bed and looked at it for a long time, mentally practising how I would get it on if a chemical or biological or nuclear bomb was dropped.

The next morning, another journalist passed as I locked my room. 'Have you heard?' he said. 'It's started.'

I spent every day of the next three weeks watching American bombers and fighter jets screeching across the sky, and tracking the little puffs of smoke that marked the latest Iraqi bunker to be blown up.

As territory fell to the advancing coalition of Kurdish fighters, backed up by US Special Forces and the relentless air assault, we were able to drive a little further into this mysterious land of Iraq, freshly captured by the Coalition forces. One day I walked around a former military base, now silent and abandoned. There were rooms full of gas masks and antidotes to various chemical or biological poisons, all years past their expiry dates. I stood a few metres from the frontline and watched the Iraqis firing warning shots towards us. I arrived at the scene of an accidental attack on a group of *peshmerga* by American fighter jets and watched the heartbroken Kurds tenderly retrieve pieces of their comrades from the ground.

At night I'd have dinner at the best hotel in town with all the other journalists and we'd swap stories and contacts. In those moments – sitting satisfied before plates of chicken and rice and a glass full of beer – it was almost possible to forget this was war. But then it would come back to us in the most horrible ways: the death of colleagues or their translators in land-mine explosions, car bombs. We searched for a way to explain each death, trying to calculate the moment when things had gone wrong, because it helped somehow to use mathematical precision to rationalise irrational death. I tried to keep a tally of risk and danger, and every day I made life or death decisions in the wake of this surreal reckoning.

One day, after a chance decision, I was at a hospital instead of a checkpoint when a suicide car bomber blew himself up and killed a colleague, injured a friend. I was standing in the hospital forecourt when the bodies started arriving and what I saw was too terrible to describe here. I called Matthew on my satellite telephone. 'Some foreign journalists have been involved in an explosion,' I said. 'But I am okay.'

I travelled north, to Erbil. Officially, it was so I could be closer to the two main fronts: one pushing northwest to

Mosul, Iraq's third-largest city and the birthplace of many of the country's senior army generals; the other moving south-west into Kirkuk, which was traditionally a Kurdish town, prized for its rich oil reserves. The Iraqi regime didn't want to lose it. The Kurds wanted it back. The Americans wanted to make damn sure they found a way to get control of all that oil. But unofficially I left because I had become haunted in Suleymanieh. Erbil had its own ghosts, but they weren't my ghosts, and so my head was clear there and I could work.

On 9 April Baghdad fell and the streets of Erbil erupted in euphoria. It was the beginning of the end. Mosul and Kirkuk fell like dominoes.

When the Iraqi Army abandoned Mosul, I drove with Ahmad and Mohammed, my Kurdish translator and my driver, across the old Kurdish–Iraqi border and into the city. We crossed a bombed bridge – piles of soil and rubble filled the gaps and provided makeshift repairs – and through swathes of empty countryside: oddly vivid green grasslands dotted with blackened military bunkers and foxholes. Stretches of road had been dug up by teams of *peshmerga* so land mines could be removed.

Ahmad and Mohammed were nervous about going to Mosul, because they would be Kurds in a mostly Arab town. In the decade or so that Kurdistan had been separated by force from the rest of Iraq, a lot of myth and hatred had been allowed to breed. Understandably, the Kurds remembered the Anfal Campaign, the uprising and violent suppression that came after it that left up to 100,000 dead, the refugee crisis with its two million homeless. They had been raised on xenophobia, a sort of survival instinct born from the horrors

Kurdish families had just barely survived. Ahmad was full of this hatred. He would tell me matter-of-factly how the Kurds and Arabs couldn't live together; how Arabs should leave their homes in Kirkuk because the city belonged to the Kurds.

It took a lot of convincing before Mohammed would drive out of Mosul's Kurdish outer suburbs and deeper into the city. But they were both curious to visit this 'other' Iraq that had been closed to them, demonised, for most of their lives. The chance to see inside Saddam's palaces – he had extravagant homes all over Iraq – proved lure enough. And so we drove on past the carved stone walls of Nineveh, the ancient capital of Assyria that had once extended all over this region of northern Iraq, past fruit and vegetable markets and into the city centre, which vibrated with tension after days of bombing, then anarchy and looting.

We parked beside the Palace of the Spear, set on an artificial lake and within sight of the Tigris River. Here, the foreboding of the city melted away and it felt like being at a carnival. The grounds were full of families; everyone was excited, animated, collegial. Entrepreneurs had set up little stalls outside the palace selling nuts and soft drinks, cigarettes.

We joined a large crowd of Iraqis traipsing through the palace, like tourists might a royal residence in Britain. We walked through large, ornate rooms with mosaic tiled floors and carved wood inlaid into the walls. The place had been extensively looted but you could still see the grandeur. There were a few things left: a large painting in a vaguely cubist style filled a wall in what had been a reception room. A portrait of Saddam, waving, was at its centre. A carved balustrade had been broken and lay partly on the floor and I tore off a tiny piece of turned wood, my souvenir of Saddam Hussein.

A sign at the entrance to the palace read: 'No President After Saddam'. As we were negotiating the crowds, Ahmad said to me, 'You know, Miss Catherine, I think that Iraq needs another tyrant.'

I didn't think Ahmad was wishing Saddam Hussein's return – the Kurds had suffered from his policies far too greatly for that. In fact, most Kurds were extremely pro-war, to the point where there were demonstrations against news organisations that they perceived to be critical of the US-led invasion. But perhaps Ahmad recognised the hatred inside himself that he felt towards Iraq's Arabs, who provided a face for Kurdish suffering.

I had a compulsion to lecture him: 'Can't you see that you are doing to the Arabs just as the Iraqi regime did to you? You condemn yourselves to misery if you think like that. You must learn to live together.' But I held my tongue. I had no right to my moralising.

Even in those days just after the overthrow of Saddam Hussein, it was clear that Iraq's mixed-up population – Sunnis and Shi'ites, Christians, even a few Jews who had not yet fled to Israel to escape persecution – was going to lead to a struggle for power during the dismantling of the regime.

We left the palace and drove through the streets. They were strewn with rubbish and rubble from smashed buildings, burnt shells of cars and makeshift barricades to keep the looters out. We found a mosque that was accepting looted goods to be returned to their owners. This was happening all across the city: a spontaneous show of civil society as Iraqis organised themselves into an improvised government to plug the gaps until a real government stepped in.

We stopped the car outside the mosque and Mohammed,

who spoke better Arabic than Ahmad, agreed to go inside and ask the imam if we could have a look around. In less than a generation, Iraqi Kurds had lost their linguistic link to their Arab brothers. The Kurds saw this as progress, the choice to abandon the language of their oppressors, but it alienated them even further from their Arab neighbours.

Mohammed returned with news: it was okay to go inside. The problem was I hadn't brought a headscarf. We debated back and forth. The imam suggested he would come outside to talk with us, but I was keen to get inside, to see the goods that had been returned, to get a feel for the place. It would be difficult and possibly dangerous to do the interview standing on the street.

Just as I was about to relent and talk to the imam outside, an old woman walked past wearing layers and layers of *hejab*. I asked her if she knew where I could buy a scarf, a *chador*. 'Anything will do,' I said.

She reached inside her *chador* and pulled off a green scarf that she was wearing underneath. She handed it to me, pulling the *chador* tightly closed again. She was poor. There were holes in the *chador* and her hands said a lot about a life lived hard. I offered her money again and again, but she refused it. I should have slipped something quietly into her hand but instead I thanked her, guilty at my bumbling, humbled by her generosity.

When I turned around to enter the mosque, Ahmad was smiling. 'Miss Catherine, when you are veiled you look very nice.'

The mosque's courtyard was filled with the detritus of a city. Fridges, filing cabinets, office furniture, couches. Even a kitchen sink. The imam led us to a small room off the courtyard that was full of boxes and books. It was well used and comfortable. He sat behind a desk and I settled into a low armchair. He was prickly and self-important and I felt anxious to win him over. But I was distracted, trying to get the green scarf to sit right. Every time the fabric moved, a pungent smell of burnt meat, onions and garlic filled my nostrils. When I was still I could feel insects crawling out of the material and making their way down the shafts of my hair.

'We have no water, and I am sorry but we cannot offer you tea,' the imam began, speaking Arabic to Mohammed, who translated into Kurdish for Ahmad, who spoke to me in English. I was concerned about the accuracy of this interview, which had all the hallmarks of turning into a macabre version of Chinese Whispers. But there was no alternative. We struggled on. The conversation was achingly slow.

The imam blamed the Kurdish *peshmerga* for the looting and the chaos. He blamed the Americans for refusing to hand control of the city to the local tribes. His anger switched back and forth on itself and there was no logic to it, just distress. 'They have robbed the bank, burned the bank. They have destroyed the museum and the central library, the university and all the offices of the government. People are being car-jacked. We have talked to people and told them, "This is your city. These are your brothers. Why steal from your brothers?" '

Just then a growl in the distance exploded into a shriek of scraping metal. The room shook. We hurried to the door and looked outside in time to see the tails of two US fighter jets patrolling so low over the city I imagined I saw the pilots inside. The noise was terrifying.

When the roar had faded the imam asked where I was from.

'Australia,' I said.

He looked down. 'Ahh. Thanks to God for what your country has done for the Iraqi people.'

'*Shukran, shukran*,' I said, obsequious. 'Thank you . . .'

Back in the car, Ahmad said that the imam had been 'making fun of us' and I felt a rush of understanding: I'd become so used to Kurdish platitudes about democracy and freedom and the importance of the war that I had failed to hear what the imam was saying.

Now I could see that his words had dripped with sarcasm: 'Thanks to God for what your country has done for the Iraqi people.' And I remembered how, as he detailed the looting and the destruction, listed the dead and those turned from their homes by ethnic tensions, he had added quietly, 'What kind of freedom is this?'

It was late afternoon. We drove past a bank where a confetti of torn notes still papered the ground from looting a few days earlier. On another corner a crowd of youths was demonstrating against the Americans who had shot into a crowd that morning and, everyone said, killed three people. One of the demonstrators saw our car and recognised us as strangers. He began yelling and ran towards us, the rest of the group close behind him, their fists in the air.

'Mohammed, for God's sake let's get out of here,' I said.

I tore the scarf from my head, suddenly exhausted by everything: by the fear and the sadness and the anger, by the fact that none of it made sense any more. I rolled the scarf into a ball and stuffed it into a pocket of my bag and we gunned it back to Erbil.

CHAPTER 13

ANNIVERSARY IN BAGHDAD

It was 6 May, our wedding anniversary. Matthew was in Jordan; I was in Iraq. It was our third anniversary but we had never managed to spend the day together and I was beginning to think we were jinxed. I was sitting in a colleague's hotel room, drinking whisky, moaning about it.

The last time I had seen Matthew was several weeks earlier in Erbil. We had breakfast together (black coffee, bread rolls, lentil soup and hard-boiled eggs) and then went out separately, as we did every day. We were together but apart, doing our different jobs and usually meeting up for dinner each evening. There was always an understanding that the job might take one of us elsewhere at short notice, and when I returned to the hotel that evening there was a message scrawled onto a page of one of my notebooks: 'Hi, I'm off to Baghdad and then to Amman. Please remember I love you very much. I'll try to ring tonight. Stay safe and well. Love always, Matthew.'

'You'd think we could have worked it out just once,'

I said, taking another swig of Ed's single malt. I was deliberately dwelling on the Anniversary Crisis. I knew it was petty but I wanted to focus on the triviality of it because I was intensely, profoundly guilty about the events of the day.

I had spent March and some of April in Iraqi Kurdistan. A couple of weeks after the regime fell I said goodbye to Ahmad and Mohammed and travelled south to Baghdad. Now the bombs had stopped falling, the government had collapsed and America was supposed to be in control. After so much debate and money being poured into the bombing, it appeared that no thought at all had been put into what happened next. The country was more or less in chaos, and gangs roamed around looting and pillaging – Ali Babas, the Baghdadis called them, in a reference, full of bitter pathos, to the tale of the Forty Thieves. There was an overwhelming feeling of a city holding its breath, suspended. People were stunned and uncertain. After so many years of being told what to do they were looking around for guidance. Everything was horror: the past, the present. Only God knew what the future held.

In the middle of all this uncertainty, there were fleeting moments of euphoria and eager attempts at democracy. Independent political parties and grass-roots organisations were springing up on almost every corner. Anyone with a cause was declaring an agenda – a sort of democratic free-for-all. I drank tea with a man who said he used to be Oday Hussein's personal artist, terrified into painting gaudy scenes of Oday, Saddam's eldest son, riding fantasy creatures to hang on his palace walls. I found him painting banners for an impromptu political party of which he was the only member. Everyone else was buying a dish to watch satellite television news channels for the first time (they were banned under the Baath Party) and hoping someone could explain what on earth was going to happen to them.

While they waited for answers, people began to pick through the rubble of their lives. Some were angry that the ordered, blinkered lives they'd had – don't look left or right, don't complain, don't ask questions, don't criticise the government and in return there will be jobs and food and schools and hospitals and roads – had been torn away and replaced by anarchy. There was no electricity, no telephones, no jobs. There was no security (although in those early days the regular terror of car bombs and fanatical violence and sectarianism had not yet taken hold). Instead, there was a great purging of the past. Memories of trauma and loss that could not be spoken about were in the open again.

Old women walked the streets with tiny photographs of missing sons, pleading at the gates of international aid organisations: 'Have you seen Ali? Please, help me find my son.' Hopes of finding missing sons and brothers, husbands and fathers, that were kept bottled (sometimes for decades) had reached their heartbreaking conclusions.

Thousands of people had gone missing while the Baath Party was in power – disappeared because of connections to political dissidents or rumours of connections or being related to people with those sorts of connections. When the Iraqi regime fell, bodies were discovered in mass graves and details of what had happened to them were uncovered in abandoned offices full of secret files.

One afternoon I found myself sitting in the basement of a once-grand villa on the banks of the Tigris River. Apparently it had belonged to some relative – a cousin or a nephew – of Saddam's. When I arrived, the place had been taken over by a group of former political prisoners and they had started an organisation called the Committee of Free Prisoners. Their goal was to collect files on those who had been imprisoned or executed and to let their families know what had happened to them and where their bodies were buried. Like all good dictatorships, the Baath Party kept careful records of every crime, every prisoner, every interrogation, every execution, every body, every grave.

Haida el-Tai was one of the former political prisoners who had helped to found the committee. He said the group had collected eight million files, although this was impossible to verify. What was clear was that the files were everywhere, stacked high along walls and across marble floors. (The rooms had, days ago, been emptied by looters.) After the regime fell, Haida and his friends entered offices once occupied by the army, information officials, secret police – anyone with authority and connections – and gathered the folder which detailed the arrests, interrogations and, inevitably, the executions of thousands of missing Iraqis.

We sat at a round table and Haida opened a white cardboard folder with a black border marked Top Secret. The prisoner's name was also Haida: Haida Saed Haid. He had been accused of working for an opposition party and his address was listed as Karbala, which meant he was almost definitely a Shia (Karbala is one of the holiest cities in Shi'ite Islam). The file detailed how Haida Saed Haid was kept in an underground jail. How his family was contacted and told never to talk about him and never to ask where he had gone 'or you will be punished'. On 17 March 1983 Haida was executed by hanging. His body was buried in grave 11235 in the T85 cemetery. Another set of documents showed where the grave was. The next step, Haida el-Tai told me, was to inform the family so that they could claim his remains.

In a courtyard outside the house several dozen people

were scanning lists stuck up along the fence. They were looking for the names of loved ones whose files had already been read and their fate discovered. If they found a name they could track down their bodies and bury them again. Even the horror of truth brought a kind of relief. Some didn't find the names they were after and, for a moment, hoped. Could they be still alive? The amount of hope was heartbreaking. Everywhere, hope and pain.

That morning I had contributed to the pain, somehow. I had fired my translator, regretfully, guiltily. Adnan was a kind man, gentle, quietly spoken, polite and very respectful towards me. He was slim and always immaculate, with carefully pressed clothes and hair brushed into precise place. He had a soft, fleshy face and was the kind of person you could pass many times and not remember. I guessed that had been an effective survival tactic in Saddam's Iraq: Adnan, The Invisible Man. Adnan was a very good translator, he knew English well and spoke it with a kind of besotted care. But he was still frightened, which meant he couldn't do his job effectively.

I planned to visit the bombed remains of Saddam's former Foreign Ministry. Enterprising Iraqis had scoured many of these bombed former ministry buildings and found documents that shed some light or other on the inner workings of the Iraqi regime. The documents were then dangled enticingly in front of foreign journalists and auctioned off to the highest bidder. At least one high-profile newspaper had landed an impressive front-page scoop this way, but I didn't have the money to take part. Instead, with Adnan's help, I was hoping to find some newsworthy documents of my own.

There was a crowd of people at the entrance to the ministry compound and a young Iraqi guard in fatigues, with a gun, attempting to quiet them. They had been told to meet there because there was a chance of jobs with the Iraqi National Congress (INC), at that time one of the largest and most influential Iraqi opposition groups, headed by Ahmad Chalabi, who had American backing and aspirations to lead the new Iraq. The jobs were a way to win favour with Iraq's millions of potential voters. The crowd was chaotic and it was easy to slip past towards the burnt-down front door of the former government building. As I made my way up the path, I noticed Adnan had dropped further and further behind.

I turned on the wide stone path, the bombed building ahead of me, the crowd of job seekers behind, and called to him: 'Adnan, come on! What's wrong?'

'We do not have permission.'

I smiled at him and told him what he must surely have already known. 'Who can give us permission? The regime is gone. There is no government any more. No one can give us permission and so unless someone stops us and explains why we should not go on, then I think it's okay for us to go inside.'

'We must find someone.' He spoke slowly and resolutely and looked down at his shoes. 'You should ask the group of Ahmad Chalabi.'

The INC was not in charge, I explained. Of course Adnan knew that too.

'Well, someone else then.' He was firm.

We continued like this, arguing back and forth. After a lifetime of obedience he was struggling to understand the boundaries of his new freedoms.

He shouted at me: 'Miss Catherine, I command you to stop where you are and not to walk a step further.'

It was more in alarm than aggression and so out of character that for a moment I was shocked into silence. When I recovered I mumbled something about being able to understand if he couldn't come with me, but that I had to do my job. 'I am sorry, but I am going inside.'

I turned and left him standing on the footpath. As I reached the steps of the building, the destroyed foyer in front of me with charred walls and ceiling and piles of broken glass and debris, and two scrappy Iraqi security guards lounging in the shade smoking cigarettes, I looked back to see if Adnan had followed me. He was frozen in the same spot, terrified.

I continued on alone, stumbling around soot-blackened rooms with bits of ceiling dangling down, picking through sheaves of documents that had survived the fire, flicking through folders in filing cabinets. I found a few faxes between Iraq and Australia that were vaguely interesting, but most of it was written in Arabic and I was oblivious.

When I saw Adnan again later I explained that we couldn't go on like that. 'I really needed you to be with me today,' I said.

'If this is what you need me to do, then you are right, I cannot,' he said. He looked at the ground and repeated his position, straightening his shoulders slightly to brace himself against the humiliation I had caused him. 'I cannot.'

Ed poured me another whisky. He was Irish and, true to all the clichés of his nationality and his profession, he had made sure to travel with a little supply of the precious amber drop. At least he was good enough to share it. We sat together on a shabby couch dotted with holes where cigarette ends had singed the fabric. The couch was brown, the carpet was brown, the bedspreads were brown. A bare bulb swung overhead on a long cord. The roar of the generator outside almost drowned out our conversation but we felt lucky to have electricity and whisky and company. We made a toast to my wedding anniversary.

The hotel manager came in with a workman to fix a dripping tap and he sat with us and had a whisky too. Then he had another one and forgot to mind his words. 'Ha! If you had asked me about Saddam two weeks ago I could never have said anything bad about him. Ask me then and I would tell you, "Our president is a very great man!".' He was on a roll. 'Do you know that we used to bug the phones and put cameras in all the rooms?' He pointed to all the spots that used to hide cameras and listening devices – behind a painting hanging on the wall, inside the bedside lamp, next to the television. 'All the maids were working for the *mukabarat*.'

It was late, almost midnight, and I was about to head back to my room when my satellite telephone rang. I had left it balancing on the window ledge so the antennae could pick up a signal.

'I'm downstairs! I've been calling your room. Where the hell are you?'

It was Matthew.

I didn't wait for the lift. I ran down four flights of stairs and emerged, dizzy, into the hotel's gleaming white-tiled lobby. In one corner was a group of men sprawled together watching satellite television. In another corner was Matthew, dishevelled after 18 hours on the road, surrounded by bags. We circled each other, unsure whether we should embrace in a public place.

'Why didn't you tell me you were coming?' I said, smiling, delighted.

'I didn't think I could make it and then we decided to just

leave. I wanted to surprise you.' He looked at me as if this must have been obvious. 'It's our anniversary. I wanted to get here on the sixth.'

We had been apart for several weeks, communicating only intermittently. And now he was here, on 6 May, with 20 minutes to spare until midnight, after a night-time dash across the desert. It was a foolish thing to have travelled the road after dark. Even in the early weeks after the fall of Baghdad, the road to Amman, past Ramadi and Fallujah, was dangerous. In those days it was patrolled by thieves, rather than kidnappers, but bad things still happened. A French television crew had arrived a few days earlier, stripped of their cash and equipment and with a terrifying tale of a mock execution. But I couldn't be angry. Matthew had made a grand, stupid gesture for love and I adored him for it.

We went back to my room and Matthew unpacked my anniversary present. He had brought a cache of food supplies: instant noodles, Pringles, bars of chocolate, coffee. It was the most beautiful anniversary present I could have imagined. But there was more. At the bottom of his suitcase, protected under a layer of T-shirts and jeans, lay a bottle of Moët et Chandon champagne. It was warm, but it scarcely mattered. We were together again, in a shitty hotel in the middle of Baghdad, drinking champagne, sucking on bowls of instant noodles, celebrating our third wedding anniversary, together.

A few days later we travelled south to Najaf, Shia Islam's holiest city and the site of the Imam Ali Mosque, which contains a precious relic: the earthly remains of the imam himself.

Ali, my driver, who had been with me from my first day

in Baghdad and who looked after me, found me food ('Catherine, you are too skinny!') and cool drinks when the days grew long and too hot, was behind the wheel once again. Two new friends, both called Majid, were squeezed in beside Matthew in the back of the car. I sat in the front passenger seat.

Ali was a Sunni and was worried about being accepted in Najaf – the mostly Shia residents had suffered greatly under Saddam Hussein's Sunni-dominated Baathist regime and may not be welcoming, he thought. He was pleased to have a name more commonly associated with the Shi'ites, especially the great imam for which Najaf was so famous and so revered. 'I have a very good name for this trip,' he said and laughed. He was always laughing.

Both Majids were members of the Iraqi National Orchestra and we distinguished between them by adding the instrument they played to their names. Majid Violin was helping us to translate interviews. (He used to receive just US$12 per month as a musician and supplemented his income by teaching music at the Music and Ballet School. But now there was no one to pay even that small salary and he had a wife and three children to support.) Majid Trumpet was accompanying us to Najaf because his family was from that holy Shia town, which was important for building trust and opening doors.

We drove in silence, gripped by the ruins of war spooling past like a real-life newsreel: lumps of burnt-out tanks and trucks; mosaic portraits of Saddam Hussein that had been shot at and mutilated; old checkpoints, abandoned, with the symbol of the Republican Guard, the core troops of Iraq's military, still visible. We passed the prison complex at Abu Ghraib, and on past Hilla where pieces of bodies were still being exhumed from mass graves and collected in little piles that were covered with white sheets, a poignant and overdue attempt to offer dignity.

After a while Majid Violin spoke up. 'All of the world thinks we Iraqis are looters and violent criminals,' he said. He was staring out the window, taking in the horror slideshow. 'I want to show that we are a people with culture.'

He leaned forward and insisted on my full attention. 'You know, after the bombing stopped I went to the Music and Ballet School where I used to teach music. I saw four or five looters and I said to them, "Tell me what you want and you can have it, but please, don't take the special things that mean so much to us." They told me it was not my business. I went to find some American troops. I spoke to one man but he said to me, "It's not my job. Get out." When I went back to the school the looters had smashed our violins. I was crying.' Majid Violin shook his head in dismay. 'I want the world to know that Iraqis have culture. Please, please, let us show you our culture and music again.'

I remembered a saying that we used to repeat all the time in Beirut. It was supposed to sum up the character of the different Arab states: 'In the Middle East, books are written in Cairo, published in Beirut and read in Baghdad.' There was no doubt that fellow Arabs understood the Iraqis' great love of learning and the superior pedigree of their ancient culture, which stretched back to the very beginning of humanity.

I also had seen evidence of it. Since arriving in Baghdad I had made several visits to al-Mutanabbi Street, a twisting lane named after a revered Iraqi poet, where you could find dozens of secondhand bookshops. Most importantly, this was where Baghdad's famous literary café, the Shabandar Café, could be found, full of Baghdadis reading those books, or writing manuscripts for new ones, and discussing politics and philosophy, history and art.

During Saddam's time the Shabandar attracted dissidents who sat together on the white-painted benches and hunched over the little wooden stools that served as tables. They filled up their glasses of tea with spoonfuls of sugar and clinked them together and smoked water pipes and whispered plans to each other, which they typed into illegal newsletters and distributed under fake names. When I turned up on al-Mutanabbi Street, the Shabandar's clientele was the same, but the whispered conversations had turned into a shout that reverberated to the café's soaring ceilings and bounced off its walls. But as we drove through Iraq's battered countryside that day, laid to waste by war, that character seemed very far away indeed.

A few kilometres outside Najaf, Ali stopped the car so that I could put on my *hejab*. I had chosen the simplest and lightest of my array of options from Iran – a black polyester shift with detailed embroidery across the chest. It only came down to my knees and so was quite comfortable to wear in the steadily rising heat of Iraq's late spring. I covered my head with a black scarf.

Under Saddam Hussein, Iraq had been a very secular place. This was one positive achievement. (He had also pumped money into infrastructure – the highways around Iraq were impressive.) But any woman entering Najaf, or nearby Karbala, was required to respect the holy cities and I was happy to comply. To do otherwise would have been like turning up at the Vatican in a G-string bikini.

Matthew and I found a room in an empty hotel on one of the streets that fanned out from the Imam Ali Mosque. The receptionist told us it used to be popular with Iranian pilgrims. We paid $10 a night for a room that was bare except for two single beds and a broken wardrobe. There was no hot water, no telephone, intermittent electricity. Breakfast was included.

That evening Matthew and I, Ali and the two Majids went in search of Grand Ayatollah Sistani's *hawza*, his religious school, where we had arranged to meet his spokesman. There were many *hawza* in Najaf, led by different senior clerics with slightly different approaches to Shi'ism. I already knew from my religion lessons with Hadi, back in Beirut, that the Shi'ites were able to use interpretation in their modern reading of the Qur'an to allow Shi'ism to be updated to reflect modern problems. And it was Sistani's skill and willingness to do that, his wisdom and years of study, that set him apart.

At that time, just after the fall of Baghdad, questions were being asked about how Iraq should be organised, who should lead the country, how groups like the Shi'ites and the Kurds – for decades locked out of the political sphere and brutally repressed – should be included in a new government. The future of the Shi'ites was particularly important. For a start, they made up the overwhelming majority of Iraq's population of 22 million. The Americans were watching all of this closely. They feared any new Shi'ite leadership would forge closer ties with their religious brothers in Iran and sideline Washington's influence in post-Saddam Iraq.

A contest was brewing between a clutch of prominent Shia clerics as to who among them should lead the country's Shi'ites. Already one of them, Abdul Majid al-Khoei, who had lived in exile in Britain and only returned after the Iraqi regime fell, had been stabbed to death as he left the Imam Ali shrine after prayers. His murderers remained unknown.

As the most senior Shia cleric in Iraq, and one of only five Grand Ayatollahs in the world, Sistani was a likely and sensible choice to become an influential figure in post-Saddam Iraq. He was highly educated and famously moderate, well versed in one of Islam's modern dilemmas: the concept of democracy and religion and how the two might intersect. But Grand Ayatollah Sistani was an old man and a famous ascetic. The rumour was that he had barely left his private rooms for seven years; partly for survival (he did not want to draw attention to himself during Saddam's time) and partly because he tried to live his life on a pure religious plane – his ego did not require appearances or public sermons or quotations in the press.

The hunt for Sistani's *hawza* got us very quickly lost in the city's tangle of ancient streets. Iraqi towns were generally quite well cared for, but Najaf seemed to have been deliberately left to run down by Saddam Hussein, who wanted the Shia to suffer for their opposition to his rule. The alleys were dirt, the buildings were broken down and rubbish lay on the ground. A group of snot-nosed children tailed us, giggling and making jokes.

We stood on the street looking around for some sort of landmark. Nothing. A group of young men, who looked like *hawza* students in their turbans and long religious robes, were walking towards us and as they drew close Majid Trumpet stepped forward and asked for directions. One of the group volunteered to show us the way and we peeled off from the main street down one of the dusty clay-coloured lanes lined with falling-down buildings and empty lots strewn with rubbish.

Our guide was thin to the point of being bony and his beige-coloured robe fell loosely from his shoulders. He had a slender face and large eyes and his chin was tipped with a meticulously trimmed beard. He was in a good mood, swinging his arms and oblivious to the destitution around him. He took out a packet of cigarettes and lit one, blew the smoke into the air with relish.

'You are smoking. But it is *haram*,' I said, and raised one eyebrow in mock disapproval.

He caught my joke good-naturedly and turned it back on itself. He puffed up and pretended to be a learned sheikh or an imam, not a mere student. 'Ah, but no!' he said, enjoying his little ruse. 'You are wrong. You see, it is only *haram* to *start* smoking.' We both laughed and he took another puff.

We fell into step. I complimented him on his beard. 'How often do you clip it?'

Devout Shi'ite men preferred a closely clipped beard, and different Shi'ite *mushtahids* (clerics who had studied to a level that allowed them to make *fatwas*, or religious rulings) had different approaches to these things. A Shi'ite friend in Beirut had shopped around until he found a *mushtahid* who allowed beards to be clipped into a goatee.

'Sometimes every day,' he said. 'I spent three years in jail for studying Shi'ism and only got out when my friends raised 94 million dinar to release me. During that time in prison my beard grew to my chest. I had nothing to cut it. Now I am proud to keep it neat.'

We had been walking for some time and emerged from the lanes onto another street. The student stopped at a wooden doorway. 'This is where you will find Sistani's Voice,' he said, a quaint way of referring to the Grand Ayatollah's spokesman. 'You must talk to him first and he will decide if you are able to speak with the Grand Ayatollah himself.'

Given the Grand Ayatollah's reticence to appear in public, we were not hopeful of success, but it was essential to try. We knocked on the door of the *hawza* and it was opened by another student. We were led into a hall where a group of about 10 or 15 students milled around waiting for prayers to begin. We were asked to remove our shoes and then to wait on wooden stools. Tea was brought. After about 10 minutes we entered an adjoining room to meet Sistani's Voice.

The room was small and the floor was covered with rugs.

The Voice sat cross-legged on the ground. Before him, carefully positioned as if on a desk, were a calculator, two religious books stacked one on top of the other, a box of tissues and a hot-pink fly swat in the shape of a heart.

I sat quietly beside Matthew as he began to question the Voice about Sistani's political ambitions. Matthew chose his words carefully, subtly, aware that in those early days few potential political or religious leaders in Iraq were being explicit about their plans. But even so, the Voice would not be drawn.

'He has no political direction,' he told us. 'He is just a religious man.'

'Why will he not come out to speak?' Matthew asked.

'Because there is not enough security. All the *marjas* [Shi'ite religious authorities] stay in their houses and we apply this method to explain that the US troops can't deliver security.'

The veiled political statement – subtly criticising the US presence – seemed as close as we would get to a candid discussion. We thanked him and walked back outside to Najaf's dilapidated streets.

It was odd, but Najaf seemed calm and almost peaceful after the anarchy of places like Mosul and Kirkuk. US troops were banned from the city because of its religious importance – to have entered would have been a provocation, an affront to its sacred history – and at that time the Iraqis seemed to have the city under control. I rarely saw a gun and I didn't feel afraid to walk alone there. We ate a dinner of kebab and bread in the gallery level of a simple restaurant that was reputed to be one of Najaf's best, and walked back to the hotel in the dark of the evening.

One afternoon I stood, insignificant, under an awning and watched as Moqtada al-Sadr, the young firebrand cleric, dashed from Friday prayers, flanked by bodyguards, black eyes flashing. Moqtada hung his importance on the link to his famous and widely liked father, Grand Ayatollah Mohammed Mohammed Sadeq al-Sadr, who had died in mysterious circumstances a few years earlier. Moqtada had his own big ambitions to lead the Shi'ites, which he would later defend with guns and a militia of faithful supporters. His head was bound in a turban – the kind worn by Shi'ite clerics and known as an *amama*. The colour of that turban, white or black, was extremely important. White turbans were much like the white collar worn by Christian priests: a symbol of religious learning. But black turbans denoted something extra: that the genealogy of the cleric could be traced directly to the Prophet himself.

Another day I stood outside the Imam Ali Mosque and watched crowds of thousands welcome Ayatollah Hakim back to Najaf from Iran, where he had lived in exile for 23 years. After a while I was so crushed and tossed about by the crowd I became afraid of being trampled. I fled to a tea shop and sat with a group of locals to watch the rest of the welcome on satellite television.

I had interviewed the Ayatollah twice in Tehran. The first time he admonished me for allowing a few wisps of my fringe to escape the headscarf. 'Catherine, your hair! Please!' his assistant had stage-whispered, urgently, sternly, before the Ayatollah would begin the interview. He had seemed gruff and impatient and I was intimidated.

The second time I met him, a year later and just days

before the first American bombs fell on Iraq, Ayatollah Hakim was in a reflective mood. He talked about the pain of exile, the murder of his family at the hands of the Iraqi regime, the dream of returning to Najaf.

'I was imprisoned for many years without trial, without seeing a judge,' he said. His voice was low and sombre. 'During the interrogation and imprisonment I was tortured, I suffered, and I saw also the death and killing of dear friends to me. Going to Iraq is my greatest wish. It will arouse the deepest and most profound feelings in me. I really want to go back to see the best things for my people.'

Hakim wasn't looking for a strictly political role – his brother was deeply involved in politics – but he was sure to find a religious one. And because of the way things worked, his followers would have looked to him to guide them towards recommended political figures.

Now I felt quite emotional as I sat in the tea shop and watched him take a place at a pulpit inside the Imam Ali Mosque, and saw how quickly that dour, pious façade melted, his voice cracked into uncontrollable emotion and the tears fell.

A few months later, on 29 August 2003, Ayatollah Hakim became another casualty of this new Iraq, assassinated by a car bomb as he left the Imam Ali Mosque after Friday prayer. He was the fourth senior Shi'ite cleric to be killed since the fall of Saddam's regime.

When the crowds from Ayatollah Hakim's homecoming had started to disperse, I returned to the hotel and sat perspiring on my bed. The roar of the generator had stopped a few minutes before and the air conditioning had gone. The lights were out. I sat in semi-darkness, claustrophobic, but without my *hejab* on and so loath to open the curtains to let in some air and daylight in case the workmen in the building opposite were able to peer inside and see me uncovered.

At dusk I walked to the Najaf cemetery: clay-coloured, enormous, and the place above all places where a devout Shia would dream of being buried. It stretched into the desert heat haze and horizon and the colours shifted and darkened to black as the sun fell. Tomorrow I was to return to Baghdad. Matthew would not be coming – he had more work to do in Najaf – and so we would be apart again.

Ali and I left early the next morning for the drive north. The day after that we drove to Tikrit and looked at Saddam's palaces and the village where he was born, which looked like a fancy housing estate rather than a village, with streets in a grid pattern lined with recently built mansions. Ali was nervous: powerful friends of Saddam still lived here, although most had fled. He was scared of being stopped and asked, 'What are you doing?' Most of the time he was bold and excited to explore this new Iraq, but the old fears were never far from the surface.

I walked around Abu Ghraib prison, until US soldiers pointed their guns at me when I accidentally walked into an area where they were carrying out 'an operation'. I spent a lot of time drinking tea with Ali's relatives in their funky 1960s houses with fruit trees in the gardens. Two of his nieces gave me a little red velour box in the shape of a heart, with a silver ring set with an amethyst inside it, 'to remember us'.

I visited a mental institution on the edges of the city. Most of the patients had escaped – the gates were broken, the place had been looted – and only the very, very mad or the almost sane had decided to stay. The mad stayed because they could not organise themselves to escape, or were locked in pens like animals. The almost sane stayed because there was nothing worth leaving for. Baghdad was in anarchy.

The conditions inside the institution were horrific too, like scenes from a film. As I walked up the long driveway from the road, there was the sound of raw, base screaming cries, hardly human, and the rhythmic clang of metal bolts being smashed up against metal gates over and over and over. As I walked closer I could hear another layer to this soundtrack: the dull endless hum of flies, and when I was nearer still I could smell the sour reek of shit and piss. And then I saw them, the inmates of this madhouse, their naked bodies writhing in a putrid cage of insanity and abandonment. They were covered in their own faeces, dripping with urine and sweat and drool, crying out in deranged anguish, and there seemed to be no one, *no* one, to help them.

'Can I help you?'

I was startled and turned to see a calm, quiet man in a grubby *jalabya*, the long shirt-dress favoured by Iraqi men, standing behind me.

'My name is Abdul Kareem,' he said and held his hand forward to be shaken.

I was wary. Was he a patient? A doctor? A looter?

'I am a poet,' he said, 'and a tailor.'

He beckoned and I followed him to a small dormitory, one of several set around a concrete courtyard. Clearly he was a patient, although not as ill as the others I had just seen. He was one of the almost sane. 'I have, just one hour before, had Valium,' he said matter-of-factly, but it explained the unnaturally carefree calm about him.

As we walked, other patients came running out of their dormitories. One was naked. 'Don't look. Don't look!' Abdul Kareem said, agitated, and I turned away to placate him but thought that nakedness was the least of the horrors here. A few moments later we passed a patient sitting on his haunches, hugging his knees and rocking back and forth. 'That man used to be one of our doctors,' Abdul Kareem said. I could see how this place would send anyone mad.

Abdul Kareem had fled the mental hospital after the regime fell, he told me, but he and a group of others had been found wandering aimlessly by an imam and returned to the institution. He had come back willingly. 'The imam had a gun to protect the hospital and he gave us food and water.' Abdul Kareem said sensibly. The imam was still looking after them, he said, but the task was too enormous for one man.

He opened a cupboard and brought out rolls and rolls of fabric that he had carefully decorated with cross-stitch. 'I hid it all in the toilet when the looters came,' he said, 'to prevent anyone stealing it.' He showed me his sheets and a pillowcase, which had also been decorated, so tenderly, with little cross-stitch images of a house and flowers in a garden. It was a sweet and almost heartbreaking gesture from a man of 44.

Abdul Kareem talked and talked. His conversation was snapshots of mismatched stories that were hard to keep track of, but after a while a picture began to emerge. 'In the past I was a political man,' he said. 'I had a political mind and many private thoughts about politics.'

He was sent to fight in the Iran–Iraq war but he escaped the army, an objector, and served five months in a military intelligence prison. When he was released in 1991 he was ordered straight back into the army and was sent to fight for Iraq in Kuwait during the first Gulf War. When that war was over, it seems that Abdul Kareem was left in a state of deep trauma. 'I used to be a normal man,' he said. 'But now I must take this medicine.' He held up a syringe filled with fluid. 'If I don't take this injection my thoughts become very fast and I can't control my mind.'

In the depths of a delusion, not long after the end of the Gulf War, he became paranoid. He believed his sister was part of the *mukabarat* and was informing on him. He believed his mother knew about it and was doing nothing to protect him. In a state of wild, delusional panic, he had attacked her and killed her. 'When I saw the blood on my mother and what I had done I collapsed,' he said, one moment of hideous clarity that he could never forget. He spoke without emotion and I could see his eyes were dull with medication. 'Now I would not kill even a chicken. I want to get well again. I want to be like any man in the street. I want to make a house, to have a family.'

He began to write poems, he said, that were critical of the regime and what it had done to him. There was enough sanity, at least, to understand that. In the institution he could continue his writing and no one bothered him; his angry words were not considered heretical, as those of so many of the poets at the Shabandar Café, they were only the harmless ravings of a madman. 'For a long time I thought it was better to live here than outside with Saddam Hussein.'

Baghdad was full of stories. I hung out with a troupe of actors and musicians at the Hewar Gallery in a suburb of Baghdad and talked about art and the future. At the back of the gallery was a café with chairs and tables set around a courtyard that was filled with plants. To one side was a series of small adjoining rooms with low ceilings and banquettes along the walls. They had a confessional feel, and during Saddam's time artists would go there and mutter to each other about their artistic journeys, their paintings and plays that could never be shown publicly because they criticised the regime or critiqued their human lives in ways that would have brought punishment. In those days conversation in cafés was whispered because you never knew if an informer was sitting at the next table. But now it was different. Like the Shabandar, the Gallery Café was throbbing with conversation, spoken loud.

The week before, this group of dissident sculptors, painters, theatre directors and writers, who had been meeting secretly for 13 years, had put on a play at the bombed-out remains of the al-Rashid Theatre. They were overjoyed at being able to show their art unfettered for the first time. 'I was full of the happiness of a newborn child,' said one of the artists. 'We are humanists and our humanity is limitless,' said another. 'Maybe in the near future we may be able to forgive them for the pain they inflicted, but our victory over them exists and it may exist forever.'

'But what about the state of the country, the city?' I asked them, thinking of the fractured political allegiances, the ruined infrastructure, the innocents who had died. 'What is going to happen next?'

'You are right,' said one. 'War destroys first the material and then the spirit of a society.' He opened his arms in a symbolic embrace of the group of friends around him. 'We are bound by the roots to the rehabilitation of the spirit. And this is indeed what we are going to do.'

Another: 'We knew that the negative was trying its best to destroy our culture and we were working so seriously, sometimes we were putting ourselves into severe danger – to the point where we believed we would die by the rope because of a report about our activities. But in our dreams we believed that one day it would all disappear like blisters on the skin and we would rebuild what has been destroyed.'

It was late. Ali, my driver, had left long ago. Matthew and the two Majids had returned from Najaf the night before and Majid Trumpet had invited us for dinner with his wife at a hip pizza place in Mansour, a wealthy suburb of Baghdad. Mansour was starting to get busy again now that the fear of falling bombs had gone, and in the evenings it was fun to walk along the main street and window shop and stop for a cool drink or dinner. There was even an internet café, the first of its kind in the city.

When I left the gallery a car slid up beside me with two young Iraqi men inside. 'Hey, get in,' they yelled and turned up the pumping American rap music on the stereo. They had baseball caps on backwards and tight jeans and they were sweet and friendly and said, 'Welcome to Baghdad'. It seems madness when I look back on it now that I would have accepted such a lift. But for a few weeks, between the end of the Baath Party and the time when sectarian violence and Islamist fanaticism and America's arrogant hypocritical occupation began to take over in Iraq, there was a sort of golden moment of hope. Of course, people were angry at the destruction America's missiles had wreaked, they were suspicious of the future, they were unsure, they were scared. But whatever they were feeling, at that time there was still room to dream about a future that maybe, just maybe, could be better than the past.

PART TWO

CHAPTER 14
PREGNANT

Matthew and I returned to Lebanon late in May, heavy with the bleakness of all we had witnessed in Iraq, and exhausted from the long days it took to report on it. Beirut was our antidote to the sadness of it all. I felt euphoric as I piled my bags into the taxi at the airport. I had been away for three months and I was delighted by how much this felt like a homecoming.

The next day I took a *service* down to the Corniche and walked along the sea front, past Luna Park and Café Raouda where the old Bedouin woman came to tell your fortune while you had coffee at a little table set around a landscaped outdoor garden, and a lone soldier kept watch under a strange little sentry post built into the rock platform below. Lebanon was always on guard, even in the most unlikely places.

Matthew and I would often talk about why we liked Beirut so much. After all, it was polluted and chaotic and noisy. Don't even start on the traffic. The politics were turbulent and sometimes dangerous. Lebanon was stifled by the past: clannish, separatist, bogged down in religious affiliations and traditions so old and so convoluted that no one could really explain why they mattered so much. Corruption was endemic, there were power cuts and bureaucracy was rampant. And despite all of that it was quite an expensive place to live. Money was pouring into the rebuilding of a glitzy New Beirut for the rich, while the middle class was disappearing and some families still lived in crumbling apartment blocks and struggled to pay their bills.

It was the little things, we decided, that we loved. The upside to chaos was that regulations were sporadic; we could drink cocktails hanging off the edge of a tower block with a view of the ocean; drive the wrong way down a highway when all other routes were closed and break the speed limit (what speed limit?). The pace of life itself was slow and rhythmic, soothing and full of things to like: a real community feel with neighbours who knew each other and people who were friendly and welcoming; wonderful restaurants, like the little place in Khalde that served fresh fish, just far enough south of Beirut to feel like an adventure but close enough so that you could make the decision to go last minute. Month after month of sunshine helped too. We would wonder out loud to each other if perhaps it was simply that Beirut's extremes exaggerated everything, made every moment seem alive.

And then something extraordinary happened. A month or so later, the ragged body I had brought back from Iraq conceived a baby. The knowledge filled me with a depth of peacefulness that I could not have imagined.

A journalist I had met in Kirkuk came to Beirut for R&R (Beirut's easy friendliness and flashes of five-star life had started to make it the press pack's favourite spot to vacation between Iraq assignments). He called it a Baghdad Baby and said that he knew of several couples who had covered the war together and fallen pregnant afterwards. He said it was a biological survival instinct, boosting fertility in the face of war, and I teased him for being cheesy and fantastical.

'It's going to be a boy,' he went on. 'Did you know that the incidence of male babies rises during wartime?'

I had planned to go to Gaza but now I cancelled the trip and fell, puzzled but willing, into my new pregnant state. I slept constantly, ate constantly and felt dreamy and reflective. I noticed that my gait had changed: I walked gently, erect, as if I had something fragile in my hands.

I abandoned my research on Jewish settlers and Palestinian collaborators and sat on our curved blue couch by the French windows and sipped tea made with fresh mint leaves and lumps of ginger and gazed down at the street. I could see Osama, the boy who helped out at the shop, carrying a bottle of gas to a neighbour. 'But I am not Osama bin Laden!' he had joked with me in his few words of halting English the first time we met, and then waggled a finger in front of his face. Whenever he saw me after that, he always stood to attention, tipped his head to the side, smiled and gave me a mock salute.

From my altered perspective, I found my mind drawn back to Iraq and the women I had met there. Their stories resonated in a new and more personal way.

One day I had visited a hospital in Baghdad. Soldiers, armed with big guns I couldn't name, guarded the hospital entrance. I walked through the empty cement lobby, past wailing families, black cloaks flapping, anxious. The walls of the stairwell were ringed by a grubby grey line where years of hands, hundreds of them, thousands, had reached for support as their owners climbed. I did the same, adding my grimy print of Baghdad dust and scum, up and up. Although I wasn't specifically looking for it, I found myself in the neonatal ward – a string of simple rooms adjacent to a wide corridor, clean enough but dull and worn.

The doctor, a paediatrician, was young. He wore a white coat. His eyes were kind and intelligent, but panicked. At night, looters regularly broke into the hospital and took what they could. 'If you come back at night you will see me with a Kalashnikov over my shoulder,' he said, incredulous at the insanity of it. I found a woman whose baby had been born in the middle of the US bombing campaign. She had been turned away from several hospitals, and had driven past burning cars, gun battles, bodies in the streets, until she found a place willing to take her. 'I asked myself, how can I possibly save this baby?' she said, and she was angry at what had happened to her city.

'What kind of New Iraq is this?' she asked me. 'The electricity is cut, the hospital is dark and hot. Can you guarantee me the future will be better? I expect it will be more miserable. Will I feel happy because my country is destroyed and there is no Saddam Hussein? I would prefer Saddam and no destruction.'

She fell quiet and stroked her baby's head. I could only imagine the hell of trying to bring up a child in this chaos.

'In Iraq there are many religions,' she continued. 'They may agree on some things but not on everything, and they will never agree who will rule Iraq. I think the destruction of our country will get worse and worse. I think there will never be a New Iraq.' She looked up at me. 'When I say that I am not trying to be pessimistic, but it is a fact. We see it every day.'

Two days after I discovered I was pregnant, Matthew left to film a story in the West Bank. Suddenly I felt so very alone. My thoughts became primeval: life, death, sleep, food and nurturing the new life inside me. Everything else ceased to exist.

I felt suspended between two lives. The old one – adventuring, reporting – had been whisked away so suddenly and there didn't seem to be enough to replace it. I wondered if I was being over-protective of myself in deciding against the Gaza trip. Yet there were times when even Beirut seemed the wrong place to be. There was no family around to share the excitement, no childhood friends to share my latest life milestone and offer empathetic advice. Everything that had tied me to Beirut – the thrill of nights out in bars and clubs, trips to conflict zones, the *edge* of it – now seemed out of reach. It was inevitable that I would begin to wonder what I was doing in a comparatively dangerous city, so far from home.

My reflex instinct was to leave Beirut as soon as possible. It seemed impossible to even consider staying to have the baby. Every time I heard of clashes on the border between Hezbollah and Israel I began to feel jumpy. There was talk of a second front opening to complicate things for the Americans in Iraq. There were stories of how Israel would retaliate with nuclear weapons if attacked by the growing Iraq-based *mujahedeen*.

A week before, I would have enjoyed debating these ideas at dinner with friends. But now I felt nervous. I felt responsible for the life inside me. I worried about whether the medical care would be of a high enough standard. What if there was a complication? Would I need to be among family? All the paranoia and xenophobia that went along with this War on Terror made me worry that the baby would have problems later getting visas to places like the US if its passport said 'Born in Beirut'. After everything that I'd seen in Iraq, I felt a deep, almost unconscious need to get far away from the Middle East. My faith in the world had been cracked. Life felt like a risk.

I became fanatical. I closed all the windows and doors to our apartment (even though it was the middle of summer) in a hysterical attempt to stop pollution drifting inside. I held my breath when I went through traffic tunnels. I barely ate when I left the house. Everything seemed dangerous: no cheese in case it wasn't pasteurised; no salad in case it hadn't been washed properly; no meat in case it wasn't cooked properly. I felt like a character in a video game, on edge, waiting to be struck down.

By chance there was a well-known maternity hospital at the end of my street, run by three generations of the same family. I asked around and got the name of a recommended doctor and made an appointment for an ultrasound.

It was unlike any hospital I had ever seen: a pretty, historical building with French doors and shuttered windows leading to Juliet balconies. I entered through gracious wrought-iron gates and along a cobbled pathway past the most beautiful bougainvillea I had ever seen, cascading over the fence. While I waited for the doctor I read old copies of *Paris Match* and *Mondanite*, a magazine that was full of snapshots of Lebanese society at different restaurants and beach clubs. I played a mental game, categorising each face and outfit: covetable or tasteless. There were plenty of both: the beautiful Lebanese women with their smooth summer tans and long black hair and stylish clothes; and those with too much make-up, too much collagen, over-adventurous boob jobs. It wasn't a magazine for the pious.

The waiting room was full. The other women were a lot like the women in the magazine: glamorous, superior. Many

Lebanese women had a haughty demeanour and I had never become used to it. It was tied into the desire for status, an idea that was almost non-existent in Australia, and it brought home to me what was meant when we called Australia 'egalitarian'. Of course we had our snobs and our society doyens, our see-and-be-seen spots and snooty doormen. But the majority of Australians weren't like that. We're casual, we're laidback, we hate to make a fuss. It was the opposite in Lebanon. People loved to make a fuss, and it was terribly important to be seen at the right restaurants, to drive the right car, to wear the right clothes. And this extended even to the obstetrician you chose to look after you during pregnancy.

I discovered that the doctor I had booked in to see was the top of the heap, *the* most fêted and sought-after obstetrician in Lebanon. His waiting room was always humming with beautiful women jostling for his attention, and he wafted past, a handshake here, a greeting there, switching seamlessly between French and English and Arabic. I dispensed with his real name immediately and referred to him as Dr T – a reference to the character Richard Gere played in a silly Hollywood film, a handsome, charming gynaecologist with a slew of glamorous, high-maintenance patients.

In the privacy of his office, Dr T was thoughtful and sincere and endlessly patient with my anxious questions. He turned the ultrasound monitor to face me and we saw a little shape dash across the screen, its arms and legs flailing. 'Look at that! You have a little Australian swimmer in there.' Dr T said in English. He was laughing and a part of me began to uncoil.

When I left the hospital it was with the overwhelming sense that I was beginning a new life. Every step seemed special and I was bursting to share my news. My friend Cheryl called and invited herself over for coffee. 'I have something to tell you,' she said and her voice had an edge to it, full of gossip to come. I couldn't wait to see her.

Cheryl was a South African filmmaker who had been in Beirut for a year or so with her husband and little boy. We met through a mutual friend and quickly became close. She had been in Afghanistan filming a segment for a documentary on Islam and I hadn't seen her for weeks. I was impatient for her visit: I knew she would be just the right person to help me through the changes ahead. We were the same age and she had a sisterly quality about her, a magical warmth. She turned up with a bag of warm croissants from the patisserie and we sat on the blue couch to eat them.

'Well,' she began, 'are you ready for this? I'm pregnant. I've just been to the doctor. I can't believe it! I must have been pregnant when I was in Afghanistan and I had no idea.'

I stared at her, incredulous. '*You* won't believe *this* but so am I.'

It seemed that Cheryl had been handed to me as some kind of miracle pregnancy buddy. She was a veteran of the foreign birth. Her son had been born in Saudi Arabia and she already had plans to stay in Beirut for the birth of her second child.

I tried to keep the pregnancy secret from everyone else for a few more weeks. I needed time to get used to the idea, and of course there was the omnipresent hovering worry that something would go wrong. But with Matthew away I was often invited out for drinks with friends and it wasn't long until suspicion arose. 'What do you want to drink?' one friend asked as we leaned against the bar at Chez André with Beirut's boho intellectual crowd, still panting from the heat outside and the walk along Hamra Street.

'Oh, just a mineral water, I think.'

'Not a beer? Come on! This is Chez André!'

'I'm detoxing,' I said, and smiled innocently and reached for a sliver of carrot.

'Well, Catherine, you have been detoxing for a long time now,' said my friend, mock-sternly. 'This is *most* unlike you.'

When I did announce that I was pregnant my status changed overnight. Everyone loves babies in Lebanon, and by extension everyone loves pregnant women. I was fussed over immediately. Leila sent around *shourbat adas ma' sabanech*, lentil and spinach soup. Ramzi's mother made me *kousa mehsi*, courgettes stuffed with minced lamb and smothered with chunky homemade tomato sauce. The message was always the same: 'This is very good while you are pregnant.'

I didn't resist when Cheryl took me under her wing and gently inducted me into the world of Beirut motherhood. She had collected a group of wonderful, warm friends – both expats and locals – and she generously began to share them with me. So, as the weeks passed I began to relax. The transition to a slower pace became easier and the care and support I received from friends and even strangers was a welcome compensation for the lack of family around me.

And then the ultrasound revealed that I was going to have a girl. The Lebanese love babies, but they love boy babies much more: boys carry on the family name, they follow their father into the family business, they are so much more valuable. So valuable, in fact, that it was rude even to suggest the bump may be other than a male child.

'Is it a boy?' strangers asked me hopefully.

'A girl,' I would answer brightly.

'Ah.' There was silence. '*Maalesh*,' came the answer at last. 'Never mind. If God is willing next time it will be a boy.'

The hospital had a weekly class for expectant mums, run by one of the team of midwives. The first hour was a discussion of labour and birth and in the second hour we did a routine of yoga stretches designed to help loosen our bodies in preparation for delivery. Dr T urged me to attend. He said I'd love Vivienne, the midwife who gave the classes. 'She's very caring,' he promised, and I had a mental image of a motherly older woman, a grandmother perhaps, who had spent her life around pregnant women and babies.

Instead, Vivienne was young and glamorous. She turned up in skin-tight jeans and a little fitted jumper in hot-pink angora, and had glossy black hair that hung to her hips. When we did the yoga stretches she could bend in ways I'd only ever dreamed about. Too bad she'd never had a baby – she already had the flexibility we were all striving for.

'Okay, girls, and now we will do our secret exercise.' Vivienne sat cross-legged before us like a guru, with her hair arranged so that it fell perfectly about her shoulders. 'Ready? Hold it for one, two, three, four, five, six, seven, eight. Do you feel it? No, Layla, that's wrong. I can see you moving your pelvis and I should not see anything. Remember, this is a *secret* exercise.'

I cringed for poor Layla. We were practising Kegels to strengthen our pelvic floor. After the Kegels we switched to stretches, to open our pelvis in preparation for birth.

'I don't need to do this exercise because I won't be giving birth naturally,' Layla said, resolute. 'I have asked for a C-section and my doctor says it's okay.'

I discovered that large numbers of Lebanese women asked for elective caesareans. Of course the Too Posh to Push set existed in Sydney too, but there was a belief among the glamour set in Lebanon that the pelvis widened as a result of a natural birth, destroying the slim hips and gentle curves that Lebanese women loved to show off at the pool clubs each summer.

Obstetrics in Lebanon was a minefield. Another of the women who attended my prenatal class was an observant Muslim and came to each of our meetings heavily covered. She had a female obstetrician and had requested a woman anaesthetist be on standby during her labour in case she needed an epidural or an emergency C-section. In the end she had her baby induced a few days before her due date so that it didn't clash with the commemoration of Ashura; I could only guess that she was superstitious about her child being born on the same day that Imam Hussein died.

There were times when I needed to escape from Beirut's traffic and noise, from being pregnant, from the clanging questions in my mind. But where? Going out of the house at all required so much primping and preening, and although I hadn't had a day of morning sickness and generally felt fantastic pregnant, there were days when I hated my new body, was repulsed by the veins that had started to appear on my stomach, breasts, legs. The summer heat got to me and I was desperate for a swim. But I felt fat and leaky and the thought of displaying myself at a Lebanese pool club was quite simply terrifying.

I found an unlikely sanctuary – al-Ajram Beach for Women Only – that was really a pool club rather than a sandy shore. I heard about the place many times before I found it, tucked behind a door in a dilapidated stretch of shopfronts at one end of the Corniche. I stepped off the footpath into a gleaming white-tiled corridor that felt clinical and spooky – like a butcher's shop or a morgue. I paid 10,000 Lebanese Lira to an attendant, who looked up absently from the book she was reading to take my money, and then I pushed through a heavy door, painted blue and white, and emerged on a little landing at the top of a long staircase. Below me was a secret world of women.

About 20 women were lounging around on white banana chairs and a group of children gambolled around them. It was a kind of anti-Beirut, a world where perfect bodies and designer swimwear didn't matter at all, and it was just what I needed. I found a chair and asked for an umbrella. In front of me was a row of women, all friends, in tiny string bikinis, taking turns to cover each other in baby oil. They lay back, their chairs angled to catch as much sun as possible. If I listened closely I was sure I'd hear the sound of hot skin sizzling.

A woman walked around asking if anyone would like a henna tattoo. Someone turned up the music and I recognised the breathless half-talking, half-singing style of Haifa Wehbe; a sort of Arab Marilyn Monroe crossed with Pamela Anderson. Everything was supposed to be fake – breasts, lips etcetera – but wow, the effect was electric. I didn't know a single person, man or woman, who wouldn't admit to thinking Haifa was s-e-x-y. She was a Lebanese Shi'ite – how's that for busting a stereotype? – and was popular all across the Arab world. The women at the pool were fans. A young woman from the crowd of sizzling friends in front of me stood up and began to dance. She was wearing a little leopard-print bikini with a matching wrap around her hips.

She held her arms in the air and swivelled her hips and shuffled her feet around in a circle, Arabic dancing to Haifa Wehbe at a women-only beach in Beirut.

I was filled with well-being. The sun was strong and although I was slathered in cream and under the umbrella I could feel the heat seeping into my body, loosening me up, burning out all the fears and tensions. I felt full of fondness for Beirut, for all its inconsistencies, its energy and glamour, its inequalities and sad memories. Suddenly it just seemed right to stay to have the baby. I would give birth in a building opposite the home of a famously flamboyant warlord politician, on a street where Palestinian and Shi'ite militias fought it out during the war. But I didn't see those things that day. I saw the crimson bougainvillea that spilled over the hospital fence. I saw the chic boutique on the corner, and the smiling faces of families bringing their babies home for the first time.

It was decided: I would give birth in Beirut. And as I lay back on my banana lounge the baby began to wriggle around inside me. I cradled my belly in my hands. It felt like my own perfect Beirut story.

CHAPTER 15

BIRTH, BRIBES, *WASTA*

One morning in late February, two weeks before I was due to give birth, Leila came by to see how I was. 'Have you decided what you are going to call the baby?' she asked.

Matthew and I had spent many months mulling over a long list of potential names. 'We have a few ideas. But none seem to fit,' I told her.

'Well, this is what I think: you must call her Yasmine.' She said it in that gorgeous Lebanese way so it sounded so exotic: Ya*ss*-m*eee*n. 'Just look at all the jasmine vines around your apartment!'

She was right. The balcony adjacent to our living room was covered with jasmine vines that twisted along the railings in perfect green spirals. They also clung to the wall outside our bedroom window and sprouted fearlessly from the garden of the old house next door. They covered the drain-pipe and tumbled over the fence. In summer the heat seemed to distil the perfume from the flowers and it blew through the apartment on the evening breeze. I knew that smell of jasmine on hot summer nights would always transport me back to the strange and happy years in Beirut; a kind of olfactory time machine. The flower's Arabic and Persian translation, Yasmine, was the perfect name for our little girl.

I had entered that wonderful period of late-pregnancy euphoria. 'You are glowing,' Dr T smiled at one of my last appointments, and I knew he was right. I felt a deep calm and contentment. I was in no rush to give up being pregnant – my fears and anxieties had gone and I was at last enjoying it – but I was ready to meet my baby.

One night a few days later, Matthew and I went for a drink at Torino Express, Matthew's favourite little bar in Gemmayze, a suburb not far from the old Green Line that had miraculously escaped a lot of the damage during the war. Its gracious 1920s apartment blocks, with huge light-filled *salons* and arched windows opening to little balconies that overlooked the street, had become highly sought after. The suburb was undergoing a revival and it seemed that almost every week one of the dank old vegetable shops or butcheries or simple clothing stores closed, to be replaced a few weeks later by a new restaurant or a boutique or art gallery. I felt torn watching the old Beirut life being turned over and replaced. Many residents were beside themselves at the loss of the neighbourhood's faded elegance and lazy charm. But the new places were also charming and they brought investment and money and life into the area. Gemmayze was already beginning to supersede Rue Monot as the best place in Beirut for a night out.

Torino was crowded, as usual. Andreas – who ran the place – was smoking a cigarette (also as usual) and had slipped outside to talk on his mobile phone away from the din of the music. The bar ran up the left side of the space and coloured bottles of alcohol were stacked on the wall behind. A DJ booth was crammed into the bay window. Our friend Vatche played there sometimes just for fun – between scripting his latest film or planning his latest video installation – and always picked quirky little self-deprecating names for himself. That night he had chalked up the name *Nicole Kidman* on a blackboard behind the turntable. There were a few tables along the right wall and a banquette ran along the back wall. The place probably fitted 30 people, if you were very lucky. Matthew and I and our little gang squeezed onto one of the banquettes and I could feel the baby moving with the vibration of the music.

'Hey, when's the baby due?' said Vatche and kissed me on both cheeks in welcome.

'Two weeks,' I told him. 'Two more weeks and then life as I know it will end forever.' I pulled a face to emphasise the drama of it.

In fact, if I was honest, life as I knew it had already ended. I'd barely left Beirut, apart from a trip to Libya when I was three months pregnant and, more recently, a short shopping trip to Damascus that had worked wonders at soothing my last-minute nesting panic. The Syrian capital was less than three hours' drive from Beirut and a shopping nirvana for those in the know. I asked around for tips and stocked up on Italian and French label baby clothes for a fraction of what they cost to buy anywhere else. I had tried to sneak in one last adventure, to Gaza, but when I confided my plans to Dr T he thwarted them sternly.

'Catherine,' he said, 'you are in your third trimester. You should look after yourself.'

'But . . .'

He smiled kindly and the words lay unspoken on my tongue. 'Being pregnant is enough,' he said.

His argument was sensible. If there were complications

and the baby came early, I'd be unable to return to Beirut: a child with 'Born in Israel' on her passport would never be allowed into Lebanon.

At midnight, when the music got even louder and the bar even more crowded, I pleaded exhaustion and weird cramps and Matthew helped me to hobble outside to a taxi and home.

I went into labour the next morning at 7.30 a.m., two weeks before my due date. Vivienne wasn't there but it didn't matter. At 3 p.m. that afternoon, 28 February 2004, Yasmine was born with Dr T and my midwife, Nisrine, cheering us on. They wrapped her in a cotton blanket and handed me my slippery, shining little girl. She gripped her hand tightly around my finger and all three of us, Matthew, Yasmine and me, coiled together and fell in love.

Matthew and I were a bit stumped for middle names but settled on two: Helen, a name that had been given to the women of my family for five generations, and Taylor, because, well, I wanted her to have a little bit more of me in there. As we sat cooing over our new daughter, we could never have predicted the troubles her name was about to cause.

When a baby is born in Lebanon the parents provide visitors with a little gift. In Beirut it is common to give a piece of chocolate that is elaborately and extravagantly wrapped. There are shops all around the city dedicated to producing these baby chocolates and it is important not to scrimp in such matters. There is a direct relationship in Beirut between spending money and gaining respect. The more you spend the more respect you earn, because you have created an image of wealth. Wealthy people are to be admired. Admired people are to be respected. 'We would rather pay more and be respected,' a friend had once explained to me.

Because Yasmine had turned up two weeks early, we hadn't organised our chocolates. Perhaps I should have dispatched Matthew to one of the favoured *chocolatiers* at the first twinge of labour, but it hardly seemed a priority. So we stayed together, snug in the hospital room, transfixed by the face of our tiny child. Guests came, weighed down with flowers and pretty potted plants and cards and tiny pink outfits, and left with nothing. We remained oblivious to the extent of our mounting *faux pas*.

The day we brought Yasmine home, Amir, our landlord, and his beautiful, elegant mother arrived with a gift: a silver platter piled high with chocolates. It was a gift to celebrate Yasmine's birth, but as Amir surely knew, he was subtly, gently, saving us from ourselves.

There were about 100 pieces of chocolate on the platter, each wrapped in either pink or lilac paper and arranged in a striped design. The pink ones were made from pieces of milk chocolate with almonds tied with pink satin ribbon. Threaded onto the ribbon was a tiny pink teddy bear. The lilac chocolates were rectangular, and instead of pink ribbon and teddy bears they were decorated with soft purple ribbon and little amethyst-coloured butterflies. But most important of all was the gold sticker on the back that read 'Perugia' – the name of the *chocolatier*, one of a clutch of highly esteemed Lebanese chocolate-makers. Thanks to Amir, I could hold my head high as I handed out my gifts, even if they were a bit late in arriving.

When it came to the big events of life – birth, death, marriage – tradition reigned. The chocolates were just a part of it. Just as important were things like the *mougleh*, a wheat pudding that was made in endless batches to offer visitors to the newborn. The preparation of all of this traditional fare required lots of family assistance, which was why, when a child was born in Lebanon, the mother of the woman who had given birth (or her mother-in-law) came to stay for 40 days. Forty seemed a magical number in Lebanon: 40 days of assistance after birth; 40 days of mourning after death. I guessed it was the same as the old Western idea of six weeks of confinement, but unlike Lebanon where these things were still observed, I didn't know anyone in the West who still adhered to the idea. Not everyone in Lebanon loved these traditions. 'It was the longest 40 days of my life,' moaned a friend who couldn't wait for her mother-in-law to leave.

With such a traditional focus on family after the birth of a child, Matthew and I probably seemed a little odd as we turned inward after Yasmine was born, shying away from too many visitors and socialising, and focusing entirely on getting to know our new baby.

When we did begin to venture out to introduce Yasmine to our friends in the weeks after her birth, we were often told '*s'm'allah, s'm'allah*', which translated loosely to 'by the grace of God'. It was considered bad luck to directly compliment a new baby and we learned that this term was a roundabout way of telling us how beautiful Yasmine was and how blessed we were to have her. But Lebanon being also a very religious society – compared with Australia, anyway – our visitors were also quick to brand her into the faith and to offer her God's protection. Although we were never asked our religion, it was automatically assumed that as Western foreigners we had a Christian tradition.

Christian friends brought Christian gifts: a charmingly distressed old copy of the Bible, written in Arabic. A delicate gold chain with a tiny circular charm decorated with the face of the Virgin Mary. Amir told us he'd visited the shrine of the Virgin at the bottom of his garden and lit a candle for Yasmine on the night of her birth. Our Muslim friends brought non-sectarian presents: a piece of turquoise decorated with the letter Y in gold. A pair of gold stud earrings in the shape of dolphins. A high chair.

I was less anxious about Yasmine's religious affiliations than her national ones. I wanted to get her passport and a certificate of Australian citizenship as soon as I could. I wanted to make her legitimate, to get her logged into the Aussie system. All I had to say that she was mine was a piece of paper from the hospital stating that I gave birth to a 'female infant' at a certain time and date. Until I officially claimed her Australian citizenship, Yasmine was stateless. She wasn't eligible for Lebanese citizenship: only babies with Lebanese fathers could become Lebanese (it was a patriarchal system). And so I made an appointment at the Australian Embassy, a large dour building at the end of Bliss Street that was ringed by guards in fatigues with big guns and concrete barriers to stop cars parking next to the building – safety measures against car bombs. As Australian citizens we had the luxury of being whisked past the queues of Lebanese waiting for visas or immigration interviews.

'Yeah, this is fine, there'll be no problem with the passport. But we need an official Lebanese birth certificate,' the clerk told us, and Matthew, Yasmine and I were shuffled out the door again with a new task ahead.

The trip to the embassy had left Matthew and I deflated. 'The only thing worse than Australian foreign affairs bureaucracy is Lebanese bureaucracy. Any kind of Lebanese bureaucracy,' I said to Matthew, moping.

We made a trip to the *mukhtar*, the mayor, to apply for a birth certificate. The mayor's office was in a demountable room on the side of a car park adjacent to the Amn el-Aam, the General Security Office. Matthew spoke with his assistant, and I waited demurely, maternally, by his side, trying to look as mild as I could. Of course it was bad news. We couldn't apply for a birth certificate for Yasmine without a valid visa in my passport, and I had let my visa lapse after Dr T's thwarting of my Gaza plan.

'Don't worry,' said the assistant. 'Just apply for an extension to your visa and it should be done in two or three days.'

To do this, I had to pay a visit to the Amn el-Aam, an Orwellian labyrinth of staircases and tiny old-fashioned lifts and doors that said 'Don't Enter' and rooms stacked with files, mouldy, dusty, crumbling. The place had old wooden parquet floors that had become loose with age and wear and clattered as you walked over them. There were lots and lots of people in military uniforms sitting behind wooden desks shuffling piles of paper and assiduously ignoring anyone who looked as if they might need some help. This branch of General Security was where Lebanese families came to register their foreign housemaids, and there were lots of dark, timid women being dragged from room to room, desk to desk, by harried employers huffing at the cost of the *icama*, the work visa.

The technique for having your query dealt with was definitely not to politely wait in line. It was best to push as hard as possible to get as close as you could to the desk of the person you wanted to see and then to wave your documents impatiently in his face or place them on the desk in front of him and keep pushing them closer and closer in little staccato movements until he had no choice but to pick them up. The expression on your face should say something along the lines of 'I am very important, wealthy and influential and certainly need to be attended to before *that* person on my left or right and if you don't recognise my inherent importance and respond quickly then I have connections that might put *you* out of a job'.

I filled out forms, got things photocopied, left my passport and was told to come back in a week. A week later I returned to the desk, pushed to the front, gave my name and the lieutenant in charge looked it up in a huge book with olive-green binding. He licked his finger and flipped the pages, which seemed so big he looked like a character from *Alice in Wonderland*.

'Ah. There is a problem.'

Of course there was a problem. My heart sank.

I was sent to another office, to an official who was slightly higher in rank. He made a telephone call and I had to fill out more forms. It seemed General Security was suspicious about what I'd been doing in Lebanon and wanted a written explanation. I explained, 'I have just had a baby.' Yasmine was with me and so I showed her, sleeping in her sling, to prove my story. 'My doctor refused to let me travel while I was pregnant,' I added, fudging the truth slightly, but the story added drama to my case.

The official wrote all of this down. 'Come back in a week.'

Somehow I knew this next visit wouldn't be any different, and of course it wasn't. The only difference was that this time the official with the big green book took pity on me, leaned towards me and whispered, 'Your case has been sent to the detectives.'

There was a recurring joke in Lebanon's expat community that we were all suspected of being foreign secret agents. It wasn't always a joke, however, because sometimes an expat would learn that someone they had considered a deep and personal Lebanese friend had harboured these sorts of suspicions. When it was discovered, the lack of trust it exposed could be deeply hurtful and troubling and throw the entire friendship into question. The problem was, because Beirut had been crawling with CIA and Mossad and MI5 agents during the civil war (many of them using covers as journalists or aid workers) there was a precedent. Times had changed, but in the minds of many this idea was not too far outside the realm of possibility.

So when the official told me I was being investigated, my suspicions immediately fell to the CIA theory. 'I'm being investigated? For what?' I demanded.

The official knew he'd said too much already. He shut tight, like a clam. 'I don't know. Come back next week.'

I had rudely blathered through protocol in my aggressive Western way. When handed this little titbit, this little secret, I should have snapped it up silently, read between the lines, and asked my next question subtly, vaguely, so as not to embarrass the man with the big green book.

I felt a bit panicked by this new development. I visited Cheryl in her cool, spacious villa off Bliss Street for some tea and advice. A neighbour dropped in to join us but she had bad news. 'To be honest I think this is not good. They are cracking down on foreigners in the country. I have three friends who didn't have their residencies renewed and were asked to leave within two weeks.'

I felt sick to the stomach. I wasn't ready to leave. I couldn't leave. My child didn't even have a passport! The Australian Embassy was its usual bureaucratic self, mired in protocol, offering no assistance, no suggestions. 'Well, we've never had a case exactly like yours. We're not really sure how it all works. So when you find out, let us know.'

As each day passed I felt myself being sucked deeper and deeper into an administrative nightmare. Steadily a realisation dawned: if I continued to trustingly follow procedure I would never get my visa renewed. I would never get a passport for Yasmine. It was time to think outside the box.

When I arrived in the Middle East, everyone came forward with tips on how to bargain in the *souk*, how to negotiate the cultural quirks, how to survive the summers. But no one told me what I really needed to know: how to use connections and how to give a bribe. In Lebanon, things often got done via an unofficial back channel. Wait for things to be done above board and you could wait forever. Instead, everything operated on *wasta*, connections. And I worked out that this constant drive to seem wealthy and influential was actually about *wasta*: the more wealthy and influential you were, or appeared to be, then the more likely you were to have *wasta*. *Wasta* could get you a job; *wasta* could get you out of trouble; *wasta* could get you pushed to the top of the queue and make problems disappear. *Wasta* could make life hell for those who didn't cooperate with you.

My problem was that I had no *wasta*.

But there was a solution to that too. If you didn't have any personal *wasta* then you could get it by piggy-backing on a friend who did. I ran through my phone book and two names bubbled to the top. The first, the son of a well-known politician, would be perfect but I was shy about imposing and decided I'd use him as a last resort if I did get a deportation order. Then there was Nabil, someone Matthew and I had met at our local gym. Nabil's father used to work in the Security Services and his uncle was still a colonel with General Security. It wasn't enough leverage to give me real power, but it was enough to at least find out what was going on.

Nabil's uncle looked up my file on the internal computer system and at last there was an answer. 'Someone told them you are working illegally in Lebanon,' Nabil said, quoting his uncle. 'They are doing an investigation which will take about eight weeks and if they find out you are working illegally then you will be given two weeks to leave the country.'

I was apoplectic. Kicked out of the country? Working illegally? Who would say that? In the weeks that followed I felt like I was being watched. I *was* being watched. There was a car that sometimes sat outside our apartment block. I was sure I wasn't imagining it. Men who no one knew went into the shop and asked Nada about me: 'What does she do?'

'I don't know. You'll have to ask her,' Nada answered, bless her.

With the spectre of an eviction notice from Lebanon looming, getting Yasmine's passport issued had gained new urgency. There was no way I would leave Lebanon without her. She was six weeks old but still without her Australian citizenship or even an official name. I was no longer willing to just wait for this situation to run its course.

Matthew and I went back to the *mukhtar* and asked if there was anything we could do to push the birth certificate through before the visa was renewed. This was our big opener to the world of bribes and I was impressed with Matthew's performance: subtle and yet unambiguous, polite and yet assertive. The key was to emphasise certain words, to employ lengthy pauses at strategic points in the conversation, to give plenty of meaningful glances. None of these things could be viewed as untoward, and yet, for those who chose, the meaning could not be missed.

'Is there anything we can do . . .' Pause. Head cocked questioningly. '. . . to speed up the process . . .?' Another pause. Furrowed brow. Earnest expression.

'Well, as you have applied for the renewal and it's being processed then it should be okay to begin to process the birth certificate in the meantime,' the assistant replied.

'Okay,' we said, scanning the assistant's face for a sign that our true meaning had been received.

And then it came: 'Are you prepared to pay an administration fee?'

'Of course,' Matthew said, nodding discreetly, graciously.

Beside him, I was almost laughing with relief. The good old administration fee (wink, wink) – we all knew what that meant. But just when I thought we were home free a new problem emerged: my name.

'You know that Taylor cannot be included on Yasmine's birth certificate,' the assistant said. 'It's not done in Lebanon. To include the mother's name – well, we see it as a kind of fraud.'

Arab names adhere to a strict paternal tradition. As in the West, it is traditional for the children to take on their father's name, as a middle name. But unlike the West, where that is a tradition rather than a law and you can add anything else in there if you fancy it, to add the mother's family name is not done in Lebanon. It is akin to trying to mask the lineage, and thus the identity, of the child.

Matthew retained his cool and tried to argue. 'In the West, Taylor is not just a family name,' he said. 'It is also a woman's first name.'

The assistant was unmoved.

I stood there in the demountable, staring at the assistant in his cheap suit and at his desk covered with kitschy souvenirs – perspex domes with plastic flowers inside, a business-card holder stamped with the insignia of some engineering company. My emotions wavered between anger and defeat. Meanwhile, Matthew was having a light-bulb moment.

'Do you watch *The Bold and the Beautiful*?' he asked. Everyone in the Middle East knew *The Bold and the Beautiful*. It was repeated on satellite television about 100 times a day.

'Of course,' the assistant said.

'Well, then you must know the character called Taylor who's always in the middle of some love triangle or other? It's her first name. It's not a family name.'

The assistant's face softened. He could tell Matthew had tried really hard to come up with that one. For the first time we stopped talking in double entendres and hidden meanings.

'Mr Matthew, I know what you are saying and, believe me, if it was up to me to decide I would not be worried. But, sir, to put Taylor on your daughter's birth certificate, believe me, it is difficult. If you insist, we can try, but it will be very, *very* difficult.'

He looked at Matthew and Matthew looked at me and it was final. We had come so far. Neither of us had the stomach for another bureaucratic battle. This was a struggle we could not win. We surrendered.

To this day I have no idea whether the administration fee was legitimate – we were told it went towards translation and photocopying fees – but whatever it was used for, the results were spectacular. By the end of the week Yasmine had a Lebanese birth certificate (without her middle names), and by the following week she had a certificate from the Australian Embassy granting her Australian citizenship 'by descent'. A few weeks later her new Aussie passport arrived with her cute little baby mug shot stamped and watermarked and official. Her name was still all wrong. The embassy would not accept her middle names if they did not appear on the birth certificate, but by that time I had lost the will to fight.

The investigation into my possibly illegal work history was completed. The irony was that while I waited for a decision, I had possibly bribed an official and committed my first illegal act in Lebanon. But the investigation declared me clean as a whistle. Case closed. It had taken almost three months but I was no longer a criminal suspect. And Yasmine was a real little Aussie, born in Beirut.

CHAPTER 16
THE PILGRIMAGE

The months passed quickly in a happy blur of motherhood. Me: hanging out with Cheryl and my network of Beirut mums. Matthew: researching stories, the latest on Egypt's Muslim Brotherhood, the Islamist political faction that was gaining ever greater popular support. That summer, between babies and Egyptian hardliners, we also spent a lot of time at the gym. Matthew and I would tag-team each morning and sometimes we'd take Yasmine along too, for a swim in the rooftop pool with views across the city and over the ocean to the horizon.

Our regular gym visits meant that we were seeing more of Nabil. We felt a great warmth towards him for his help in smoothing my visa woes and as the year progressed our morning chats (huffing conversation on the treadmill, disjointed sentences between repetitions on the weight machines) began to evolve into a deeper friendship. One day Nabil told us that he was planning to make a pilgrimage to the Church of Our Lady of Bechwat and the chapel beside it, in the village of Deir al-Ahmar on the edge of the Bekaa Valley. Would we like to go with him?

The chapel had long been an important pilgrimage site in Lebanon, but a few weeks earlier it had gained an even greater significance. A ten-year-old boy claimed to have seen a miracle: the famous statue of the Virgin Mary in the chapel had blinked. There were even photographs purporting to show the statue with its eyes open and then closed. In the weeks following the miracle, crowds of around 5000 a day flocked to the site hoping to witness the vision, to pray and ask for blessings. The boy who reported it was a Muslim from Jordan, and the fact that he was not Christian, not even Lebanese, had given the miracle greater weight in the eyes of many because, the argument went, he had no reason to make it up. The pilgrims were a mixture of Christians and Muslims, because Mary is also revered in Islam as the mother of the Prophet Jesus, although she is not considered a virgin.

We were keen to join Nabil. It took a while to organise ourselves, but one Sunday morning several weeks later we waited for him in the lobby of a hotel around the corner from our apartment. It was early, 7.30 a.m., and the late autumn sun shone the day's first thin, pale rays across empty weekend streets. Without the intense hustle and jostle of the weekdays, the backstreets of Clemenceau had a ghost-town stillness. It was an effect enhanced by balls of crumpled paper and other rubbish blowing down cracked footpaths, and stray cats venturing from their hiding places to creep through gutters and across ledges in search of scraps of food.

I was just about to order coffee when Nabil burst through the doors. He was in a buoyant mood. '*Yalla*,' he said as he hurried Matthew, Yasmine and me onto the street and into the back of his battered Jeep, apologising for the mess and the draught from where the windows didn't close properly.

We drove the short distance from Clemenceau into the heart of Hamra and began looking for a parking spot as close as possible to the St Francine Church. The plan was to join a bus of Filipina housemaids, all regular churchgoers, who were using their precious single day off a week to make the pilgrimage to the chapel.

Nabil was religious in the way of many Lebanese: religion was important as a sectarian stamp, a means of marking difference, as much as for the faith itself. But I could tell he was sincere about this trip. He had serious reasons for making it: reasons dug up from the rotten depths of Lebanese history, where hatreds were inherited and memories were long.

A friend of Nabil's, Nadim, worked as a bouncer at a nightclub. One night Nadim refused a group of Palestinians access to the club. It was a provocation that drove its own emotive wounds deep into the soft and still-tender memories of conflict between the Maronites and Palestinians. That night the Palestinians pulled out knives, their honour insulted, and a fight broke out. Nadim telephoned Nabil for backup, and in the course of the brawl that ensued Nadim got badly slashed. The two friends raced to the hospital but it wasn't until one of the doctors saw Nabil bleeding that he realised he'd also been hurt – a knife injury deep inside his liver. His blood pressure plummeted and the last thing he remembers before passing out on the gurney was praying: 'Jesus, please, save me. I don't want to die.' The pilgrimage was his chance to give thanks for his life being saved.

The Filipina maids, about 50 of them, were also eager pilgrims and had arrived long before us. I squeezed on board the bus and claimed the last seats, side by side in the back row. Yasmine was an instant hit and was passed from seat to seat; tickled, tossed, admired. About 20 minutes later Nabil, puffed from parking the car and running to the bus, settled beside us.

As the coach began moving a group of three of the maids

shifted to the front and began singing hymns, accompanied by a guitar. A Filipino priest gave a short sermon and then another of the maids began reciting the rosary. All around me women were earnestly counting beads and praying: 'Hail Mary full of Grace, blessed art thou among women and blessed is the fruit of thy womb, Jesus . . .'

It was a two- or three-hour drive from Beirut, over Mount Lebanon. The journey would take us to the northwestern edge of the Bekaa Valley. The air that morning was bracing, invigorating. It wasn't long until I could look back and see Beirut's grey sprawl stretched across the coastal flatlands below. The Mediterranean lay like a metallic grey soup behind it; dull without the energy of summer sun glittering on the waves. Inexplicably, perhaps, I loved that view. From above, the city appeared supernatural; the crazy development of high-rises spanned a neutral spectrum from white through pale grey to black. Hanging above it was a ring of putrid grey-brown pollution. Unlike so many other cities, which from this perspective offered a graduated silhouette that built and built until a cluster of skyscrapers emerged at a single distinct point – the city centre – Beirut was a uniform mess, like rows of chipped and blackened rotting teeth. If you looked very carefully, you could see its city centre appear like a scar, a razed space full of memories. The view was repulsive and yet compelling.

After an hour or so we reached the snow line. Great piles of snow stretched from a brown icy slush at the kerb to blinding white powder covering hillsides and rooftops to the horizon. We drove past banks of shops, closed for the weekend, although an occasional restaurant was open selling chicken *sharwarma* or *saj* with turkey, mint, pickles and melted cheese folded inside. Yellow taxis on their way to or from Damascus, huge old American models from the 1970s and 1980s, roared past us.

We descended fast into the Bekaa Valley and along its wide, potholed roads. From time to time hessian tents, home to Syrian or Bedouin seasonal workers, sprang up in clusters. Tattered children played in the dust outside or loitered shyly at the doors. Goats were kept in filthy, muddy pens. Bright washing hung from the tent poles. We passed through villages slung with political posters, mostly of prominent figures from Hezbollah, or the young earnest faces of dead fighters from its Islamic Resistance.

From time to time there were checkpoints manned by Syrian soldiers rather than Lebanese. Stylised stencil portraits of Hafez al-Assad were painted in black on lumps of concrete, side by side with more of these concrete lumps painted roughly in the Syrian colours – green, red, black – and little sentry posts with piles of cigarette butts lying on the ground or scuffed into the dust.

Ahh, Syria. The country was magical. The sweetest people, kind and generous and without the brash, keep-you-on-your-toes sophistication that you found in Beirut. Syria was crammed with labyrinthine castles with fat histories of Crusader battles and Roman ruins that you could walk around free of other tourists or the touts that fed from them. You could pick up ancient things like pieces of clay pots and carved lumps of stone, turn them over in your hands and feel the past. In Damascus, the *souk* swallowed you whole and you could time-travel down its dark alleys, past spice stalls, and tread where history had happened.

But in Lebanon, the Syrian regime was collecting enemies. Syria had a long memory: its leaders remembered when Lebanon was part of Greater Syria, until Ottoman and then Western conquerors tore it away and remade the map to suit themselves. During the Lebanese civil war Syria had been invited in by the Christian Maronites to help them fight the Muslim militias. But war is fickle. Allegiances shift. After a while the Syrian troops turned against the Maronites, and allied themselves with the Muslim militias. When the war ended, Syria didn't want to leave. Alliances had shifted again and Lebanon's new Maronite president was friendly to Syria. Damascus filled Lebanon with its troops and security forces and put checkpoints up around the country – to protect the Lebanese from themselves, they said – and started to control the way politics took place.

The ordinary Lebanese were starting to become more vocal about their wish that Syria would leave. The country was splitting down sectarian lines: Shi'ites, Hezbollah supporters, continued to support Syria; while many Christians, Sunnis and Druze were against. I'd often catch Nabil telling jokes in which the punchline was the humiliation of some hapless Syrian character.

The final leg of the journey to Our Lady of Bechwat went through the Christian village of Deir al-Ahmar, indistinguishable from all the other Bekaa Valley villages apart from the fact that it was dotted with churches instead of mosques and there were no stencils of Assad.

When we reached the village we didn't stop, but continued to drive up a gently winding slope to the site of the shrine. We got off the bus and our little group split immediately from the crowd of maids, who were heading to the main church for a Sunday service.

The miracle statue was inside a stone chapel that was off to the right as you approached the main church. Portable metal fencing had been used to channel crowds of pilgrims into the chapel in the heady days after the miracle first happened and it still lay around at odd angles. There were few visitors that day and I walked straight inside. Immediately the cold, thin air of outside was replaced and I was wrapped in incense and warmth. It hit me like a drug and I felt my body, which had been tensed against the cold, loosen into the chapel's quiet, womb-like interior.

The chapel was just one room, made entirely of stone. The internal walls had not been plastered over and the stone blocks, relatively consistent in size, formed horizontal rows that flowed in layer upon layer around the chapel. There was a bank of wooden pews encased in a wooden fence and worshippers were routed, left and right, to the altar. The famous statue of the Virgin was nestled in an alcove to the left, protected behind a mesh enclosure. There were perhaps eight or ten worshippers in the chapel and most were deep in prayer, their heads bowed and their hands cupped in front of their faces.

I walked as close as possible to the Virgin. The statue was about one and a half metres high. Her robe was painted a bright, almost electric, blue and decorated with dozens of raised stars in various sizes, each painted gold. The Virgin had long, straight dark hair, her head was tilted slightly forward and her eyes, those famous blinking eyes, were cast down. She wore a gold crown on her head and in her hands carried a gold-painted cross.

I peered intently, as sceptics do, to see if I would also witness a miracle. And as I stared the dimness of the room seemed to close in on me. The Virgin became surrounded by a pulse of light; darkness filled my peripheral vision. The straight lines that marked the separation between the rows and rows of pale stones began to waver in and out of focus, an effect made more dramatic as the straight lines clashed with the curve of the chapel's chancel. I began to lose my sense of perspective. It was almost like vertigo. The Virgin herself seemed to be leaning towards me, closer, closer, and I decided not to fight it, or rationalise it, but to allow myself to fall into this holy embrace. It was easy to understand how others believed they saw miracles here.

Beside me, Nabil was silent, at prayer, and in my heart I reached out to him. Most of the time he presented a slightly cocky air, trading off his impressive physical presence, but it didn't take much intuition to sense the vulnerability beneath it. He had modest dreams – to buy an apartment, to fall in love, to keep a job and maybe even find one that paid a decent salary. But even this was a struggle. Nabil's family wasn't wealthy. The connections he'd used to help me with my visa problems weren't significant enough to make much change for him. Without *wasta* or family wealth, nothing was certain in Lebanon.

I walked back outside with Yasmine and we waited for the others in a sunny corner that was protected from the wind. A few minutes later Nabil came out and joined us, blinking in the sunlight, sighing as if he had been through something.

'So!' I began, trying to sound light-hearted. I could see he felt embarrassed by the welling of emotions. 'What did you pray for?'

'Oh, I don't know,' he answered, trailing off and looking down at his feet. 'I prayed for better days than these.' He tilted his head slightly, raised his eyebrows, and gave me a wan smile.

We walked across to the string of small souvenir shops selling prayer beads, credit-card-sized pictures of Lebanon's saints, and reproductions in various sizes of the Virgin statue. Nabil filled a plastic bag with different things and paid for them, and then he pulled out a small wooden diptych with a picture of Christ on one side and a picture of the statue of the Virgin on the other. The pictures were stuck to two pieces of wood with the bark still attached and had been carved into arches, and the entire thing was thickly lacquered. The hinge in the middle allowed the two images to be folded together like a book. 'This is for you,' he said, and held it towards me. I thanked him, stirred by the depth of his feeling, and held his gift tightly in my palm.

'The maids want to be here for three or four hours,' Nabil said.

Three hours sounded like a long time; there wasn't really anything left to do. I walked with Matthew across the plaza that separated the church from the chapel and found a private, sunny corner to feed Yasmine her lunch. I could hear a guitar being played and the maids singing folksy hymns. Yasmine was restless. There was no grass for her to play on and anyway, it was too cold to be outside for long. Nabil was right, we could not wait here for the maids to finish. We had to find a way to get back to Deir al-Ahmar on our own. From there we hoped it would be possible to find a taxi or a bus to take us back to Beirut.

'What about hitching?' I suggested.

Nabil looked sceptical, but really it was the only way. We half-heartedly hailed a few cars, without a response. Hitch-hiking in Lebanon was an extremely rare and derided activity; something only for the very poor or the desperate.

'I think we are desperate,' I reminded Nabil.

He mumbled something about how he should have brought his car and I instantly regretted my comment. I could tell he was feeling the weight of his responsibility as a Lebanese to ensure his foreign guests had a pleasant and trouble-free day out.

'Come on, Nabil,' Matthew said, 'don't be so serious. We don't mind hitching. It will be fun.' A rickety old Mercedes came roaring towards us. I nodded encouragingly towards Nabil. 'This is it,' I said.

Nabil waved down the car and explained our predicament. A man and a woman sat in the front; they broke into grins and gestured for us to climb in. Matthew and Nabil filled up the back seat, squashed in next to a box of vegetables and fruit. Yasmine and I squeezed into the front passenger seat beside the woman: a crazy dangerous thing to do, but there was no choice. They were a hillbilly pair, members of a tobacco-farming family from Deir al-Ahmar. At first I had mistaken them for husband and wife, but they were siblings and when you looked more closely it was impossible to miss the likeness. Both had tanned faces scored with deep laugh lines, and large hands, almost cartoonish, that they waved and clapped and used to sweep aside bits and pieces to make room for us all to fit.

At Deir al-Ahmar the tobacco hillbillies careened up to the home of the local taxi driver, honking the horn and waving those large hands in the air. But the taxi driver had gone to Beirut for the day and had not yet returned. The tobacco hillbillies shrugged – no point worrying about what can't be changed – and invited us for tea while we worked out what to do.

We pulled up beside an empty field enclosed by a barbed-wire fence. An unpaved driveway ran along one side and at the bottom was the house. It was made of concrete and appeared incomplete. A staircase ran up the outside of the building but led to nowhere, an invisible second floor not yet built. We entered some sort of large garage, which was empty but looked like it was used for tractors and farming equipment, and were ushered into a small living room to the left.

It was furnished with three couches, one along each of three sides of the room, and there were rugs on the floor. In the middle of the room was a stove with a small door on one side to add blocks of wood. The stove had a little platform where a teapot could be kept warm, and we sipped a sweet, subtle brew of dried flowers as we talked – the usual conversation of mixed-up bits of broken language, with Nabil stepping in frequently with translations.

The glow of the miracle statue had spread out from the chapel and over the area. Residents of Deir al-Ahmar clung to their Christian credentials with pride; that they had been blessed with such a powerful sign from God seemed confirmation of their piety and righteousness.

'You know, Mary has always protected us,' said the brother and shared one of the village stories, told and retold until you couldn't tell where the line between truth and myth was drawn. 'During the war, if the Syrians were about to attack, a fog would descend. This meant they couldn't see clearly enough to attack us.'

'That's right!' His sister picked up the thread, expanding, embellishing. 'And then we would look into the clouds and we could see Mary's face smiling at us. It was she who protected us.'

The pot of tea emptied and the logs in the stove burned low. The problem of our return to Beirut had not been solved and Yasmine was looking tired and unsettled. I began to pray quietly that maybe Mary could help us too. Nabil and the tobacco hillbillies discussed our predicament intently and it was decided that the only way we were going to make it back to Beirut before nightfall was to take a mini-van from Baalbek.

'We will drive you to Baalbek!' said the brother, springing up from the couch and smoothing his trousers.

'Yes, we will drive!' said the sister.

I was thoroughly charmed by this crazy laidback pair. They handed out their generosity blithely, unselfconsciously. We took up our positions in the car and sped across the Bekaa Valley floor, past fields where I'd seen marijuana growing just a couple of years earlier, but which had since been destroyed by a new government crackdown.

It was only 15 kilometres from one side of the Bekaa to the other and so it wasn't long before we were in Baalbek. We looped around the Roman ruins, which glowed yellow, lit up at night, and stopped at the front of the Palmyra Hotel with its faded turn-of-the-century grandeur, four-poster beds, views of the ruins from the balcony, and original Jean Cocteau sketches on the walls, done when the artist was a regular at the Baalbek Festival in the 1950s. I loved to stay there with visitors from Australia and listen to the staff tell stories of when Charles de Gaulle came to stay and other tales of grander times. But there was no time to stop today.

White mini-vans were passing all the time. 'Beirut?' yelled the brother as one van passed, and swerved towards the kerb in preparation for a stop. '*Yalla*, Beirut,' yelled the driver. Suddenly there was no time for goodbyes either, for heartfelt thanks. We scrambled out of the car, shouted our gratitude for the transport and tea and stories, and climbed into the van, doubled over as we shuffled up the bus to find a seat. When I'd settled myself and Yasmine, I looked out the window and saw the tobacco hillbillies careening back to their farm. The car was almost on its side as it swung around the corner, those giant hands waving excitedly out the windows.

The mini-van sped along the valley floor in the opposite direction. When we reached Chatura we turned and started to climb out of the valley. Very soon there was snow on the ground again. We rode the saddle of the mountain and then, just before we began to descend, we saw the famous Beirut view in the distance below us.

'Look,' I said to no one in particular. 'We've almost made it.'

'Yeah,' said Nabil smiling again. 'Now that really is a miracle.'

CHAPTER 17

ASSASSINATION, REVOLUTION

That year, we flew to Australia for Christmas. We were glad to escape the depths of winter and indulge in our first long Aussie summer holiday since we had moved to Beirut. When the parties and the presents were all over, Matthew and I piled the car with suitcases and beach gear, strapped Yasmine into her little car seat, and drove north to Seal Rocks. We rented a house with a big verandah, surrounded by bushland and a short walk from the beach, and just exhaled.

That first beach holiday with our little girl felt like time-warping back 30 years to my own childhood in the 1970s: trudging through the dunes to get to the ocean, hunting for pippies in the sand, collecting shells in our buckets and using them to decorate enormous sandcastles that were incredible feats of amateur engineering. Matthew felt it too. We woke every morning to the chirp of cicadas and days filled with the smell of eucalyptus leaves in the sun, the squeak of clean sand underfoot and barbeques every night. The Middle East and all its complicated politics was far away; it began to feel like I'd dreamt it all.

And then reality came crashing through. When we returned to Beirut at the end of February, we flew into a city that had been utterly changed for us in almost every way.

For a start, we were no longer living in our beloved apartment in Rue d'Amerique. Before we left for Sydney we had given it up, regretful but resigned, and moved to a larger place in Achrafieh that allowed Yasmine her own room. If I am honest, I should add that we were also fearful of the enormous construction project – 13 floors of luxury apartments – that was being prepared on the site of the car park opposite, where Abu Khalil used to live his plain and genteel life. He had already left, back to Tripoli, on his putt-putt step-through scooter that blew black smoke from the exhaust as it revved up the hill towards the hospital where Yasmine was born.

Sad as we were to leave Amir and the garden, and our little neighbourhood in Clemenceau, it was clear our new place offered a range of other benefits: as well as a room for Yasmine there was space for an office, and the biggest luxury of all – access to a supply of generator electricity in the event of blackouts. The electricity was siphoned from a generator owned by a larger, plusher apartment block opposite ours, for which we paid a small monthly fee. It was delivered to us via an ingenious tangle of wires that ran up an electricity pole and spanned the full width of the street then looped and dangled above the footpath to our block.

Our new building was a rather uninspiring-looking concrete block, boxy, almost Russian-looking. The swaying lift was so tiny it fitted only four passengers at a push. The sides of the gondola had been pierced with something and you could trace the trajectory to an exit point on the other side. Every time we caught the lift Matthew and I debated what could possibly have caused such marks – furniture? bullets? – until our new neighbour Mary confirmed our most sensational imaginings. The marks were from a gun battle during the war, she said, and shrugged as if this was clearly the most obvious and normal of answers. We nodded our understanding and played cool.

Once inside, the block's bland exterior and battered lift gave way to an apartment filled with comfort and light and an intoxicating view into the lives of the neighbours around us. It was a real Beirut view, with ultra-modern high-rises sandwiched next to crumbling two-storey villas. When I stood on the balcony, six floors up and with only a waist-height railing to protect me, I felt as if I was falling into that view, floating through Beirut both inside and apart from the city.

Our new home took us from the multi-sectarian bustle of Clemenceau and neighbouring Hamra to within a few metres of the old frontline, inside the eastern sector of Beirut, an overwhelmingly Christian area. I swapped English and stumbling Arabic for my schoolgirl French – the preferred second language in Christian suburbs. The political posters changed too. The posters of Amal and Hezbollah that were all around Clemenceau and Hamra were nowhere to be seen in Achrafieh. Instead, the neighbourhood was papered with Lebanese Forces posters.

We were right around the corner from Rue Monot, and only a walk away from the shiny new ABC mall, Beirut's first undercover shopping centre, which was crammed with great boutiques and little cafés. The main street of Gemmayze was down the road, and at lunchtime there was probably no better spot in Beirut than Le Chef, a packed little restaurant with a nicotine-stained mural along one side and sagging shelves stocked with cans and jars of food on the other.

Le Chef was fronted by Charbel, who had an uncanny knack for remembering faces and names and making you feel like a regular even if it was only your second visit. Le Chef served up lashings of cheap home-style Lebanese recipes, cooked by Charbel's father in a mezzanine kitchen at the back. This was the sort of food that Lebanese mothers and grandmothers cooked – comfort food that was almost impossible to find in the fancier places around Beirut. Even before we moved into the area we regularly slipped down to Le Chef for lunch and feasted on *mougrabieh* (tiny balls of pasta topped with chicken, lamb and gravy) and *moulokieh* (chicken with spinach-like leaves topped with onion and vinegar sauce and croutons). These meals were so steeped in nostalgia you could almost see the smiles on the faces of the diners as they rolled the familiar flavours around in their mouths. Over time the flavour of this food became entwined with our own happy memories of life in Beirut and brought with it a deeper sense of home.

We hadn't had time to unpack before we'd left for Sydney and so when we returned to the apartment – owned by a Canadian–Lebanese friend who had offered to rent it to us while she was in the US to finish her PhD – it was filled with boxes and bags: four years of collected things. The carpets we had bought in Syria and Iran were rolled up in a corner. The wooden mirror inlaid with mother of pearl that we found at Basta – a knot of shops in Beirut that were home to a treasure trove of antiques and priceless junk if you had the patience and the eye – rested against a wall. Because of this, the place didn't yet feel like our own, and so this return to Beirut was a strange homecoming.

While we were away, something else had happened to make it even stranger: Lebanon's political minefield had taken a new and deeply shocking turn.

On Valentine's Day 2005, shortly before we were due to fly home to Beirut, I was lying in bed in Sydney early one morning when I heard my mother talking to Matthew in the hallway. Scattered words: 'Bomb . . . Beirut . . . killed . . . prime minister . . .' Matthew came quickly into the bedroom. 'Hariri's been assassinated,' he said, and there was an edge in his voice. 'He was blown up in a massive car bomb.'

We had experienced car bombs and assassinations in Beirut already: one year it was Elie Hobieka, an influential member of the Phalange and Lebanese Forces militia who became a politician when the war ended. Another time it was a Hezbollah member. But Hariri? Mr Lebanon! This was the most significant assassination since the end of the war.

Hariri was voted in as Lebanon's prime minister in 1992 and he kept the job for 12 of the next 13 years. His vision and determination (and, some would add, his corruption and nepotism) had more or less defined Lebanon's postwar revival. He used his enormous personal wealth (billions of dollars made doing business in Saudi Arabia) and his impeccable connections (friendships with the Saudi royals and French president Jacques Chirac) to attract billions of dollars in foreign investment to Lebanon. He used the money to turn the city's destroyed central district into a vibrant centre again. Before his death Lebanon really felt as if it was getting back on its feet: tourism was booming, international musicians had begun to put Lebanon on their touring schedules; there was even talk of a Beirut Grand Prix and a bid for the 2024 Summer Olympics. Glossy travel magazines had started listing Beirut as one of their top ten cities.

For voters, one of Hariri's most appealing qualities was the fact that he was among the few senior Lebanese politicians to be untainted by wartime affiliations to militias and massacres. While the war raged he was too busy making money in Saudi to get involved. Not that he lacked political *savoir faire*. He had donated US$12 million to the victims of Israel's 1982 invasion of Lebanon and helped to lay the foundations for the Taif Accord that ended the Lebanese civil war. There was method in all of this, of course: Hariri was building his credentials in readiness for his push into politics. His relationship with Syria alone showed that he knew how to use political expediency: for years he supported Syria's military presence in Lebanon, but at the time of his death, just over a year after his resignation as prime minister in protest over the reshaping of Lebanon's constitution to allow President Emile Lahoud a third term in office, Hariri was developing a comeback campaign. It featured criticism of Syria's manipulation of Lebanese politics as its central agenda. Lahoud was Syria's man and Damascus was keen to keep him in office. Hariri had received several death threats – attempts to intimidate him into abandoning his campaign. So when he was killed, it was natural that suspicion would fall on Damascus.

Matthew and I knew the political response to Hariri's murder would be immense. But what neither of us was prepared for was the emotional reaction of the Lebanese, and the way the fallout from the assassination would suddenly make Beirut a much more dangerous place to be.

The morning after our return I was up early and waved down a *service* taxi to take me to Clemenceau. I wanted to stitch myself back into the city and needed the familiar reassurance of a visit to our old apartment block, to say hi to Nada and Asmat in the shop, to do a bit of browsing in Piaff, my favourite boutique. But most of all I wanted to visit Amir.

Clemenceau wasn't far from the spot where Hariri's motorcade had been blown up and I hoped Amir could recreate the moment for me.

As the taxi took me across the city that day, portraits of Hariri were everywhere: giant posters hung from the sides of buildings or were strung up across major thoroughfares. Smaller pictures were papered 10, 20 at a time over bare walls. He had been laid to rest in the grounds of a huge new mosque (built with Saudi money and Hariri's overt support). It was overwhelming, huge and not at all in the Levantine style. Before his death most Beirutis hated it, but afterwards it became a sort of monument to Hariri. His body lay beneath a great mound of earth covered with flowers and surrounded by candles that had dripped a carpet of wax in a ring around his grave.

An electronic counter had been placed on the edge of Martyrs' Square – the huge empty space in the centre of Beirut that had been razed after the war and was still waiting to be redeveloped – next to the site where Hariri was buried. The counter ticked over the number of days since his assassination, next to a banner that read 'The Truth'. Mourners had graffitied messages on nearby hoardings and over the stone base of the Martyrs' Statue, some in English, some in French, some in Arabic: 'We'll never forget you.' 'Thank you for a new Lebanon.' 'You will not die when you are in our hearts.'

The site quickly became the focus of a nightly pilgrimage. Hundreds of Beirutis of every religion would gather there to pray and light candles. Coaches were hired to bus in more political pilgrims from towns and villages outside Beirut. Once their respects were paid, they wrapped their leather jackets and scarves a little more tightly around their shoulders and went out for dinner, or to a movie. It was a little act of defiance that said 'Whoever did this, our spirit will not be bowed'.

When the *service* dropped me in Rue d'Amerique I scouted around for Amir and found him, as usual, tending to his plants and organising the impressive collection of antiques that he had stashed in the spare rooms of his villa.

'Amir! Oh, how *are* you?' I almost ran towards him, dispensing with the usual greetings, suddenly hungry for news of what had happened. 'Where were you? Did you hear it?'

Amir told his story. He had been clearing out a room of his villa with Susan, the eccentric English yoga teacher who lived down the road, when he heard the sound. 'Catherine! It was terrible.' He made a sucking noise, pursed his lips and drew breath so it hissed, and then 'Boo-oom!' The force of the blast was so violent that it blew out the back windows in one of the old houses. 'We were terrified,' he went on. 'Of course, we thought it was the Israelis bombing again. Then we thought, No, the noise is too big, it has to be something very close. Jumblatt! They have blown up Jumblatt's house.'

Walid Jumblatt, the Druze leader whose Beirut home was just a block from our Clemenceau apartment, was a key leader of the anti-Syria push and had also been receiving death threats. Jumblatt was so concerned for his life he had set up a little roadblock outside his house, manned by his personal staff of bodyguards.

Amir continued the story, his eyes wide. 'But when we went to the balcony to look, we could see a huge, *huge* cloud of black smoke and it wasn't coming from Jumblatt's house. It was coming from the Corniche.'

The Lebanese had two reactions to these sorts of things: a cascade of fear, tapped from a deep well of memory. Years of war could do that. The other reaction was to forget fear; to reduce the magnitude of things. Amir belonged to this latter group. He headed out straightaway, in the direction of the smoke, and had almost reached the site when he heard a rumour that another bomb had been planted and was about to go off. His courage failed. He ran back up the hill, towards home.

We walked outside to the garden behind the old villa and sat in a pair of wrought-iron chairs overlooking the fountain. Amir had a newspaper published the day after the assassination, and he spread it out on the grass and pointed out the pictures of the explosion. Hariri's body featured, splayed and swollen, charred, and yet undeniably him. His white collar and tie were the only pieces of clothing that had not been singed from his body. The image was too terrible to look at for long, even though a blanket was covering the hole in his stomach.

He could sense my horror. He folded the paper shut and put it under his arm. 'They have to show it, because it is the only way to prove to people that he is really gone,' he said.

A few days later, on 28 February 2005, Yasmine turned one. We held a little party for her in our new apartment, but her birthday was overshadowed by the political upheaval that was brewing across the country. Lebanese civilians refused to accept the attack on Hariri and rallies began to overtake the city. That morning, thousands gathered in Martyrs' Square to rally against the assassination and I put Yasmine in her stroller and walked down with Matthew. As I watched, surrounded by Lebanese Army soldiers with guns and tanks, and emotional protesters, I began to wonder if we should have stayed in Sydney. Was a country reeling from an enormous car bomb that had killed a former prime minister and 20 bodyguards and bystanders, and on the brink of some kind of revolution, the right place for Yasmine? But what I didn't know was that the heat was about to be turned up.

There had been no formal answer to Lebanon's most pressing question: who killed Hariri? But the demonstrators were in no doubt that Syria had ordered the murder. People were beginning to call their demonstrations an independence movement, and they demanded Damascus pull its troops and its secret police out of Lebanon once and for all.

A few days later, Hezbollah – which supported Syria's role in Lebanon because Syria supported it – gathered hundreds of thousands into Martyrs' Square in reply. It was a slap in the face for the nationalists: Hezbollah's effort brought up to 30 times more people into the street, and the next day's newspapers estimated that 500,000 had attended. Syria's President Bashar al-Assad was quoted saying that the images of Lebanese nationalists rallying against Syria had been manipulated: photographers had zoomed in close, he said, to make it appear as if there were large numbers of objectors.

The burgeoning independence movement was furious. Something had to be done. They could not be beaten. Emails were sent out, phone calls made, the word was spread and another rally organised for 14 March, exactly one month after Hariri's death.

By mid-morning on the 14th there was a steady stream of demonstrators marching down our street and down Rue Monot, and trucks blaring nationalist songs through loudspeakers drove up and down. Some people wore the Lebanese flag wrapped around their head like a bandanna or around their neck like a scarf. The streets were filled with tanks and soldiers on alert to control the crowd. Matthew was filming, so Yasmine and I walked down separately with the demonstrators.

By lunchtime up to one million people – a quarter of

Lebanon's population – packed Martyrs' Square. 'Zoom Out' read one of the placards in the heart of the crowd, an unabashed taunt at al-Assad.

It seemed to me that the response wasn't just about Hariri. People were shocked by his violent death but this was more than a political reaction. It was emotional. It was as if that explosion had transported everyone back to the darkest days of the civil war. All of the anger and sadness that had been bottled up for years, for decades, was pouring out.

As the campaign to rid Lebanon of Syria's influence gained pace, so did the movement to unite the Lebanese, to rid the country of this undercurrent of sectarian tension that the civil war hadn't resolved and the end of the civil war had never reconciled. 'Lebanon United, Never Again Divided'; '100% Lebanese' screamed the placards, references to the pain of the civil war and the Lebanese people's refusal to allow it to happen again. You could buy pendants that featured a Christian cross and Islamic crescent fused together.

A tent city sprang up in the centre of Martyrs' Square. Every night Christians, Muslims and Druze sat together and planned a united future. It was impossible to miss the symbolism: hundreds of thousands of people rallying for peace, for reconciliation, for independence from outside interference, on the spot where a decade or so before the same people, or relatives of those people, had been killing each other. The demonstrators called it the Cedar Revolution, the Beirut Spring. They joked it was a Gucci Revolution because of all the glamorous housewives who had joined the demonstrations. Whatever they called it, they were sure that it was the beginning of better days. The protest had unseated the government, new elections were to be held, and plans were being made for Syria to withdraw its troops and secret police. A few weeks earlier this would have been an unthinkable victory.

But somehow I felt uneasy. As I wandered through the tent camp – the apparent source of this unity – it became clear. The message was forgiveness and togetherness, but the participants had set up under the banners of particular sectarian militias and political parties. It seemed to me that the echoes of the civil war's divisions had never reverberated so loudly.

A few weeks later, the bombing started again.

As March progressed small bombs began to explode with chilling regularity. Our move from Clemenceau to our new place in Achrafieh had been badly timed. A great deal of the criticism against Syria's presence in Lebanon came from Christian groups and factions, and the bombing campaign had so far focused exclusively on Christian suburbs. We had landed into the heart of it. A siege mentality had started to build. Just a few days earlier a sign had appeared at the entrance to my apartment block: 'Due to the recent events we ask that all residents and visitors leave their name and telephone number on the windscreen of cars parked in this street. Cars without the owner's details will be reported to the police.'

There were those who wanted to use Hariri's murder as a chance to purge the past, to reconcile differences, to move ahead with a fresh and united agenda, but the old fears were all around. I worried that the peaceful Beirut I had come to love was about to be lost once again.

CHAPTER 18

VIGILANTES, SUSHI

One night, Nabil and I rode over to Sin El Fil, the neighbourhood where he'd grown up and where he still lived, because he wanted to show me how the residents of the area had banded together to hunt out potential bombers. 'I tell you, Catherine, if so much as a firecracker goes off here, we will retaliate,' he said as we got into the car, and he rubbed the handgun in his pocket.

The bombs were getting closer and closer to the city centre. The latest was only 15 minutes from downtown Beirut and an area neighbouring Sin El Fil.

'People feel the bombing is getting too close to where we live.' Nabil tried to explain the anxiety that had ripped through his neighbourhood. 'The bombs are received as messages.'

So far the bombs had each been small, designed to terrify rather than kill. They had gone off in the dead of night in car parks and shopping centres, and each time the casualties had been one or two innocent foreign workers, asleep in makeshift accommodation. The message was pretty clear: criticism of Syria would be punished, and it was suspected that Syrian agents were behind them.

Nabil said that Sin El Fil residents did not trust the Lebanese government to protect them. Residents had decided to take unilateral control of who came and went, and had set up checkpoints in and around the suburb. Each was manned by a group of vigilantes made up mainly of men who had experience fighting during the civil war. They had returned seamlessly to old duties. Guns were taken out of cupboards and dusted off. It was as if no time had passed at all since the civil war. More than anything I'd seen in my years in the country – more than the battered infrastructure and the shrapnel-marked buildings – the speed of this reaction brought home just how deeply the war had scarred these people. Hariri's US$13 billion renovation budget had been unable to heal these emotional wounds.

Sin El Fil was a working-class Christian suburb and a stronghold of support for the Lebanese Forces (LF) – an affiliation of Christian militias dominated by the Phalange. Like most of these militias, the LF had sunk into the background since the end of the war, but its members were still around and the smell of threat in recent weeks had provoked them back into action. The organisation's flag – white with a green cedar tree ringed in red, symbolic of the blood LF fighters had spilled – flew from buildings here and there.

I could see that Nabil and his neighbours had a right to protect themselves, but the guns made me uneasy and so did the speed with which the old wartime affiliations had been reinvigorated, and I told him this.

'Why the guns? Why the flags? It's a bit provocative, don't you think? Shouldn't you talk out your differences?'

Nabil was exasperated, but kindly. 'For a start, no one has

claimed responsibility for these bombs. Who do we talk to? The people here feel targeted and decided, no, we are not going to be sitting ducks,' Nabil said. 'Look, this is more of a show of power, to say, "We are here, we are able, and we will defend ourselves if we are attacked." We hope it will be a deterrent. As well, you know, I think people need a place to release the pressure, the stress.'

We drove past the Beirut River (optimistically named, I had always thought: it was nothing more than a concrete canal with a trickle of filthy water at the bottom), not far from the suburb of Chiah where the first shots of the civil war had been fired exactly three decades ago. We veered off the highway and into Sin El Fil's residential streets. The suburb was built on a hill. The streets were quite narrow and lined with modest apartment blocks.

Suddenly there was tension in the air. The footpaths were almost empty. Nabil fiddled around on the dashboard and pushed a laminated piece of yellow cardboard towards the windscreen, so that what was written on it could be seen from outside. It was official-looking, with a red stamp.

'What does it say?' I asked, struggling to make anything out in the darkness.

'Basically, it's a document to prove my identity,' Nabil said. 'The residents here have organised these cards so we know who owns the cars parked in the street.'

Before us was a roadblock – hunks of concrete positioned so cars were forced to slow to a crawl and drive in a zigzag through a kind of maze. Nabil flicked on the interior light so our faces could be seen clearly. Never had I experienced anything like this in Beirut. It was like being back in the West Bank, or Baghdad.

Nabil wound down the window, exchanged pleasantries with a young man, and explained quickly where we were going. We were waved on. 'Now,' Nabil said gravely, 'we are inside the Protection Zone.'

Groups of men were gathered on almost every street corner, peering into cars. They stopped anyone they didn't recognise and asked for identification. I was safe with Nabil because he was well known there. We parked the car in a side street and walked across the road to one of the groups. Nabil greeted the men with soldierly formality. 'This is Catherine,' he said. 'A friend.' The men nodded in unison.

Nabil had a shift from midnight until 3 a.m. but it was only 11.30 p.m. so he had some time to kill. We walked together to a flight of stairs leading up to the Boulangerie el Raheb, the Monk Bakery, and sat on the steps side by side. The men were out in the street on their patrol shifts or just hanging around, talking and strategising. The women were inside brewing coffee to bring to the men, mixing up familiar recipes for late-night dinners.

Nabil took out a cigarette from a packet of Marlboro Light. He offered me one and we sat together, blowing smoke into the darkness.

'You know, Catherine, during the war everyone took cocaine and hashish. But this revolution is being fuelled by caffeine and nicotine!'

In Lebanon there was a silent agreement that no one talked openly about the war. As a foreigner, it felt like bad form to ask too many questions. At first I found this very strange. Even in the places where trauma was usually dealt with – in art and academia – it seemed that Lebanon's civil war was still too raw to be fully, freely discussed. After all, many of the major players were still active in politics and public life. It was too early to point fingers or to analyse the situation. Everyone was fearful of where it might lead.

But after Hariri died something snapped. It felt as if the outpouring of emotion over his murder had created a forum in which to release other kinds of grief: for youth lost in fighting, for loved ones dead too early, for a ruined city. And as we sat there, in an eerie half-light, Nabil began to talk about the war.

He was born during the fighting, in 1978.

'You can't possibly remember much,' I jibed, wanting to prevent him repeating the well-worn myths, exaggerations and hatreds. I wanted an authentic tale.

'The early and middle part of the war, you are right, I was too young. I don't remember much from that time,' he said. 'But from 1986 I remember everything. And that is too much.'

He paused and looked around him, and I could tell there were images replaying in his head like old film.

'For example,' he went on, 'I remember there was a car bomb in the street, just down there.' He pointed to a small road, barely wider than an alley, that disappeared into the darkness off the main street. 'It was a Friday morning. We had no school because the situation was unstable. I remember my youngest sister had been recently born and she was sleeping. My mother put a mosquito net over her crib. When the bomb went off the window in her room broke and shards of glass came down on her. If my mother had not put up the net she would have been cut to shreds.'

The whole street ran to the site of the blast. Nabil went too. 'I remember one man, he was standing by his car with the door open as if he was about to push it closed. But his entire body was burned. He was black, charred. He was dead.'

'How does a child deal with things like that?' I asked him, gently.

'That didn't affect me much,' he said and masked the emotion building on his face by taking another drag of his cigarette. He blew out the smoke and cocked his head to feign nonchalance. 'The first time you see a dead body, sure, it affects you.' He flicked cigarette ash in an arc over the steps and onto the road. 'But the first time you see a man killed in front of you, that changes you forever.'

I didn't want to ask. I thought I knew what he meant. I had seen plenty of dead bodies. When I first started out as a journalist I was often rostered on the midnight to dawn police shift, chasing ambulances and police cars to car accidents, murders, fires. Then, when I lived in Vietnam, death hadn't been the clean, packed-away thing it was in the West and I'd seen families washing their dead at the temple before burial. At funerals in the West Bank and Gaza it was a similar thing – the body of the martyr carried high above the crowd in full view. I remembered Jenin camp, watching bodies being pulled from the rubble. In Iraq, there were more corpses; one, the body of a fellow journalist, a shocking and haunting image I would never forget. But I was grateful I'd never seen anyone killed in front of me.

We fell silent again. We stared at the road and half-watched as the vigilante team stopped cars and chatted to the drivers, waving them on before returning to tables and chairs filled with friends and family to play cards and smoke cigarettes and *nargileh*, share pots of tea and coffee. The street activity was lit by uncovered light bulbs swinging on long cords, or by torchlight, which cast an ethereal glow over the scene. Neon crosses and pictures of Jesus suspended over the road compounded the effect. Miniature shrines, built into little glass boxes like a diorama, were placed regularly around the streets – on corners, tucked into elegantly shabby foyers or the sides of buildings. Most represented the site of a wartime bombing or the death of a loved one. They each contained small statues, perhaps 30 centimetres high, of Lebanese saints or of Notre Dame, Our Lady, standing with her arms held slightly apart from her body, palms facing heaven-ward, in a pose that Matthew joked was the 'search me' look. As we sat there in that strange light, with midnight approaching and the Lebanese Forces flags outnumbering the Lebanese ones, the past was all around. I tried to understand it.

'Right here. This corner.' Nabil spoke suddenly, jolting me from my thoughts, and patted the steps where we were sitting. 'This is where I saw someone killed for the first time.'

A chill ran over me and I looked at the pavement, trying to find some trace of it: a drop of blood, a tear. 'What happened?'

It was during the final stages of the war, one of the bloodiest. Two Christian militias – Samir Geagea's Lebanese Forces (the group that Nabil and his family still supported) and General Michel Aoun's Nationalists – were at war against each other. The tragic irony was that at the time, 1989, the Aounists were fighting to get the Syrians, who were allied with Muslim factions, out of Lebanon. But the Lebanese Forces, feeling under pressure, had allied themselves with Damascus and so fought against their own Lebanese Christian brothers in support of Syria's right to remain in Lebanon. In the end, the Arab League intervened to stop the fighting and an accord was drawn up to bring peace. But Aoun refused to accept it and fled into exile in France. Not long after, Geagea was sent to prison, where he languished still. And the rest of the mafia politicians and warlords had just carried on, their war crimes forgiven as part of the general amnesty that was supposed to bring a kind of resolution to war's untidy ends.

There was always a campaign of sorts underway to have

Geagea released from prison, and in the wake of Hariri's assassination and the Cedar Revolution and the mood of reconciliation and compromise it had at first created, that campaign had been stepped up. It was beginning to look as if the campaign to release him might actually succeed this time. LF supporters were angry that Geagea was still in jail when so many of his contemporaries with equally brutal histories had been allowed to remain free. Not just free: many were high-profile businessmen or elected members of the Lebanese parliament.

Nabil continued his story. The Aounists had set up snipers on the top of a building about one kilometre away from where he lived and regularly fired down on the street to terrorise the residents, most of whom were LF supporters. 'During the war, sometimes it was impossible to leave the house to go to get bread or water and things that you really needed to live,' Nabil said. 'So the members of the Lebanese Forces used to do it. There was a rope that ran from here to there.' He pointed first to the balcony of an apartment opposite where we were sitting, then to another apartment across the main road, about 20 metres away. A long black sheet was rigged up on the rope so that it could be drawn across the road like a curtain. If an LF fighter was doing his rounds buying bread and water for the neighbourhood, he could draw the curtain so the Aounist sniper was unable to line him up for a shot.

'How ingenious,' I said, ignoring the grisly purpose and smiling at the brilliant simplicity of the idea.

'So one day,' Nabil continued, 'I was in my usual place, hiding behind the sandbags in the foyer of my apartment building, watching what was happening on the street. And I saw this guy, this LF guy, he's full of life, joking around. He says, "I'm going over without dropping the sheet."'

I looked across to the apartment foyer. It wasn't hard to imagine Nabil's wide-eyed boyish face peering out from behind the sandbags, knowing his mother would be furious if she found out where he was.

'I saw the LF guy start to cross the road and then, suddenly, he fell. I thought it was a joke. I didn't hear the sniper. Then about two seconds later we heard the crack of the rifle. Because it was so far away there was a time delay.'

The fighter lay bleeding in the street. 'But you know the ugliest thing? When anyone tried to get to him, the sniper would shoot again and again, and that guy, he just lay there and lay there and I watched him as he bled to death.'

Nabil looked down at the ground and shook his head. Then he unzipped a little pouch he always wore fastened around his waist and pulled out a rosary and began moving his fingers quickly over the beads. He turned his face to me and continued talking, his fingers still rubbing the beads. 'That was in 1989. I was 11 years old. You know, Catherine, every one of us has a story like that. Every fucking Lebanese has a story like that.'

A few nights later I was having sushi with Matthew, Leila and Ramzi at The Sushi Bar in Achrafieh, with all the beautiful people. It was the usual Beirut conversation: politics, and questions about the future, and reviews of the latest bars.

I told them about my night with Nabil and how shocked I was by how quickly people had begun to rally so publicly around their particular militia king. 'Where's the unity gone? Where's the nationalism? Isn't that what one million people came into the street to protest about?' I asked.

'Exactly,' said Leila, and took a sip of sake. 'You know they are comparing Lebanese politics to *The Lord of the Rings*? Remember the Hezbollah rally? The young Christian kids are calling them the Orcs! All in black, the Orcs, get it? Then they call Aoun Gandalf. Can you believe it? They said, "The Orcs may seem powerful now but wait until our Gandalf returns." '

Ramzi had heard it too. 'Well, if he's Gandalf, at least he's becoming more secular,' he said, smiling quietly. 'During the war they used to call him Jesus.'

CHAPTER 19
AN ENGAGEMENT IN SHATILA

Another summer in Beirut began, but this year politics hovered over everything. Elections were due in June and bombs were still exploding. The future was in flux and I prayed that a more stable Lebanon would be the result.

It was almost three years since the photographic workshop in Shatila. One morning I met Alan for a coffee at Paul, a café in Gemmayze that baked great bread and baguettes and pastries (the *tarte au citron* was my favourite) and had achieved cult chic status. I'd often go there with Yasmine and the Beirut Mums. Paul was *the* spot for the ladies who lunched and I loved people-watching there. This was where you'd see that fascinating breed of Beirut *madam* dressed (literally) head to toe in European designer gear, perfectly manicured, perfectly coiffured, perfectly made up and chatting to her friends in French.

It was hot that day and I'd made the mistake of walking through the backstreets of Achrafieh to get to Paul. It was a walk I loved – narrow streets and Art Deco apartment blocks painted in pastels, gates hiding overgrown gardens with little stone fountains. As a result of the walk I was sticky and uncomfortable. I was relieved when I immediately spotted Alan, and I slipped into a chair beside him, hoping to make myself invisible.

Alan had news about Samar, one of our former students. 'She's engaged,' he said and raised his eyebrows sceptically. After all, she must now be only 19. 'But she seems happy. I don't know . . . The guy is a Palestinian from Holland.'

I had chased up some of our former students to see how they were getting on, and had already caught up with Lina and Ahmad. Lina was happy: she had done some acting in a film put together by a foreign NGO. 'I am realising my dream to become an actress,' she told me with great excitement when we met in Shatila one day. On another occasion we went to a women-only beach, Costa Brava, and swam in the sea together, with huge fabric curtains strung across the water obscuring the view to the horizon and hiding us from the prying eyes of passing fishermen and daytrippers.

Dear sweet little Ahmad seemed to have fallen through the cracks. I had gone to visit him shortly after the photographic workshop and had found him working in his aunt and uncle's shop. He stood up when he saw me enter and held his arms wide, mimicking the proprietorial welcome of the head of the house. He slowly clasped his hands around my head and kissed me hello one, two, three times on the cheek, and I had been once again charmed by this boy, forced old by circumstance. But that was three years ago and things had changed. His aunt and uncle had grown tired of his increasingly aggressive and rebellious behaviour and they had kicked him out. I found him in an internet café one afternoon emailing his 'girlfriend', he had said, boastful. He was jumpy and nervous and his face had grown old. Our conversation was awkward, more so because a little crowd had gathered around him. He struck a pose and tried to act tough. I went along with it, loath to humiliate him, but I couldn't reconcile the Ahmad I'd known with this scruffy, suspicious youth, though I could see the vulnerability beneath it. I tried to rationalise it. Was it just a normal teenage phase? The processing of a difficult life? A pure cry for help? The maturing of a no-good personality? I felt sorry that I hadn't been more of a friend to him. My regret was pure middle-class guilt and I felt guilty even for that. Could I have changed anything? Who knew, but I could surely have done more than I had. In a flurry of remorseful phone calls I tried to put him in touch with a youth worker who scooped up kids like him and tried to set them straight, give them back hope of one kind or another.

And now, Samar. Alan gave me her telephone number and I called later that day. Her sister answered and I left a message. A while later there was a text message: 'Sorry I can't call. I have no credit left.' I rang back and she was relaxed and easy on the telephone. I told her I'd like to visit to see how she was and we agreed to meet in a few days' time.

I called a favourite taxi driver but he'd had a car accident. 'I am at my village,' he said over a crackling mobile phone line. 'I can't drive for a week.'

'Oh dear. Were you hurt?'

'It's no problem for me. But my car!'

I called my local taxi company instead, but when I saw the car slide into a parking spot in front of my apartment block it dawned on me that I'd made a mistake. Most of the drivers with this company were Christian and – the real problem –

most had been members of the Phalange. The Phalange was responsible for the massacre of Palestinians at Shatila in 1982 and a great hatred and fear continued to brew between the two groups. What was I thinking? There was no way this guy was going to take me to Shatila. But it was too late to change plans now; I was already running late.

I climbed into the back and saw the driver had the usual collection of rosary beads looped around the rear-vision mirror and pictures of St Maron (the priest who founded the Maronite Catholic order) stuck over the dash. I asked him to stop at a little sweet shop nearby so I could buy some *petits fours* to give to Samar. It would be unthinkable to arrive at someone's house in Lebanon without a gift – sweets, chocolates, flowers, these were the usual things. The sweets were bought by weight and I asked for one kilogram. The baker lifted the tiny biscuits, honey, nuts, flakes of pastry, one at a time from silver trays and laid them carefully into a box stamped with the name of the shop. He tied a ribbon around the package and placed it carefully into a bag.

I got back into the car and we pulled away from the kerb. 'Where to?' the driver asked.

'I am going to Shatila, the Palestinian camp,' I told him.

There was silence. 'Where?'

'Shatila. You know, the Palestinian camp near the Kuwaiti Embassy.'

He caught my eye in the rear-vision mirror and repeated my request, incredulous. 'The camp *Palestine*?'

'Yes,' I said, deadpan, holding my breath.

He turned around to face me and raised a finger, wagged it back and forth and spoke in English. 'I no go Shatila camp!'

I didn't put up a fight. I'd known this was coming and I'd probably been stupid and insensitive. We agreed that he would drop me at the Kuwaiti Embassy and from there I would walk down the hill to the camp.

I couldn't remember where to find Samar's house, but I knew it was nearby, veering off the market street that bordered Shatila. Yet the street itself emerged before me, perfectly preserved in memory; it was just the precise location of the alley to Samar's home that was missing. I called for directions as I passed the massacre memorial. I was walking past the rubbish dump when the line connected. 'I can't remember how to find your place,' I said.

'Don't worry. I'm coming to get you,' Samar said. 'Just keep walking as you are and I will see you. I'm coming from the other direction.'

I kept walking. Past the mobile telephone shop that sold snap-on covers featuring the Hezbollah flag and pictures of Nasrallah with his fist raised; past torn posters of Sheikh Yassin, the Hamas leader killed in an Israeli air strike a year earlier, and others of Yasser Arafat who had died a few months before; past a fabric shop with rolls and rolls of coloured cotton on display; past a guy frying balls of *falafel*. I had to weave back and forth to avoid the puddles of mud and being hit by the cars and bikes and vegetable carts. And then in the middle of this world of mud, rubbish and broken breeze blocks I saw Samar coming towards me wearing a candy pink headscarf. She stood out like a light bulb.

'You've changed! You've become a woman,' I joked with her, but it was true. In three years she'd turned from a chubby teenager into an elegant young woman with a slender figure and perfect cheekbones.

'Yes, you are right,' she said, smiling, then, unable to contain her good news: 'Do you know I've become engaged?'

'Alan told me. Are you happy? Samar, you are so young!' I couldn't help it, my instinct was to disapprove. I knew it was more or less an arranged marriage; Samar had known him for only a few days before they became engaged.

'I know, but this is a good thing,' she said, and she looked at me, her face glowing with certainty.

We walked together along the main street, then turned into an alley on the left, little more than a body width, and then right again into a small dirt courtyard, maybe two metres squared, with doors leading off in all directions. Each of the doors opened into a tiny apartment and one of them was Samar's home.

We stepped into a small room, painted white, with tiles on the floor. It had been renovated since I'd last seen it – it was almost a cave back then, without paint, without a proper floor. Samar's father had died when she was tiny. Her mother did what she could, but the family was very poor. 'I hated inviting people to my house then,' Samar confided when I admired the improvements. 'People would never say anything but I could tell that they felt sorry for us. I could see it, you know, in their eyes.'

Now, there were couches and chairs lining three walls. On the fourth, a door led to another room and I could see Samar's younger brother asleep on the floor. In a corner stood a chest of drawers with photographs and other familiar household knick-knacks arranged on the top. Samar excused herself and went quickly to a shop nearby and bought two small bottles of mango juice. She poured them into glasses and we sat to talk.

'Engaged, huh!' I began.

Samar jumped up and shuffled a pile of photographs. She selected one and thrust it towards me. 'That's him,' she said, pointing to a tall, well-built man with a handsome, gentle face.

'Ooh, Samar, he's very good-looking,' I said, and we laughed.

'But, Catherine, really, he is very nice,' she told me, suddenly serious. 'I never planned to get married. Believe me! But something happened to my head. I don't know . . .'

Samar's fiancé was much older than her, 29. His name was Abed. He was an engineer and lived in Holland and had Dutch citizenship. He met Samar on a trip home to Shatila (his family were Samar's family's neighbours) and the two of them had sat together on her mother's couch, in the same room where we were now sitting, and they'd talked and talked. After that first meeting they had crossed paths a few more times, and one day he visited Samar's mother. 'I want your daughter to be my wife,' he said.

Samar's mother passed on the request but Samar was suspicious. She wanted to be sure he was the right man for her, that they had an intellectual connection. She questioned him about the kind of wife he was expecting.

'If you were sitting in a group with your friends, talking, and you knew that your wife was not following the conversation, what would you do?' she asked him. 'Do you want a wife who sits silently or who participates in the conversation?' she said. 'Do you think it is important for your wife to be your intellectual equal?'

Samar liked the answer she received. But she wanted to know more. 'I asked him, why me? Why now?'

Abed had lived in Holland for 10 years and he was once married to a Dutch girl. They got on very well but his Dutch wife was older, she wanted different things. They decided to separate but they were still friends. Abed wanted to be married. He wanted a family. He wanted to stay in Holland but life there could be lonely, there could be racism, you worked long hours, he missed his own people. He wanted someone who understood him and where he'd come from. 'Don't marry me because you think Europe is a paradise,' he'd told Samar. 'Life in Holland is difficult. It can be a miserable life there but I know it can be better. If you agree to be my wife, you will be the first step in my new life.'

I asked Samar what her family thought. She was reflective.

'My mother told me if you say no, you will still face problems and happiness in your life. If you say yes, it will be the same. So this is your choice.' She wrestled with the decision; leaving her family would be terribly difficult. 'I asked myself, who will make me happy when I am sad? Who will make me laugh when I cry? How can I leave everyone, my whole family, my best friend, for just one person?'

Samar got a piece of paper and a pen. She drew a line down the centre of the page and on one side she wrote down all the reasons why she should accept Abed's proposal and move to Holland. On the other, she wrote all the reasons why she should stay. 'I decided I had the chance to win more than I would lose,' she said.

She was quiet for a while and looked over at her mother, who was sitting opposite but was unable to speak a word of English and so was oblivious to our conversation. Then Samar spoke again as if her mother wasn't there, the foreign language giving her a privacy that proximity did not.

'Sometimes you feel you are in prison,' she said. 'I just – want – to – breathe.' She drew out the word, *breeeathe*, and it was impossible to miss her meaning. She turned her face towards me. 'You know?'

CHAPTER 20
ONE JUNE DAY

The day began like many others: I woke to the sound of Yasmine calling from her cot. I got up and carried her into the kitchen. I made her a bottle of milk and myself a mug of coffee and we both went back to bed. I drank my coffee and Yasmine lay back on the pillow drinking her milk and examining her toes.

Matthew had left for Sydney to edit a film on Hariri's assassination. It was just Yasmine and me and so together we watched the news: the Dutch said 'no' to a referendum on the European constitution; a car bomb in Iraq.

As we lay there, the city ground into life. Car horns cut through the morning's peace, I heard jackhammers on a construction site in the distance. A dog barked; the Sri Lankan maid in the apartment opposite threw a carpet over the balcony and then came the dull, rhythmical thud, thud, thud as she beat out the dust with a broom. The morning sun streamed through the balcony doors and the heat grew. I read Yasmine a book, and we played football with the big green ball with the bears on it. I made chicken stock. At 9 a.m. Gracie, our maid, arrived.

I had resisted hiring a maid for a long time. Partly because it felt strange and indulgent, but also because I felt uncomfortable with how maids were held apart from the rest of the society, as if subject to a kind of apartheid – hiring one seemed to condone it somehow. They had their own cafés and restaurants and bars, and their wages were ranked according to nationality. Ethiopian maids were the cheapest, then Sri Lankans, and Filipinas were paid the most. You saw advertisements in the local papers that promoted 'Sale Time' on housemaids: 'Ethiopians: Only US$100 a Month!' But slowly I had relented. First I hired a regular cleaner, and then when Yasmine was born Gracie had come as a regular babysitter at night, then for some half-days that soon became full-time plus two evenings of babysitting. Gracie was a loud, bustling presence and Yasmine adored her. She insisted on calling me 'ma'am', no matter how many times I told her not to, and every day she arrived with gossip and conspiracy theories and old wives' tales.

'Look at Yasmine's forehead,' she said one day. 'You see how it's round? It means she will have a lot of patience, but when that patience comes to an end she will get very angry.' Another day as I was fastidiously documenting Yasmine's every move: 'Never take a picture of a sleeping baby. It's bad luck.'

Gracie was a survivor and I admired her toughness. She had come to Lebanon towards the end of the war when she was just 19. A friend from her small, poor Philippines village had told her they could get jobs and excitement and money if they went to Lebanon. 'I thought, why not?' Gracie told me. They set off together and caught a boat from Cyprus into the heart of one of the darkest periods of the civil war: when Aoun and Geagea were fighting each other over Syria's future in Lebanon. She cowered in her apartment while bombs fell around her. She survived on her wits: found work as a housemaid, fell in love with a married Lebanese man and bore him a son. He set her up in an apartment and forbade her from working. 'I will support you,' he said. But Gracie would have none of it. 'I told him, I want my independence. You can't stop me from working.'

She left him and went back to work, made enough to put her son on a plane home to the Philippines, and continued working, sending gifts and money to her brother and her parents. She met another Lebanese man, married him, and bore him two sons in quick succession. But this time she had found a man who allowed her to be herself. Every Sunday she took the bus to Jounieh, a Christian area north of Beirut, famous as the site of the Casino du Liban and Super Night-clubs, where some of her Filipina girlfriends worked as nannies for rich families, and they hung out together. 'Ma'am, it's important for me to be with my people, to speak my language, to eat my food,' she said.

Just before lunch on that June day, Gracie and Yasmine went for a walk to the courtyard garden of a nearby church that had become an informal playground for the neighbourhood kids. Yasmine had a great time being fussed over every time she went to the church yard – the only blue-eyed blonde among kids with lush curly dark hair and long-lashed brown eyes.

I headed out to meet Nabil for *lemonada* and *saj*. I hadn't seen him since the night I'd joined him and the vigilantes in Sin El Fil and I was anxious to know how he was getting on.

He looked well. The warm weather had made his skin glow and it was obvious his body had more or less recovered from the fight he'd been in before we went on our pilgrim-age. But his mood was dark. When we got to the restaurant and chose a table upstairs by the window, he stared past me at the traffic below. He couldn't find work, had been six months in and out of new jobs. He'd worked briefly as a driver for a pimp, and he joked about it uncomfortably. He had quit after a month. And yesterday, he'd quit another job, this time as a security guard, but the pay was low, US$340 a month. Nabil ran through a list of his monthly expenses to underline how paltry the salary had been. I made sympathetic noises. 'I can't live on that,' he said. He felt taken advantage of. His pride overcame him. He left.

'You speak French, Arabic and English. You have a degree. I'm sure you can find work doing something,' I said, and began to brainstorm suggestions. But Nabil wasn't in the mood to be positive or entrepreneurial. He felt defeated, and although I didn't mean it, my barrage of ideas had come across as somehow unsympathetic. He just needed an ear. We ate our *saj* and sipped our drinks in silence.

'In Lebanon there is no middle,' he said after a while. 'There is only rich and poor. And 40 or 50 per cent of the rich get their money from illegal things – drugs and money laundering.'

This wasn't all true, of course, although there were stories, gossip, rumours, repeated and exaggerated in cafés across the country. The private jet that had flown from Baghdad to Beirut with the sons of several high-profile Lebanese politicians and US$12 billion in cash on board – the proceeds of a sale of arms to Iraq. The owner of a well-known boutique who used the shop to launder money from his Bekaa Valley drug business.

Nabil was full of bitterness and defeat. He took a bite of his *saj* and chewed, sullen. 'Look, Catherine, I was thinking of going to Iraq. A friend of mine is going next week and he says you can earn $US4000 a month.' His eyes were wide, incredulous. 'In three months I can earn a year's salary. I can earn $50,000 in a year.'

I could see he was hooked on the idea. It was easy to

understand why. Three months in Iraq and his financial troubles would be over. He could put a down payment on an apartment. He could propose to his girlfriend. He could plan his life.

'They pay a lot because it's dangerous,' I said. 'You could get killed. Being Arab won't help you. Quite a few Lebanese have been kidnapped, you know.'

'When your time's up, it's up. I could be killed walking across this street,' he said, gesturing to the road outside.

I'd heard this line so many times before in Beirut. I put it down to the fact that it was the only way to rationalise why some people had survived the war and others had died. Nabil had lived through the war. He knew how random death could be.

Just then, sirens. Sirens everywhere. Traffic everywhere. Everywhere chaos.

'What's going on?' I asked. 'Is there a fire? Has something happened at the shopping centre?' We were only a short distance from the ABC shopping mall. I thought of Yasmine. I didn't know where she was and I felt a knot of panic in my stomach. It was everything I could do to contain it.

'Please, Nabil, let's find out what's happening,' I said, and there was an urgency in my voice that shook him into the present. He called to the waiter, who explained that there had been 'another bomb'.

'The bomb has just been *found* or it's gone *off*?' I asked, irritated by the lack of details.

'It's gone off,' said Nabil, tuning into a television mounted on the wall to his left. A reporter was being interviewed from the scene via telephone. 'I think one person has been killed.'

The sirens grew louder. Several ambulances and fire trucks passed. The stream of traffic coming down from the ABC mall thickened.

'Look, Catherine, don't worry. It is just a small bomb,' Nabil counselled and shrugged off my concerns. 'We didn't hear it so it can't have been more than 20 or 30 kilograms.' He knotted his brow in thought and then added with a sort of conclusiveness: 'Maximum.' These were the kind of macabre facts that many Lebanese had at their fingertips.

'Nabil, I don't know where Yasmine is,' I replied, ignoring his attempts to placate me. 'I have to find her.'

I dialled Gracie's mobile but the lines had been blocked. This was common after a bomb. We paid for our food and drinks and Nabil drove me home via the church. I kept dialling, and now Nabil, too, was dialling Gracie's number on his telephone. I got an SMS message from Leila, who knew I lived close to where it seemed the bomb had been detonated: 'I have been trying to call you. Are you okay?'

This meant the lines were back up. I dialled again and at last Gracie answered. 'Don't worry, ma'am, we are almost home,' she said. I could have cried with the relief of it.

The streets were all blocked off. There were sirens and traffic jams and people running. 'Do you feel safe?' Nabil asked, as we tried to find a route through the chaos.

'I'm not sure,' I said. 'I don't feel like a target but I'm scared of being in the wrong place at the wrong time. I'm scared for Yasmine.'

'Listen, Catherine, I can lend you a gun.'

'What would I do with a gun? What use is it if a bomb goes off anyway?'

'Just to make you feel safe. You don't have to keep it out; you can hide it and it will make you safe to know it's there.'

'It's not normal for me to have a gun, Nabil. I don't think it would make me feel safe.'

'It's just a handgun.'

'Oh great, just a handgun.' I laughed and it relieved the tension I felt. 'Were you considering lending me a Kalashnikov or perhaps an M16?'

That afternoon I walked to the place where I guessed the bomb had gone off. It had killed Samir Kassir, a well-known and respected columnist for one of Lebanon's biggest daily newspapers. Who was responsible for his death? He was strongly anti-Syrian so, of course, in the current political climate the first suspect was Syrian agents. This felt like a serious escalation in the campaign of bombs that had been going off regularly, randomly, since the demonstrations against Hariri's death. It was the first time a bomb had gone off during the day and it was the first one since Hariri to target a high-profile personality.

When I got to the bomb site my heart leapt. It was much closer to home than I had imagined; outside a supermarket I visited with Yasmine several times a week. The irony was that I had switched from shopping at the big French chain supermarket to this one during the last spate of bombs, because I'd thought a little neighbourhood place would be safer. I stood at the police cordon for a long time and looked at the wreck of Kassir's car, a small white Alfa Romeo, which was now wrapped in plastic. Police and soldiers milled around the site, picking over bits of evidence and preventing people crossing the yellow police line.

Everything that had happened in the past few months – Hariri's death, the bombing campaign that had escalated and escalated – had led to this: another targeted assassination of a well-known figure. Strange as it may sound, I felt shocked. The Beirut I'd come to know wasn't *this* place, the violent, chaotic city of the past; it was a city of great kindness, enormous fun, chic style. But now the old image of Beirut as a dangerous and bombed-out place was becoming reality again. I felt frightened. This bomb had been way too close and all my bravado about learning to live in the moment was no preparation for it. I began to think about many things: the unpredictability of life; the crime of what had happened; the fate of Lebanon; the constant reopening of the wound of memory; the circularity of politics. I thought about how easily Yasmine and I could have been walking past that spot when the bomb went off. And for the first time I began to think seriously of going home.

That night I met Leila for dinner. She had suggested a new place in Hamra with a funky 1970s design that reflected the heritage of the complex it was in – one of Beirut's most famous buildings and beloved by architects the world over for its clean Modernist lines and exterior spiral staircase. We slid into one of the chocolate leather banquettes that lined the walls and sat under the glow of about 20 large silver pendant lights that hung in formation from the ceiling. Our waiter was very young, very sweet, and kept encouraging us to try the new dishes on the menu.

'What a day,' said Leila. She rolled her eyes and blew the air through her lips, long and slow like a kind of sigh.

'How do you feel about what's happening?' I asked as we clinked our glasses and took a sip of beer.

'You know, Catherine, the war started and I still don't know why. And then it ended and I don't know why that happened either.'

At first I thought she had avoided my question, but when I thought more about it I realised she had given a perfect answer. The future couldn't be predicted, and the years of brutality and horror of the Lebanese civil war couldn't be rationalised. Political and military facts would never be enough to explain it.

Leila began to talk and the stories tumbled from her. There was the Shi'ite guy who couldn't make it home because of fighting and so asked if he could stay in a neighbour's apartment for the night. The man agreed and the next day the Shi'ite man's family began to arrive. By the end of the week there were 15 people living in the neighbour's flat. 'And then do you know what the Shi'ite guy said?' said Leila, laughing almost uncontrollably at the insanity of it. 'He said, "Look, you are alone, only one person, and we are a family of 15. Don't you think it's better if you find another place to live?" He kicked the guy out of his own apartment!'

Then there was the story of the young militia fighter who was terrified and wound up on drugs. He came to Leila's family's apartment, screaming, 'They are coming. We're all gonna die. We're all gonna die.' He was hysterical. He screamed to Leila's father, 'If you leave this building without fucking taking me I will find you and I will kill you.' Years later there was a knock at the door. It was the young fighter, older now, calmer. They recognised him immediately. 'I remembered you,' he said. 'I just wanted to come and say hello and to see if you had survived it and to know how you are.'

And the woman on the fourth floor who got through the war with Valium and whisky and cigarettes, which she would hold with a pair of tweezers so she could smoke each one right down to the butt without burning her fingers, and how she shook uncontrollably from the effects of the Valium, and the whisky, and the fear.

We laughed and laughed that night. We laughed because we had to. Leila, because today had brought back bad memories and old fears. Me, because I was out of my comfort zone and felt scared about protecting my little girl. But there was nothing we could do and so we kept laughing and we had another drink. And then we had another one, laughing still.

After dinner we shared a cab and I dropped Leila off at her apartment in Ain El Mraisseh, behind the mosque that overlooked the Corniche. I watched her from the taxi as she clicked across the footpath in her high heels towards the lit-up rectangle that marked out the foyer to her apartment block. Living in Beirut was like living with a lover who suffers from bipolar disorder, I thought as I watched her open the door and disappear inside. There were good times, but you couldn't ever truly forget about the bad, or shake the uneasy feeling that they might return.

The taxi swished past the barricades that still sealed off the grisly site where Hariri had been assassinated, and through the tunnel that swept from west to east Beirut. We were about halfway along when I heard the thump of drums and tambourines. There was a crowd of people standing in the middle of the road in the middle of the tunnel. The taxi driver slowed the car; both of us were suspicious. What new insanity was up ahead?

We came closer and I could hear shouting and dancing and saw that people were throwing flowers at the passing cars. The crowd was laughing and milling around a group of five or six cars parked at odd angles in the fluorescent glow of the tunnel.

In the heart of it all, a bride and groom danced, exhilarated. I wanted to shout out loud with the relief of it and the thrill of such joyful madness. I sank back into the taxi's leather seats, smiling. It felt good to witness such defiant happiness; to see Beirut so alive.

CHAPTER 21
BELONGING, LEAVING

Summer was slow to arrive that year, but one Sunday not long after the car bomb I woke to blue sky and the cool winds gone and the air like hot breath on my skin. It felt like a liberation. Beirut was its best in early summer and the entire city hummed with the thrill of the approaching day.

We didn't yet have plans to leave Lebanon but maybe I knew, deep down, that it was to be our last summer. I had an urge to savour every moment. I got up early that morning and sat on the balcony with my bare feet resting on the railing and let the sun tan my toes. I ate pistachio nuts and drank coffee and mused about what to do with myself. A little pile of nutshells gathered on the table next to me and I was absently stacking them one inside the other when the telephone rang. It was Nabil.

'We're going for a picnic in my village. A group of friends is coming, some with babies. You'll enjoy it,' he said, enthusiastic. 'I'll pick you up in an hour.'

'Will that be Lebanese time or Western time?'

I borrowed the joke from a Lebanese friend who had married an American and constantly tussled with him over the meaning of punctuality. It turned out to be Lebanese time. Nabil was almost two hours late when he arrived in a borrowed car. 'There's no way my car would make it as far as my village,' he said.

Nabil had never lived in the village, which was tucked into the rolling hilly country behind Sidon, except for a short stint to escape fighting in Beirut during the war. But it was the place his ancestors came from and his grandfather still lived there and for that reason he called it 'my village'. It was typical of the Lebanese to keep one eye on the past. Lebanon was divided into different regions, each with their own character and religious connections, and so the link to village was a mark of identity as much as anything else. Village life was still the old-fashioned Lebanese life: local specialties like homemade *arak* and olive oil, fruit trees in the back garden, tea made from dried flowers, the smell of bread being baked the traditional way. At first I had admired the sentimentality, the strong sense of heritage and belonging. But after a while I grew tired of the constant harping about this golden perfect past, and it began to feel stifling rather than romantic. I saw the bind to heritage as just another way the Lebanese had come up with to categorise themselves.

Nabil drove Matthew, Yasmine and me back to Sin El Fil and we bought *mana'oushi* from the nearby bakery where Nabil had seen the Lebanese Forces fighter gunned down during the war. I felt callous for my criticisms. The past was here, too, I thought. It was impossible to escape it. We ate our snack and washed it down with espresso and then hung around in the street and waited for the group to gather.

The plan was to take three cars and drive to the village in convoy so Nabil could guide everyone through the web of back roads. We shared the car with Nabil's friends Maryam and Elie and their baby daughter, who was a few months younger than Yasmine, and somehow we all squashed in together. The route took us up into the mountains, and after a while the landscape opened up; the clutter of shops and car workshops that lined the road further down the mountain were gone and I could look out across worn dome-shaped hills that sank into shallow valleys. After we had been driving like that for about 30 minutes Nabil pointed out his village, clustered on the crest of a hill opposite.

We descended into a final dip, past groves of olive and fruit trees, and climbed that final hill, at last entering the village's narrow streets and alleys. Everything was pale, bleached. The streets were empty and silent except for the hum of insects. An old church made from weather-worn stone stood on a small rise to one side of the main street. Nabil directed Elie straight on, past the church, past his grandfather's house – painted white with a flat roof and roses growing along the fence – and then we veered left and descended down a steep, winding and broken track.

'Don't worry!' Nabil was laughing at our gasps as we seemed to plunge into the gully below. 'I know this road like the back of my hand because I usually travel down here at night. We come at four in the morning to hunt boar.'

We found a picnic site on a flat area of grassy land down by the river. Hills surrounded us and the silhouette of the village was just visible above us on one side. It was like being inside a crucible – the warmth of the sun and the chirp of birds and insects and the smells of the countryside were all concentrated in that hollow. Every sense was arrested, heightened. These simple things, tossed together, forged something magical, as if an alchemist had conducted the day.

When we were settled, I left Yasmine and Matthew

lounging on the grass and drove with Nabil back up the track to the village to borrow a saucepan from his grandfather. We wanted to use it to deep-fry some potato wedges. But it turned out that his grandfather had gone out for the day and so we went next door and asked for one from a neighbour. We walked in on a big family lunch to welcome a sister, a daughter, home from America.

One of the family, Miled, asked me inside as soon as he saw I was a foreigner. It was a kind of Middle Eastern default position: always offer hospitality to a stranger. I was curious, the lunch looked wonderful. The family was crowded around a large table that swayed slightly under the weight of dozens of dishes. A huge golden retriever lolled at their feet and you could feel the happiness in the air. But we had our own lunch to prepare and I declined the offer, again and again as is customary, until Miled accepted my refusal. Nabil and I took the saucepan and went back to our picnic site.

When we got back Nabil and several of his friends left to go hunting, promising to return with food for lunch. It was really just bravado. We had brought with us more food than could possibly be consumed and as the men left for their hunting trip, the women gathered to prepare lunch. Elie stayed behind to make a fire in a metal trough, a sort of portable barbeque. He collected kindling and lumps of fallen wood and let the fire burn low until the trough was filled with a carpet of silver ash and lumps of glowing embers.

Maryam had brought bags of lamb and chicken, marinated and cut into cubes for kebabs. There were discs of flat bread, and potatoes that we sliced thickly to make the wedges and fried in oil heated over a small gas burner. Someone else had brought a whole fish that we laid on a latticed griddle over the coals.

Elie took an armful of wooden skewers down to the river

and rested them in its cool wash, soaking the wood so it wouldn't catch fire on the barbeque, before bringing them back for us to use to thread through chunks of meat.

We poured salt and olive oil over the lamb cubes, rubbed it into the flesh. Then we began skewering the lumps of meat. We kept one piece of fat aside for each skewer, and turned them into kebabs. We used thin, round skewers for the lamb and flat ones, about a centimetre wide, for the chicken. After five or six pieces of meat had been speared, we squeezed the lot together so the meat held firm against the stick.

The marinade covered our palms and oozed between our fingers and we grimaced little faces at each other, shook the excess onto the grass. We worked silently, happily, the sun warm on our backs and our minds relieved to be free of the city. We laid each completed kebab inside the plastic bags: one for lamb, one for the chicken with garlic and paprika marinade. We took turns cleaning our hands with water that Elie brought from the river, and then carried the bags over to the barbeque.

After a while we heard voices. 'Where's Nabil?' The men were back from an unsuccessful hunting trip but Nabil was not among them. 'I don't know. Hey! Where's Nabil?' The question ricocheted back and forth.

'He's still out there,' one of his friends replied. And then, teasing gently, 'He says he is not coming back until he gets a boar.'

A short time later, I saw Nabil's smooth brown head bobbing above the tall mountain grasses; he was moving easily, not like someone dragging the carcass of a wild pig. As he came into view I saw that although there was no boar, he had not returned empty-handed. Three small birds hung limply from his left hand. He was proud and told me I could be in on the kill; he had reserved one of his little birds for me to eat for lunch. I told him I was revolted. 'God knows what parasites they are carrying,' I said. But he ignored me, good-naturedly, and turned to his audience, bathing in his moment. He posed for pictures with his three dead birds. He swung the gun down from his shoulder and held it by his side like a walking stick, one leg forward, knee bent, hips at an angle. With the other arm he held the birds aloft in some sort of victory stance and smiled as the camera clicked.

The little birds were plucked and skewered together on a stick, all three, arse to beak. They were laid beside the kebabs, where they sizzled and spat from the heat of the coals and shrank into little spiky, blackened shapes.

While the food was cooking we set up a camp. We laid blankets and sheets under some trees and between lumps of rock that we used for backrests. Matthew took Yasmine down to the river and I heard her squeals of delight as the water rushed over her bare feet. He threw flowers into the cascade and she laughed and pointed as they disappeared downstream. When they returned I dried her little feet with a towel and she sat in my arms as we rolled the barbequed kebabs between pieces of soft flat bread and peeled the flaking white flesh of the fish from the bone, and ate sprawled under the trees, sharing cups of *arak* and home-made lemonade, basking in the tender warmth of the day.

After lunch everyone urged me to try shooting. I felt morally opposed, somehow. At first I thought it was just a stupid Western middle-class position, but perhaps I was fearful of being corrupted. With bombs going off around Beirut and Nabil and his friends ready to fire in defence as they patrolled their patch each night, I couldn't manage to make the switch in my mind between guns as playthings and guns as weapons. We reached a compromise. Maryam and some of the other women were shooting at bottles on a rock and I decided to give that a go. Nabil offered me his rifle, the one he used to kill the birds. It was his pride and joy. He said it exactly like that: 'You know Catherine, this gun is my pride and joy', and he patted the barrel, smiling half at me and half to himself.

Matthew grabbed Yasmine and took her safely away and amused her with wild flowers and a collection of smooth river rocks while Nabil explained the basics of how to line up a shot. It was my first ever time shooting a gun of any kind and I saw it was fairly easy to find the right aim. But the gun was heavy and I had to fit the butt firmly into the flesh beneath my shoulder, just above my armpit, to stop it jumping backwards and injuring me when I pulled the trigger. As I bent to synchronise my eye with the target I could see the muzzle waver slightly and the angles seemed all wrong and I couldn't seem to balance it and stop it moving.

Everyone was waiting. In the end I just took a breath, held it, fired; and as I did I closed my eyes against the roar of the blast. When I opened them a fraction of a second later I saw fragments of green glass flying through the air. I was a crack shot!

Oh how quickly my ethical angst dissolved. I was addicted. It was like being at a fairground. I shot at bottles, at plastic cups, I was unstoppable. I didn't want to share the gun. Nabil joked: 'Now you can get a job in the Lebanese Forces.'

After the welcome-home lunch, when his family had fallen asleep, Miled walked down to the river to join us. He was in his mid-fifties with a pleasantly worn face and tired eyes that had seen too much. He smoked as we talked, and explained that he lived most of the year in Russia and worked at a casino in Moscow. His wife was Russian. They had a son. He liked to come back to Lebanon during the summer. He missed Russia but he also missed Lebanon. It was a hard thing, finding a place to belong, he said. But in Lebanon work was difficult to find, there were memories and not all of them were good. He let the statement hang, waiting for me to follow it.

We talked about 'the situation'.

'There will not be another civil war,' he said confidently. 'We know what war is.' He flicked roughly at the ash of his cigarette and looked at the ground. 'Anyway, who will give us money this time? It's not like before. There's no one from outside to give us money.'

I wondered if he was right. The line-up of foreign forces willing to interfere in Lebanon's civil war all those years ago was still more or less hovering on the sidelines. Iran and Syria were still supporting their interests inside Lebanon via Hezbollah; Israel could guarantee US support to do whatever it wanted or needed to do in Lebanon; the Palestinian leadership may have left Lebanon but hundreds of thousands of refugees still lived here, angry and poor – the most radicalising of combinations; the Lebanese diaspora had influence that stretched from France to Canada, the US and Australia via Brazil and Africa. I wasn't so sure. It seemed to me that Lebanon still had plenty of outside forces more than willing to get involved again. The only question was whether the Lebanese would turn against each other.

Miled asked where I lived. I told him Achrafieh, just to the east of the old Green Line. 'We have just moved there from Clemenceau in the west,' I added, because I didn't want to be classified as favouring one side or another.

'I know it well,' he said, still looking at the ground. 'I used to fight there during the war.' He took another drag of his cigarette and raised his eyebrows. He looked sheepish, and

I realised he thought I was judging him after all we'd said about the futility of war. 'At that time we believed in what we were doing,' he said after a while. 'We could see no other way. But what has it brought us?'

I mumbled something about learning to live together. And as he walked off I saw that he had a limp.

The warm afternoon was soporific but I didn't want to sleep the day away. I suggested we drive back to Beirut via Lady Hester Stanhope's villa in the little village of Joun, not far from Sidon. It was a bit of a detour but the days were getting longer and I wasn't ready for this day to end – and anyway, I'd been dying to go there for months.

Lady Hester was born in 1776 in Kent, in the pretty English countryside. She was the favourite daughter of a wealthy and eccentric family: her father was Lord Charles, Third Earl of Stanhope, and her uncle, William Pitt, became prime minister of Britain.

Her life could have continued like this: privileged, cloistered, unremarkable except for its status. But at 27 she was orphaned and penniless: her passionate but irresponsible father had given away his fortune to French revolutionaries. She had no husband to save her.

Her uncle invited her to Downing Street and she created a role for herself as his social and political hostess. She was very good at it and became known for her wit and gregarious conversation. When Pitt died in 1806 Lady Hester was 30. Despite her string of admirers she had never married and without the lure of her uncle's status she was not such an attractive match. Lady Hester found herself alone once again. She'd lost her influence, her money, and she had no family.

Instead of settling, defeated, into unmarried middle age, she fled London in search of adventure.

She travelled with her cousin to Constantinople, and when he returned to England she continued east. Her boat was shipwrecked off the Greek island of Rhodes and she lost everything. In that moment, it seems, something overtook her. She shed her role as an aristocratic Englishwoman and began to wear a bizarre mix of men's clothes, often being mistaken for a Turkish boy. She travelled through Egypt, Palestine, Syria (where she was the first foreign woman to enter the ruined Roman city of Palmyra) and lived in several homes across Lebanon. Eventually she built a 36-room villa at Joun and spent a fortune growing and maintaining a large and beautiful garden around it. She hosted emirs and sheikhs and became well known.

Lady Hester's eccentric and extravagant ways became more eccentric and more extravagant. She studied alchemy and astrology; hired Albanians to guard her compound and staffed it with African slaves, who she treated badly. She paid a local chieftain to start a private war against the murderers of a French consul she had liked. She maintained a camel caravan, which she used to transport water to the villa from her favourite spring. Her debts grew, her enemies grew, her friends disappeared. She walled herself inside her home, dismissed her servants – who took whatever furniture was left in her house in lieu of a wage – and died, aged 63, alone and penniless, tragic. It was 1839.

We made our way from Nabil's village back to the coast road before turning right and climbing back into the mountains towards Joun.

The road was narrow. On both sides were plantations of corn, bananas, oranges. Bamboo and palm trees bent in the breeze. After about half an hour there was still no sign of the villa and I began to worry we'd made a wrong turn.

A little way further on we spotted a man walking in the garden of a large house and we stopped him to ask for directions. 'I know the place,' he said. 'I used to go there all the time when I was a kid. But do you know it's ruined? There's nothing there to see now.' He waved dismissively as if the matter had been settled.

Matthew placated him. 'It's my wife's idea. She really wants to go there.' The conversation was being carried to me on the breeze and I smiled brightly from the car window in response. The man in the garden was spurred by my enthusiasm and after explaining the route he began to tell us about the site. 'It's in two parts,' he said, spreading his hands out in front of him, creating the borders of an imaginary map in the air. 'You can see her tomb but you have to walk about 50 metres from the buildings, out this way.' He moved one hand in a straight line out to the right.

We thanked him and continued, through the centre of Joun and onwards, higher, and we could look down on bare hills and unfinished houses. The sides of the road were busy with picnicking families enjoying the cool, clean mountain air. A group of young men had set up a *nargileh* bar on the side of the road, in the middle of a little group of trees. The stereo of their car was turned up to provide music. They had no customers but they were pacing around, smiling, entrepreneurial, and tried to wave us over as we drove past.

We stopped at a police station to ask for more directions. There was a television sitting in the centre of the reception desk. A bed, recently slept in, was to the right. It was clear not much crime happened here. When the policeman turned up he was still pulling on his uniform over a pair of rumpled shorts. He offered to accompany us to the ruins.

The remains of the home were on the crest of a nearby hill, he said. We passed through a valley filled with olive and fruit trees, and as we climbed out of the valley what was left of the compound appeared quite suddenly in front of us. 'Congratulations!' I yelled in Arabic, to whoever, as much in relief as celebration. The policeman laughed and I was opening the door before the car had even come to a stop.

In front of us was a high smooth wall made from blocks of honey-coloured stone. I remembered that towards the end of her life Lady Hester had walled herself inside her compound; this must be what was left of it. Yet the man from the garden was right. The place was in ruins. I had read that most of the damage had occurred during an earthquake that hit the area in 1956. Before that many of the rooms were still somewhat intact, although decrepit. It was impossible now, without an expert guide, to understand how the house had been laid out and there'd been no attempt to save what was left.

I stepped through the remains of a doorway and into what might once have been a reception room, now choked with fallen stone and weeds and saplings trying to survive in the rock crevices. I climbed over the debris and out a window on the other side. I was feeling somehow reverent. I wondered which room was Lady Hester's bedroom, the spot she had died, so alone and defeated.

I sat down on a piece of fallen stone, and looked out at what were once the grounds of the house. The remains of the gardens sprawled across a large flat area, maybe the size of a football field, and were now wildly overgrown. But you could still see, dotted here and there, coloured flowers that I assumed were once tended and contained into the famous gardens. The area dropped away quite suddenly, melting into hills and mountains. In the distance was the sea.

I walked the perimeter of the house, stumbling through overgrowth. Beneath were the remains of catacombs, arches once used to store food or livestock, now dank tunnels covered in moss.

I headed away from the house to try to find her tomb. Her body had been exhumed years ago and reburied in the grounds of the British Embassy's summer house. Just the previous year, when the Embassy was planning to sell its summer residence, her bones had been cremated and her ashes scattered over the site of her former home, this place. The walking was difficult – the grasses and weeds were shoulder-high in places and the ground was uneven. I lost my enthusiasm; what would I find anyway? A piece of broken marble lying over a hole? With her remains cremated and scattered, there was no point maintaining a gravesite, and so the tangible evidence of Lady Hester's many years in Lebanon were slowly fading to nothingness. When the old villa finally crumbled to dust what would remain to show that she had been there at all?

As I stood watching that view of mountains, sea and sky, it wasn't at all hard to understand why Lady Hester had fallen in love with Lebanon. I, too, loved this ancient, battle-worn country, with its passionate and friendly people, its beautiful scenery. We had been in Beirut for more than four years and in that time we had watched the city bloom again.

Lebanon had taken me on a journey, too. One day not long before, I had been searching for something in the back of a cupboard when I pulled out a wicker basket filled with odds and ends. Inside was a metal bullet casing that I'd picked up from Kirkuk in Iraq on the day it was abandoned by the Iraqi army. Beside it was a rubber bullet – a sphere of metal the size of a marble, covered in black plastic – that I'd found three years earlier in Ramallah during one of the Friday confrontations between the Palestinians and IDF. Lying next to the bullets was a pacifier with a little bunny on the front that I'd bought for Yasmine when she was tiny, and the hospital bracelet she'd worn on her wrist after she was born. This odd collection seemed to define my Lebanese journey. Did having a child mean that things had changed? The recent months had brought the fear of random violence closer and closer. Although I had been trying to ignore it, questions were beginning to gnaw at the back of my mind. Was it still safe to stay?

As the afternoon closed in I had an overwhelming feeling of coming to the end of something. I felt the pull of Australia, of family, of the safe and comfortable fit of home. I could hear Matthew and Yasmine playing in the shade on the other side of the garden and I felt an urge to be close to them. They called out to me and we found the others and walked together back to the car. The engine kicked into gear and as we began the drive back to Beirut I knew that it was the beginning of my journey home.

PART THREE

CHAPTER 21
RETURNING

We left Beirut later that summer, amid whirling uncertainty. On my last night Leila, Ramzi and I went for sushi at our favourite place in Achrafieh and afterwards we drove downtown and had coffee and dessert at an outdoor café. There were demonstrations in the city that night, and a large group of young men – many from the Amal movement – were riding around Beirut in cars and on motorbikes in a show of solidarity with Syria. The security services were nervous – would support spill over into attacks on Christian suburbs? The roads that led into Achrafieh from the west and from the area around Martyrs' Square were being guarded by the Lebanese Army in tanks and military trucks. When Yasmine and I boarded the plane to Australia the next morning – Matthew had left a month earlier for work in Sydney – I felt that maybe we were leaving Beirut just in time.

During the year that followed, life in Sydney fell into a familiar and comforting routine: trips to the beach, barbeques and visiting grandparents. I fell pregnant again and when

Joseph was born our expanded family brought profound joy. Matthew and I sold our apartment and bought a new house big enough for our little family; we spent weekends at the hardware store and collected lemons and mulberries from the trees in our new garden. The space and environment of Sydney and the closeness of family were what had been missing in Beirut, and the connection to land and people brought a deep and unquestioned sense of belonging. I often hankered after the adventure of my old life – I missed it hugely – but I felt certain that our decision to return to Australia had been the right one.

And so that first year home passed quickly. It felt as if a lot of things had changed, but the news from the Middle East stayed the same. The crescendo of hope that had accompanied the Cedar Revolution continued to fade; sectarianism and political divisions grew.

Apart from the regular horrors in Baghdad and the endless tragedy of the Palestinians (now they were at war with each other), every few months we'd hear that another leading Lebanese anti-Syrian figure had been assassinated and Damascus remained the prime suspect. But it wasn't just Syria that was causing havoc in Lebanon. The political flux had brought all the old names back in control of Lebanese politics and it was easy to be suspicious.

When war broke out between Hezbollah and Israel on 12 July 2006, the feeling of reliving the past was overwhelming. Israel bombing Beirut evoked the horror of 1982. I emailed friends in Lebanon to see how they were. Every morning my inbox was full of heartbroken replies, forwarded emails suggesting news reports or blogs to read, or messages from lobby groups collecting money and other things.

Dear Catherine, Talk is of a ground invasion. My initial shock has turned to frustration and anger – why this and why now and why the civilians??? Every day I say to myself that we are lucky to be safe.

Catherine, A recent poll in one of the papers says that some 50% of the 20–40 yrs age respondents don't believe their futures lie in Lebanon. That says it all!

Dear Catherine, Basically, from your old flat in Clemenceau you would have heard it all and also felt it. Take the Hariri explosion and multiply it tens of times on a daily basis.

Dear Catherine, My parents and I came up here to our village in the mountains three days after the bombing started and we are, thankfully, safe here so far. The situation is terrible and heartbreaking. This country was just beginning to get back on its feet and now Israel has destroyed everything. It will take decades for us to recover and I don't know if we have it in us to start all over again.

Catherine, The situation is just so fucked. Everyone is being very stoic about it, even though the fear, dread and sadness is all too clear as our beloved country and city are blown apart before our eyes.

Catherine, At first we were angry when Hezbollah announced the abductions of the Israeli soldiers. We realised they were taking us down a dangerous path. But when the Israeli Defence Forces (what a misnomer) began their onslaught and their strategy of collective punishment, I think the Lebanese became united against a common outside aggressor. The resentment against Nasrallah is still there for doing this to us and for not being transparent in his allegiances. Maybe I am wrong, but I think there will come a day of reckoning.

Catherine, I listen to the Voice of Lebanon, the same station we used to listen to all the time during the war. Their 'flash news' music is permanently seared into our memories. Now, as before, between each news flash they play Fairouz. It's just so heart-breaking.

I knew I had to go back.

Matthew came home one night with a plane ticket in his hand. 'I'll look after the babies,' he said as he passed it to me. 'This is something you should do.'

There were dark patches of freshly laid asphalt on the runway at Beirut airport that covered up the places where bombs had fallen. Inside the terminal it was still pure Beirut: advertisements for expensive jewellery stores, a billboard with the face of some Lebanese pop star promoting an album, details of the upcoming Beirut Marathon. Outside was the same too: a jam of jostling taxis and cuddling families.

I would be staying with Kate, another American photographer friend. Kate had kindly dispatched her favourite driver to pick me up at the airport. Atef held up a sign with my name on it and we pushed through the crowds to his waiting car. It was almost the end of October, time for the weather to change, but the sun was out that day and it was hot. 'The sun is shining because you have returned to Lebanon,' said Atef in that quixotic way the Lebanese have, as he loaded my bags into the boot of his car. Despite everything it felt good to be back.

I was hungry for evidence of the 34-Day War, as the summer's brutal conflict had become known. As we rode towards Kate's place in Achrafieh the diamond advertisements and the pop stars disappeared and were replaced by giant pictures of Hezbollah's leader, Hassan Nasrallah. On one building, photographs of crowds at a Hezbollah rally had been stuck up on all four sides, forming a huge cube celebrating the Islamic Resistance. Posters proclaiming a Divine Victory against Israel flew from lamp posts along the new highway from the airport.

I had met Kate three years earlier in Iraq. She had covered wars and horror relentlessly for eight years – war in Afghanistan, earthquakes in Pakistan, war in Iraq – but for the past year or so, Beirut, despite all its uncertainty, had provided a kind of stability, a pleasant base to return to. But now war had followed her here too.

'How did it compare?' I asked as we sat in her kitchen a short time later while I drank cup after cup of coffee to ward off jetlag.

Kate had always been more daring than me, bold enough to sit in trenches with Kurdish fighters while bullets and grenades exploded around her; making trips with US soldiers into the wild and dangerous Afghan countryside, where she had recently survived the explosion of an IED (improvised exploding device) that targeted the convoy she was travelling with. She was in the thick of it in Lebanon too. Her heartbreaking photographs of dead children and destroyed villages, and the story of her friendship with a distraught Shi'ite family who had lost a child in the bombing, proved that. She had returned many evenings to this apartment and lain in bed listening to the missiles hit Beirut's southern suburbs.

'At night the bombs were two or three miles away but it

felt as if they were right next to you,' she said. 'It was pretty bad. It seemed worse than others somehow.' She wrinkled her brow in thought. 'I don't know, I guess it was more emotional for me this time. With the other wars I was visiting, I could leave; but Beirut is my home.'

The next morning I woke early and sat on the deep covered balcony overlooking the street and wrote notes to myself. The road outside was still and almost silent. The warmth of the day before had disappeared and rain fell softly from a low grey sky. Even so, the air was pleasantly warm and I could sit there with my bare feet cooled by the tiles and the green tropical lushness of potted plants all around.

After breakfast Kate and Atef and I drove south to Bint Jbeil, a village close to the Israeli border in the far south of Lebanon. It was the heartland of Hezbollistan, as the cynical liked to call this region, and had suffered some of the worst and most sustained attacks during the summer's short and furious war. I wanted to see for myself the damage that had been wreaked on beloved Lebanon. Central Beirut had been virtually untouched by bombing, but as we left the city that morning and travelled the road to Sidon, it became clear that all was not as before. Bombed and burned buildings began to appear, and as we went further I saw how bombs had torn up the road itself, or destroyed bridges and flyovers. In some places makeshift repairs had begun, but in others we were forced to turn off the highway and negotiate the narrow and often winding side roads.

As we drew closer to Sidon the signs to the beach clubs that had offered resort-style luxury and glamour began to appear – Bamboo Bay, then Ô Cap, La Voile Bleu – little familiar things that made you think all was as before and mocked the reality. The story went that one of the newest and most luxurious clubs had suffered US$10 million in damaged infrastructure and lost business. Missiles had hit oil storage facilities along the coastline and an environmental disaster was in train; filthy leaking oil still clung to the rocks here and there, but most of it had sunk to the bottom, suffocating fish and sea life up and down the coast.

There were banners attached to electricity poles and street lamps promoting Hezbollah. 'Our soldiers are working to get you back to your villages with your head held high' they read. But the political reality of the war was also clear. Hezbollah had its posters, but the unofficial lookouts that used to be scattered around Lebanon's south were gone, replaced by UN tanks and Lebanese Army checkpoints. This was the agreement brokered in the peace deal: the Lebanese Army and UN would be deployed along the Lebanese–Israeli border and Hezbollah was required to leave. It was hard to work out what was going on below the neat surface of UN resolutions and handshakes between important international figures. The fact was that the villages of southern Lebanon were almost all Shi'ite villages and most residents were fervent supporters of Hezbollah. It was ridiculous to assume that the organisation no longer had a presence there.

And people were still dying every day from war-related accidents. Kate sat beside me with a pile of the previous week's editions of the *Daily Star* newspaper on her lap, catching up on reading.

'A young mother and her one-year-old baby son were killed on Saturday as their car plunged off a badly damaged bridge in the Bekaa Valley. The bridge . . . was targeted in an Israeli air strike during the summer's 34-day war,' she read aloud.

There were also deaths from unexploded ordinance, especially cluster bombs that lay around in paddocks, deadly, waiting, then ripped off the limbs of children who were attracted to their bright colour.

'It says here that Israel used phosphorus bombs,' Kate said and she leaned across the back seat towards me and pointed to a photograph showing a woman in a hospital bed with strange blood-black spots of various sizes all over her skin. 'They can't work out what else could have made these burns.'

There was a lot of debate about the use of white phosphorus in bombs and whether it was legal or illegal because of the horrible injuries it inflicted.

As we entered Tyre, the seaside town where I had once wandered entranced through the remains of an elegant Roman city built right out to the very edge of the coastline, Kate pointed to a plot of churned earth by the side of the road. 'That's a mass grave,' she said, and explained that dozens of the bodies of those killed in air strikes had been buried there in a rush when the morgue could no longer cope. A little further on I saw a man carving gravestones, chipping away details of lives lost onto pieces of flat grey rock, and on several he had added the Hezbollah symbol. I supposed they were to mark the graves of dead fighters.

We turned into the mountains and began the climb inland to Bint Jbeil. My ears popped. Evidence of conflict was everywhere: the blackened shells of cars, blackened buildings, tents set up by the UN High Commission for Refugees to house the displaced, pathetically old-fashioned Lebanese Army tanks lined up by the side of the road. As we entered Bint Jbeil, which had been home to about 20,000, the true scale of what had gone on was laid out before me.

The centre of the village was completely destroyed in

parts and the white stone of the houses formed a carpet of rubble, flattened, ruined. In the main square shops were operating and people were standing about in the ruins, trying to carry on as normal, but you could see the confusion on their faces. It was weeks since the town had been the focus of some of the war's most intense battles but in places the stench of corpses was still overpowering. I felt my nostrils flare as we passed and I cast a questioning look at Kate. 'Bodies,' she nodded, certain because she had smelled it so many times before.

We drove up to the hospital and I found a surgeon standing outside, with a tired face and worn hands and a cigarette in his mouth. Abdullah Jouni was born in Bint Jbeil and grew up there but had long ago moved to Beirut. He came back during the war to find his mother and his sister and got pulled in to work at the local hospital. The staff were overwhelmed by the injured and the dying and they needed him.

'The nights here were terrible,' he said, and chain-smoked another cigarette. 'There was no water, no light, no phone. People were hiding in their homes and hoping they would be safe. On the nights we had no bombing the only sound you could hear was of cats and dogs eating the dead. It was like living on another planet.'

Abdullah shook his head and gave a long and tired sigh. 'We received nothing from the Lebanese government. The people here are Lebanese! They are human. But someone did bring food and water. We found it out the back of our houses in the morning.' He didn't say it but I caught his meaning. It was Hezbollah.

Kate, Atef and I drove back to Tyre and found a place to eat. We shared plates of fattoush, hommous and grilled rings of calamari. I washed it down with a sweet orange soda and we joked ruefully about how wonderful Tyre would be in peacetime as a destination for foreign tourists, with its warm climate, great food, spectacular Roman ruins and pretty coastline. I gazed out of the restaurant's huge tinted plate-glass windows. The sun had almost set. Palm trees laden with unripe dates – bunches of bright yellow and orange – swayed in the early evening breeze and the Mediterranean Sea lapped gently at the sandy shore behind them.

The 34-Day War did something else to Lebanon that summer that was perhaps more terrible than the psychological and physical damage wreaked by US-funded Israeli missiles: it exposed and entrenched a political and ideological split inside the country.

The division had always existed, but since the end of the civil war in 1990 it had lacked an issue to rally around, and for the entire time I had lived in Lebanon it was fairly easy to pretend that the Lebanese were forging ahead on the same path. Old hatreds and rivalries were in the background, discussed only quietly. But the months after Hariri's assassination, and the elections that followed, had created two starkly opposed political alliances in Lebanon. One they called the March 14 Coalition, a group of political parties that supported the ideas of 14 March 2005, when one million people had rallied in the street to demand Syria leave Lebanon. The Opposition was the pro-Syrian groups who had mobilised their own half a million supporters. The situation pitted Aoun, Hezbollah and Amal against Hariri's son and political heir, Saad, Jumblatt and Geagea.

The situation was already tense before the summer war. But after the war, it was as if a centrifuge had been spun:

emotions towards Hezbollah became more and more polarised. There were those who hailed the group as heroes, victorious against the mighty IDF; deserving of a larger political voice; the only honest politicians in the Lebanese parliament; the only group capable of protecting Lebanon against Israeli 'aggressions' (as they called Israel's occupation of Syrian and Lebanese land, its overflights, attacks); the only political group who really looked after its people. Then there were those opposed, who believed that Hezbollah's agenda had more to do with the interests of Lebanon's Shi'ites, Iran and Syria than those of Lebanon itself – and had been the catalyst for the Israeli invasion. They believed Hezbollah must adhere to the UN Resolution 1559, which called on it (and all other militias in Lebanon) to disarm. It was time for Hezbollah to give up its weapons, to become a normal political party, they said.

These two views had exposed a large and maybe unbridgeable gulf between the Lebanese.

I had been calling Nabil, but his telephone was switched off. 'I am away!' he told me when at last I managed to get through to him.

It seemed that the summer war (and a new love with whom he really saw a future) had mellowed Nabil from the gun-toting vigilante he had been a year earlier. 'Well, the situation here is basically going from worse to worst,' he said. 'Everyone is trying to make the best of things before all hell breaks loose, and unless some miraculous solution presents itself, it's pretty much 1975 all over again.'

He was silent for a few moments and I heard the click of a cigarette lighter and a crackle as the end of the cigarette caught alight.

'I am seriously considering leaving the country for good,' he continued. 'I have lost faith in all politicians because I am starting to feel that the Lebanese people are pawns in a giant chess game that officials and politicians enjoy playing after having a very expensive lunch together and exchanging pleasantries at the expense of the Lebanese people.'

I was looking forward to catching up with Amir, my old landlord. There had been almost total silence between us since I'd left Beirut, which I blamed on Amir's rejection of email and the internet. 'Send me a letter from Australia,' he had said before I left. 'I love receiving mail.' I understood the sentiment but, really, I never had time for paper and envelopes, stamps and trips to the post office!

I found a group of Syrian workmen in one of Amir's old houses and one of them telephoned Amir. 'Someone is looking for you,' he said. A few minutes later Amir was there in front of me. There was a moment of hesitation as he registered my features and absorbed the fact of my surprise appearance. 'Oh my!' he exclaimed and we embraced, laughing, delighted to see each other again. He looked well. His hair was longer and it suited him.

'What are you doing?' I asked, and swept my hand to take in the room around us, its walls stripped of plaster and paint, the faux ceiling that had contained a small but cumbersome mezzanine level gone.

'I'm renovating,' he said, stating the obvious. 'I'm going to fix up the place and rent it.'

It would be magnificent when it was completed. The centrepiece of the house was two huge formal rooms, with massively high ceilings and decorated floor tiles, which would be stunning when brought back to their original grandeur. They opened to a marble staircase that led down to a small entrance courtyard protected behind a high, vine-covered wrought iron gate.

Amir led me into the kitchen and opened a box of Arabic sweets, like Turkish baklava only better, subtle and more sophisticated, full of chunks of cashew and pistachio stuck together with flower-scented syrup and encased in layers of flaky pastry. He made Arabic coffee and placed the lot on a small tray – the sweets, silver coffee pot, cups – and carried it into the garden, and we sat together and began to talk about the war.

'It was terrible,' he said, and laughed regretfully. 'You wouldn't believe how loud the bombing was. You panic in your bed. There was very, very little water, food was scarce. The worst thing was that we had no petrol. You would wait in line for hours and then they would give only a small amount. I used to go at 3 a.m. and pay more so I did not have to wait.'

We sipped our coffee, nibbled our sweets.

'The thing was that we didn't know how long it would last. It was really a trauma, I can tell you. In the morning you wake up and the dust was all over you from the bombs during the night. The smell! Everyone left. Everyone!'

'Why did you stay? I thought you would escape into the mountains,' I said. Amir's family owned a beautiful home in the mountains not far from Bikfaya, an area that had been shielded from the worst of the conflict.

'I had to look after the property,' he said and nodded towards the two old houses and the apartment blocks.

The bombing in the south of Lebanon and Beirut's southern suburbs had displaced up to one million people – a quarter of Lebanon's population – and while some of them were dual citizens of other countries and eligible for evacuation, and others were able to stay with family and friends or rent places somewhere safer, many families had nowhere to go. They were housed in underground car parks, mosques, churches, parks and school halls. Others squatted in abandoned properties, and Amir was worried his apartments and two old houses would be taken over as many others in the area had been. The civil war had taught the Lebanese to be wary of such things. Some squatters came and then never left and there were few legal avenues to combat it.

Instead Amir invited the kids of refugee families into his garden to play. 'Some of them had never even seen a garden,' he said, and shook his head with pity. 'There was a lot of compassion.'

Amir went inside and returned a few minutes later with a newspaper. I remembered how, 18 months earlier, we had sat in that same garden and he had shown me the images of Hariri's assassination. Today the image was not of splayed bodies and a blackened crater; it was of great canyons of rubble strewn with household things – bits of furniture, photographs, books, a child's teddy bear. This was what remained of a swathe of the Dahiyeh, Beirut's southern suburbs, which had been targeted heavily in missile strikes because the area was packed with Hezbollah supporters, offices, infrastructure and secret stores of weapons. The damage was horrific, and even though the strikes had been targeting Hezbollah it was impossible that innocent people had escaped suffering.

It was early afternoon. Amir had his renovations to oversee and we kissed goodbye and I wandered out on to Rue d'Amerique and called Atef. 'Can you take me to the Dahiyeh?' I asked him. 'Of course, *habibte*,' he said. 'Where do I pick you up?'

I knew the Dahiyeh quite well because over the years I'd gone there repeatedly: to meet with Hussein Naboulsi, Hezbollah's foreign media manager; to visit Hezbollah's Martyrs' Association, Hezbollah-run schools, Hezbollah's Al-Manar satellite-television network, the Hezbollah martyrs' wives, Hezbollah MPs and the Palestinian camps.

As Atef drove me into the area we passed shops selling electricity generators or cheap furniture – sofas and mattresses piled up on the footpath. The roads grew narrower and the concrete buildings that lined them higher. The streets were busy, just as I remembered, but as we drove deeper into the area razed spaces where buildings had once stood began to appear. In other places buildings were half-standing, the concrete-slab floors lying together like slices of bread, or you could see what fire had left, charred interiors, fingers of soot striped on the buildings' façades.

I was struggling to get my bearings. 'Do you know where we can find Al-Manar?' I asked Atef. I knew the streets around the television station fairly well and hoped from there I would be able to put together the puzzle of this ripped-apart suburb.

'It is in front of you,' Atef said. 'There.' He pointed to a flat area of nothingness where a lone security guard, probably from Hezbollah, paced around, a handgun stuck in the pocket of his jeans, trying to look inconspicuous.

I got out of the car and began to walk around, stumbling over rubble and piles of possessions that someone might soon be desperate enough to claim. As I turned a corner I saw two women standing, unsure, at the edge of one of these piles of debris. The entrance gate to their apartment block was locked shut and they were attempting to access the stairwell from a door at the side of the building. The neighbouring building had been bombed into a void, and although the worst of the rubble had been cleared there were still piles of it spilling onto the roadway.

I followed them, stepping over see-sawing lumps of concrete and into the stairwell. Hovering uncomfortably in the back of my mind was always a fear of stepping on some unexploded ordinance and so I trod carefully, choosing a path that looked as if it had been used before. A film of grey dust was everywhere and I could hear the women ahead of me as I climbed up and up. The block had been abandoned. Pictures of Nasrallah decorated the front door of almost every apartment. Others had scrawled notes that gave telephone numbers or details of where the occupants had fled.

I found the women on the fifth floor. Nada, who was 25, had lived there with her parents and three sisters. She had returned with her Aunt Zeinab to take photographs of the damage in order to lodge a compensation claim with the Lebanese government. The government grant was good, she said, but it was slow and disorganised compared with Hezbollah, which had already given them A$10,000 in cash to put towards rent and furniture while it was decided what to do with the block – demolish it or repair it. This would also be paid for by Hezbollah as part of a massive plan to reconstruct and landscape the entire area.

The apartment was a mess. What the bombs had left, looters had taken. Aluminium window frames, light switches and fittings had all been torn out by scrap-metal sellers. Even the kitchen and bathroom fittings were gone. A balcony off the kitchen that had once been enclosed by a metal railing was now totally open, a death trap. The place was unliveable.

I offered sympathy but Zeinab was jubilant. 'Buildings are nothing!' she said and hit the walls with her fists. It was the expected response, rehearsed, and designed to pass on a message that Israel could not cow these proud and pious people. Hezbollah would protect them. Nada nodded her agreement, but frankly she did not look so certain.

'We left when the bombs hit Al-Manar. We went to stay with relatives in Chiyeh,' she said, naming an adjacent suburb. 'We came back the next day. We thought it was over but at 3.30 a.m. they started bombing bridges. The sound, oh, I am dying once I heard it. It was incredible.'

'You feel that it is right next to you,' said Zeinab.

'We thought, *khalas*,' said Nada, 'enough. And even though it was the middle of the night we put everything in our truck and we ran. We were so afraid. We didn't know when the bombing would come to us. We stayed in a house north of Beirut with six other families and every day we thought, Today it will end, until 34 days had passed.'

'Why do you think the war happened?' I asked, curious to know if they would blame Hezbollah's miscalculation in kidnapping the Israeli soldiers. Even Nasrallah had apologised for it.

'Easy,' said Zeinab. 'The war was to take Hezbollah out because we are the strongest force in the world.'

'What does Hezbollah mean to you?'

'Hezbollah is everything, and in this life if there is no Hezbollah then we will be oppressed,' she said. 'They use weapons to defend us in a strategic way.'

Zeinab and Nada wanted to finish taking photographs of the apartment to send to whatever Lebanese government office was responsible for providing their compensation money.

'We have to go,' said Zeinab, apologetic, polite. 'But see it. And remember.'

CHAPTER 22
THE NEW BEIRUT

One evening I met Leila and another friend, Roula, in Gemmayze for dinner. The restaurant was busy and it felt as if no time at all had passed, as if I hadn't left Beirut and there had been no war. We were dressed up and the music was good and we drank wine and snacked on plates of tapas. You could say that, in a way, life was normal.

As we shuffled in to our booth seats, Roula and Leila questioned me warmly about life in Australia, about Joseph and Yasmine, and Matthew, but I could tell they were struggling to keep their minds away from their own lives. Compared with Nada and Zeinab in the Dahiyeh, my friends had survived the Israeli attack relatively intact. But that didn't mean it had been an easy thing. It wasn't war itself that was getting to them; it was the potential for more war, the way it had dug up bad memories of the civil war, and the fear that they wouldn't be strong enough to get through such a thing a second time. They had no idea what the days, weeks, months ahead would hold.

'This was a psychological war,' Roula reasoned, taking a sip of her wine. 'Your life stops. We were lucky not to be really involved and yet we are psychologically frozen.'

Leila told a story. 'One day I heard this big noise, loud but not as loud as an explosion, and it was one of those packages the Israelis dropped with the leaflets inside. Beirut was empty that day. The sea was flat. It was quiet and I looked out and saw all of these pieces of paper fluttering down, catching the light and shining like silver. It looked quite beautiful, like rain, but on these leaflets was a message saying that the Israelis were going to bomb us.'

She turned to me and touched her hand lightly on mine, hoping, I suppose, that the emotion in her face and the power of her touch would help to convey to me how it felt to know that your city was about to be attacked.

'That night I went to bed but you can't really sleep, because you are just waiting, waiting, waiting for this bomb. To be honest it is better when you don't know. In the end I slept close to the patio because if something happened I wanted to feel it the moment it happened.'

The Lebanese television stations were reporting the war live, 24 hours a day. 'As we heard a bomb we would rush to the television to find out where it was,' said Leila.

'Oh yes, we were addicted to TV,' said Roula.

'I would flick between the stations, looking for the best coverage,' said Leila, and she looked over at Roula expectantly, waiting for her to confirm a similar experience, and they laughed at how this banal little ritual – watching television – had taken on such enormous significance.

'I am bitter about what's happening,' said Roula, suddenly serious. 'If I can leave I will. I am not interested in experiencing this for a second time. I just want to know how I can get out of it without being affected.' She paused, thoughtful. 'You forget how much is already in you. One night I had a dream that a bullet came in the window. In my dream I saw it rolling around and even though it was a bullet in my mind it was a bomb. It was rolling and rolling and I was chasing it. It was always just out of reach. It rolled under the bed and I couldn't catch it. Then my brother came to me and he said, "Don't bother. It's too late." It exploded and I woke up and I thought to myself, Oh my God, this is *in* me. When I woke up I was smiling. I was happy. It is only a dream! But at the same time I was affected.'

Roula went on. 'People argue that you should stay and challenge the situation, this is where you belong, you are Lebanese, you have to admit it and this is your fate. In parallel to this is a fear of the unknown. There is the feeling of home, the warmth of home, and you wonder if even the bombed home is better than no home. It is extremely hard to leave to go somewhere you don't belong. But for me, whatever the price, it's better to go. I will leave that statement to someone else, even though I know that means Lebanon will lose the young, the interesting and educated people who have a chance to get jobs elsewhere.'

I was sitting quietly, reaching for pieces of tapas, sipping my wine, listening. Roula and Leila spoke eloquently, vividly, and I felt drawn into this other world of war and survival; their stories of uncertainty resonated so much more clearly and told me far more about how much the war had cost Lebanon. Perhaps it was because I could identify with them. Roula and Leila were Lebanese versions of me: my age, university-educated, well-travelled. I could easily put myself in their place or imagine that a different twist of fate could have left me in their situation.

'One day a few years ago I asked my father why he didn't take us away from Lebanon during the war, when we were kids,' Roula said. 'I said to him, "In the end you were willing to sacrifice your kids!" I felt a bit . . . I don't know . . .' Her voice trailed off in reminiscence. 'I wanted to know why he made us take that risk. I was very judgemental. My father said, "Do you think we knew it would last 15 years? Every time we thought, this is the end, it's almost over." I thought about what he said and I could understand it, and it haunts you. This time I began to wonder, what if it's still not over? What if it keeps happening again and again and again?

'There are little things that stay with you, little traumas. Like candles. Candles for me are not romantic. We used candles all the time during the war because there was no electricity.' Roula fell silent and I could tell she was looking for a way to lift the moment. 'This is why we love neon here,' she said suddenly, a teasing justification for Lebanese bad taste. 'Neon is the ultimate light.'

I was looking forward to visiting Hadi, my Hezbollah friend, and we agreed to meet one afternoon at his shop. I was excited to see him, but although his welcome was warm, it was subdued and he seemed more vulnerable than ever. As we sat for our customary coffee and exchanged pleasantries, he told me the saddest but most honest thing I had heard since arriving in Lebanon.

'We are living in a very critical and sensitive moment. The whole country is split into two halves,' he said. 'They call us the Syria/Iran axis and we call them the American/Israeli axis. So that means there are no Lebanese any more.'

He was right. Neither group had the pure interests of Lebanon at heart. Each was appealing to the preferences of powerful outside forces or to their own unrealised ambitions. There was a horrible circularity about it. It was impossible not to feel fearful that these external manipulations would add so much pressure that it would spark another civil conflict.

'We have no choice but to unite the government. Lebanon must form a national unity government,' Hadi said. Hezbollah, Aoun and Amal believed they had been sidelined by the twisted-up political process in the June 2005 elections, despite the fact that support for them was high. Hezbollah was now leading a push to be given a greater percentage of parliamentary seats and a consultation process to iron out the differences was scheduled for the following week. On the surface this seemed fine – national unity sounded like a noble goal – but to think that a government could be remade after democratic elections exposed the immaturity of Lebanon's democracy and the weakness of the state that it had created. The real reason, some people believed, for Hezbollah's insistence on a government of national unity was to use political numbers to block the trial of suspects in the killing of Hariri.

'If the consultations fail,' said Hadi, 'then our axis will take to the street and topple the government. This is not a religious thing – Aoun is a Christian, Hezbollah are Shia. But Lebanon must be ruled by consensus.'

'People say Hezbollah miscalculated in July,' I said to him.

'If we had thought such a thing would happen, we would not have done it,' Hadi said, repeating Nasrallah's line, his eyes wide with innocence. 'We thought Israel wouldn't want to ruin its tourism season. We thought they were stuck in a war in Gaza. We thought the political situation didn't permit Israel to attack Lebanon. And we had previous experience that had turned out well. When we captured Israeli soldiers in the past they began negotiating with us on the second day. Our conclusion is that Israel planned to attack Lebanon all along.'

'But why would they attack, Hadi?' I said. 'Isn't it only because Hezbollah continues to attack Israel for the return of the Shebaa Farms? Is what happened in July and August worth it?'

'The Shebaa is Lebanese land,' he said referring to the small parcel of land that remained occupied by Israel. 'It is our legitimate choice and right to liberate it by all means. There is a point when the resistance must hand over its arms, but not until the state and army is able to take over. We want a strong government able to defend the people, but don't forget that the reason we have a resistance is because we have an occupation.'

I said goodbye to Hadi and walked outside. Of course he was right that Lebanese (and Syrian) land remained occupied by Israel. No matter how you looked at it Israel's response to Hezbollah's actions was out of all proportion. The situation was dire. But I had never felt so alienated by him, and it felt as if the honesty we used to enjoy was missing. He was talking to me in riddles. What did he mean by 'a strong government'? Did he mean a government Hezbollah could control?

I was thinking about these things when I bumped into an acquaintance on Hamra Street who I had lost touch with and not seen for a long time. We peeled off from the bustling street and found a café and ordered drinks. She was a real Beirut girl, worldly and educated, and had spent many years in Australia during the 1980s while her father finished a PhD at the University of Sydney. She was depressed about the situation and worried for the safety and sanity of her children.

'I came to realise something during the war this summer that I feel ashamed had never occurred to me before,' she said, swirling a straw around in a glass of fresh lemon juice. 'In Beirut we have felt for the past ten years that the war was over. We have enjoyed a more or less normal life. We could go out and go to restaurants and movies and it was safe most of the time. But I realised during this war that for the people of the south, life has never been normal.'

It was true. When the Lebanese civil war ended, the Israeli occupation of the south of the country continued until 2000. For the past six years landmines and overflights and tit-for-tat attacks between Israel and Hezbollah had continued. The region was poor. A lot of infrastructure had been rebuilt by Hezbollah but it was still far from perfect. Technically there was peace, but echoes of war and the threat of more war were everywhere, constant.

It was a simple point but it helped to explain a lot of things. As I rode home that evening it occurred to me that for the Lebanese Shia, the Islamic Resistance was not simply a military issue or even a political one. It was emotional. Hadi had told me so many times how he grew up with a deep and ingrained sense of oppression, and although I could accept the position it was impossible for me to truly understand him. I realised that for the Shi'ites, Hezbollah was the one thing they felt they could trust and they were not ready to give it up. If the Islamic Resistance was disarmed, who would be there to protect them? I had heard the line so many times but at last I felt I was beginning to understand it.

I began to wonder if the brewing crisis would somehow become a violent reordering of things. Since 1932 – the last time Lebanon had an official population census – the country had lived a kind of fiction. That 1932 census stated that Lebanon was 51 per cent Christian and 49 per cent Muslim. It said that the Christian Maronites were the largest sect with 29 per cent of the population, the Sunnis were 22 per cent and Shi'ites 20 per cent. Lebanon's political system was carved up in line with these statistics – the presidency and various security roles were given to the Maronites, the prime ministership to the Sunnis, and the parliamentary speaker was always a Shi'ite. But more than 70 years later it was absurd to believe that the figures of the 1932 census stacked up, and no one did. It was widely assumed that the Shi'ites were now the largest confessional group in the country – a 1985 guess put them at 41 per cent and rising and the Maronites probably made up less than 20 per cent of the population.

What did that mean? Should a new census be ordered and the country's rulers swapped around to take into account the new reality? The alternative – to abandon the confessional system and encourage the Lebanese to vote and participate in politics according to national issues rather than religious affiliations – would require an enormous leap of democratic maturity. Were the Lebanese ready for it?

As I rode through the streets of Beirut that afternoon, passing through Hamra and across the old frontline into east Beirut, I felt depressed about Lebanon's prospects. I could not see a way forward and it began to feel as if some kind of confrontation was inevitable. More than anything, I thought, the people of Lebanon needed to forget about political affiliations and sectarianism and decide once and for all what it meant to be Lebanese.

The uncertainty whirling around Lebanon had made me remember Henri and the American Dream and my rose-tinted predictions more than five years earlier that he would have no use for his US passport. As I was walking past his bar late one afternoon, I was caught by an urge to drop in to see how he was and if he remembered me.

The American Dream was the same more-or-less empty place. Through the dim light I could see one patron on a stool, leaning over the bar, and behind him serving the drinks was a man I didn't recognise.

'Is Henri around?' I asked him, and the man shook his head.

'He's travelling.'

'Where has he gone?' I pushed, hoping I suppose that he would say America.

'He's in Cyprus,' the man said as he poured a drink for his only customer. 'The Americans evacuated him during the war and now he has a problem with his heart so he's stayed over there for an operation.'

'He was evacuated during the war!' I said. 'By the Americans?' and the man nodded.

'He left on the ship?' I asked again, wanting to confirm all the details. 'Using his American passport?'

The man nodded again and smiled, amused that this apparently simple information had interested me.

I was vaguely concerned to hear of Henri's health problems, but it sounded as if he would be okay (the barman wasn't worried) and a little part of me smiled for him. Perhaps it wasn't the American dream he had been hoping for but at least the US passport had brought him a benefit of one kind.

'Stay for a drink,' the barman encouraged, but I refused him. It wasn't the same without Henri, without Matthew by my side, and anyway I had a meeting to get to.

I went outside and found a *service* taxi to take me to Beir El Abed, a poor, chaotic and mostly Shi'ite suburb of Beirut that rammed up against Hezbollah's Haret Hreik stronghold. I had a meeting with Ali Fadlallah, who had lost five members of his family, including his mother, during the summer's war with Israel.

I waited for Ali on the footpath beside a strip of shops built into the base of bland concrete apartment buildings that also housed a religious school. You could feel winter in the air. It was just after 5 p.m. but it was already dark and the shopfronts glowed neon across the footpath where I was standing.

Cars, taxis and motorbikes rushed wildly back and forth along the street in front of me and horns were blaring. In the middle of this peak-hour commotion some families had begun to venture out for an evening walk and, later, a bite to eat.

When Ali arrived, he led me around the corner away from the lights and noise of the main road. The side street was almost in darkness and I had to tread carefully to avoid tripping on the torn-up asphalt. Pools of muddy water – from the rain a few days earlier – filled ruts and potholes. The street stretched out before us and I could see several razed spaces where buildings had once stood, destroyed in missile attacks a few weeks earlier. Teams of workmen, hired and paid for by Hezbollah, had cleaned up most of the rubble but there were still small lumps of stone and concrete scattered about. The sides of some buildings dangled in precarious and macabre mobiles of hunks of concrete attached to metal rods, like flesh on bones.

Ali beckoned and I followed him into the foyer of his apartment block. More lumps of rubble covered the entrance-way. There was no light and the lobby was in darkness and my eyes were taking time to adjust. It was difficult even to find the place where the staircase began, and so Ali took out his mobile phone and used the light from its screen like a torch.

There was a photograph on the screen, an image of a man. 'Who is this?' I asked him, and he said the picture was of his martyred brother, a Hezbollah fighter. And so we climbed like this, the strange and ghostly glow from the mobile phone fanning out around us, the Hezbollah martyr forever watching over his brother, helping to guide his steps.

In late July Ali's mother, Maryam, his 16-year-old sister, Zahra, sister-in-law, Yamama, and nephew, Houda, who was only three, were killed in an Israeli missile strike. The basement shelter where they were hiding – in the village of

Aainata in the far south of Lebanon, not far from Bint Jbeil – was flattened all at once and Ali's family, along with other visiting friends and neighbours, must have died immediately. Their bodies lay under the rubble for 20 days until the ceasefire made it possible to reclaim what was left of them.

That summer Ali also lost a brother, Amir, a Hezbollah fighter who was killed in the battle with Israel. Ali believed Amir had joined another brother, Ahmad, who had died in 1999 also fighting Israel. Death everywhere, a part of life: a mother, two brothers and a sister, a sister-in-law, a nephew, friends and acquaintances. All of this and Ali was only 20.

The Fadlallah family was split up that day, with some living in the rented house in their ancestral village and others in Beirut where there was work and tertiary education. Ali's father had survived because he had fled the village earlier on the day of the strike, unaware that the rest of his family had stayed behind. Ali had survived because he was living in the family's apartment in Beirut, where I was now sitting.

Ali had never been a fighter, he said, and did not want to be. 'I want to study, to finish my education,' he told me, and I believed him. He spoke softly, gently, and was quiet and composed, but you could feel a great weight of sadness about him. His eyes were full of uncertainty and questions and he had a fragility that made the right or wrong of Hezbollah irrelevant; I wanted to reach out to him. He was dressed carefully in jeans and sports shoes, a tight fitting black jacket with Dolce & Gabbana written all over it, but I don't think it was genuine.

He took me on to the balcony and from high up you could see great canyons of devastation that stretched across entire blocks.

'That was the headquarters of Sayyad Nasrallah,' he said, pointing to a gap between two buildings, still standing, and on into the distance where the whole area had been flattened. 'And there,' he pointed across the road to another demolition site, 'is where I used to work.' Ali had a job in the marketing department of a telecommunications company. 'There was a bakery there and I used to love their *mana'oushi*.' He shook his head. 'It will never be like before.'

We moved back inside and sat in the living room, completely bare except for two sofas and two plastic stools used as tables. A bare bulb hung from the ceiling but no light came from it. Two candles stood on the plastic tables so we could see each other. They lit up the walls of the room and I could see photographs of his martyred family, their smiling faces, from happier times, staring out; the edges blurred slightly to make them seem otherworldly, beatific. In the background were fields of flowers, and Hassan Nasrallah smiled paternalistically, almost godlike, from a corner of the frame.

Two of Ali's surviving siblings joined us: his older sister, Rajaa, and older brother, Hamza, and in the semi-darkness coffee was brought, cigarettes offered, water poured, a box of chocolates opened.

'We are sorry we are unable to offer you hospitality,' said Hamza.

I smiled at him, incredulous. 'Look at all that you have provided,' I said and swept my hand along the length of the two plastic tables covered in things to eat and drink.

Ali grew up in Aainata, which was inside Israel's security zone until May 2000 when the IDF withdrew from Lebanon. He doesn't remember the Lebanese civil war – it ended when he was just three or four years old. Instead, he remembers a happy childhood, climbing trees and building treehouses, helping the family plant vegetables, exploring the caves that snaked through the region's rocky mountains, tormenting his mother. 'I love my village very much,' he said.

'I hate to leave it even for an hour. I was born there, my family was there.'

But that summer Ali was in Beirut. He was finishing his studies in hotel management and working at the telecommunications company. He had a crush on a girl who lived in an apartment a few floors below his, and was daydreaming about falling in love and getting married and moving to the United States to work in a big hotel. 'We criticise the US government because it supports the Israel lobby and allows Israel to kill our people,' he said. 'But I am not trying to criticise the people of America. I would love to live in the West, to try all different kinds of life.'

And then war came. 'I was in east Beirut when I heard that the airport had been bombed,' he said. 'I called my friend and he told me that Hezbollah had taken two prisoners and that the roads had been cut. I knew that the Israelis would have no mercy.'

It was 4 a.m. when the first missile hit Ali's street. 'The noise was extremely, extremely strong,' he said, lost for the words to adequately describe it. He went to the balcony to investigate and a second missile hit, sending pieces of concrete and debris flying. 'One tore my shirt,' he said, pulling theatrically at his jacket, acting out the moment. It was too dangerous to remain – the buildings around him were falling like dominoes – so Ali went to stay with friends in another suburb. It was safer there, and every day he called his mother and sister in the south and begged them to leave Aainata.

'My mother told me she would prefer to die in her own house than on the street trying to escape,' he said. I looked at him, curious; surely she must have tried to save herself? 'We are the kind of people who are very attached to our memories, our land, our house,' he said, trying to explain, and I nodded. But there was another reason.

Ali's mother was 60 years old. She didn't carry a gun but, regardless, she was a revolutionary. In the early 1990s she had spent two months as a prisoner in the notorious El Khiam prison in south Lebanon (run by the South Lebanon Army, a proxy for the Israelis, and famous for torturing its inmates). Ali's mother was imprisoned for supporting the fight against the Israeli occupation. This time, she saw it as her duty to remain in Aainata. She cooked for the Hezbollah fighters – often it was a traditional dish from the region of tomato and burghul wheat – she welcomed them into her home to wash, to eat; tended their wounds. Ali believes this is why the family was targeted: the day before, two fighters had been seen entering their home.

'Do you remember the last time you spoke to her?' I asked softly, and Ali clicked his knuckles and squeezed his hands together so that the skin stretched white over his bones.

'I called her the day before she died and she told me to take care and I said to her, "It is not me who must take care, it is you in the heart of the battle," ' he said. He spoke his words slowly and looked down at his knees; he was trying very hard not to cry. 'We are going to win,' she had told him and began ululating down the phone, that joyous and almost hysterical sound of celebration that is a favourite with women across the Arab world. 'Very soon you will be back in the house where you were born.'

'What does it mean to lose your mother?' I asked him.

'We are used to it,' Ali answered. 'All our lives we have experienced people dying.'

'No,' I said. 'You can never get used to losing your mother. Ali, it only happens once.'

He was quiet for a long time and lit a cigarette. He scratched his face and then turned to me. 'I used to have a huge love for her,' he admitted at last and his voice was shaking. 'She used to be my friend, my sister, everything to me. She called me the Naughty Guy and I would call her *Um Karim*, the Mother of Karim, after her firstborn son.'

Ali fell quiet again and smiled weakly, shook his head. 'My sister, Zahra,' he continued at last, 'I was very attached to her too. She was engaged to be married and would have turned 17 just three days after she died.'

'How will you survive?' I asked him. I looked around the bare room, the street outside empty and destroyed, his dead family on the walls, his sister and brother – older and tougher than him – watching, critiquing his replies and my questions. He looked so young and vulnerable sitting in that empty room, the candle flickering in front of him.

'I want to tell you one thing,' he began. 'The Shia of Lebanon, we feel that we can take consolation from our sisters, our brothers, our uncles and aunts who try to reimburse us for such a loss. During our phone calls before she died, my mother would tell me to continue with a normal life, to continue my education.'

'Are you angry?' I said, and he answered me with a mixed-up logic of appeasement and retribution.

'I want to tell you that it is not the thing to take revenge. Even though I lost my mother, my sister, we are ready to talk. We have to reply if they attack. We would like a peaceful life.'

'But many people say Hezbollah began this war,' I told him. 'It was Hezbollah who captured the Israeli soldiers. And what about your weapons? Maybe it is time for Hezbollah to give them up and become a normal political party.'

'It is my opinion that these weapons protect me,' he said. 'They helped me to get back my land, my trees, my memories. I am the type of person who says an eye for an eye. If someone hits me I will hit back. At the same time I am not the one who starts it; on the contrary, we are trying to defend ourselves.'

I sat quietly in the semi-dark, listening.

'But for sure I feel very depressed by what has happened,' Ali continued. 'For sure I feel scared of wanting to call my mother and dialling the number just like I used to do but no one answers. You know, my mother would always bake for us *marmouk*. It is a kind of bread that is a specialty of our region. Each week she would send it up to Beirut for us to eat.' Ali sucked in his breath and blew it out again in a sigh. Then he spoke very softly, 'And now there is no one to send us bread any more.'

In the taxi on the way home I talked to Howeida, who had come along with me to translate, about the futility of war, the definition of innocence. Howeida had her own theories. 'I give Ali two or three more years and he will be just like his brothers,' she said, meaning that his vulnerability would turn into rage and he would join the Islamic Resistance and become a fighter. 'They have to think about the future because what is the future of weapons? They have to think about what comes after this. It is no kind of life in the Dahiyeh.'

It was Friday, the day before I was due to leave Beirut and fly back home to Sydney. During the past few days I had begun to feel as if the stray ends of my Middle Eastern journey were, one by one, being tied up. Saddam Hussein's trial in Iraq had delivered its verdict and he had been sentenced to death for his role in the murder of 148 Shi'ites from Djail in 1988. The BBC's Beirut correspondent, Kim Ghattas, said the Lebanese were watching closely because they were preparing to try those accused of Hariri's assassination. Ghattas said the sentence facing Saddam would reassure the Lebanese that international tribunals had teeth and could force brutal leaders to be accountable for their war crimes. A few days later the Republicans lost to the Democrats in the US mid-term elections and Donald Rumsfeld was at last swallowed by his failures in Iraq.

That night my friend Ahmad, who had lived up the road from me in Clemenceau, had a dinner party. He had just returned from the US where he was now based and had brought with him to Beirut a white truffle. It featured in a rich but delicious dish of mashed potato and beef and we all swooned as we tasted it. Ahmad had put together a table of foreign journalists, other friends and family, and it was impossible to escape politics. It was a beautiful evening and the conversation was energetic and intelligent but I just couldn't pull myself into the moment. I was sad about leaving Beirut and my friends, and yet I missed Matthew and my babies and it was starting to become painful.

I walked out onto Ahmad's terrace and looked down on the street where I had lived for four years. To my right I could see our old apartment with a light on inside. To my left, the hospital where Yasmine was born. It was late and the street was quiet, full of the past: old civil war ghosts mixed up with my own happy memories of peacetime.

I could hear voices and the clink of cutlery on porcelain coming from the dining room behind me. It was impossible to predict what would come next for Lebanon. But what was the point of attempting to foretell the future? There was only ever this moment. The Lebanese spirit was alive in Ahmad's apartment that night, and as I turned from the balcony to walk back inside I heard the sound of people laughing.